BIOGRAPHICAL STUDIES
IN MODERN INDIAN EDUCATION

BIOGRAPHICAL STUDIES IN MODERN INDIAN EDUCATION

BY

HENRY V. HAMPTON, M.A.

*Formerly Member of the Indian Educational Service
and Principal and Professor of Education
Secondary Training College, Bombay*

Biography Index Reprint Series

BOOKS FOR LIBRARIES PRESS
FREEPORT, NEW YORK

First Published 1947

Reprinted 1970 by arrangement with
Oxford University Press, Inc.

INTERNATIONAL STANDARD BOOK NUMBER:
0-8369-8042-5

LIBRARY OF CONGRESS CATALOG CARD NUMBER:
78-136647

PRINTED IN THE UNITED STATES OF AMERICA

PREFACE

ALTHOUGH there are several books in which the main events in the history of education in India during the British period are recorded with reasonable accuracy, there are few—if, indeed, there are any—which deal, save in a cursory fashion, with the men who caused these events. Clearly, every historical event, certainly every important one, is the result of the precedent thought of individuals, and in the following pages I have attempted to show that the most memorable events in the chequered history of Indian education in the nineteenth century were, as Sir Henry Sharp has pointed out, 'linked with the names of striking personalities'.[1]

I make no claim that the studies which follow comprise a complete history of Indian education from the time of Warren Hastings until Lord Curzon became Viceroy. My aim has been to focus attention on certain outstanding men who devoted much thought to the educational problems of their day and who, whether they achieved success or not, have left a lasting impression on the educational system of the country. At most, therefore, I claim that this book is an introduction to the history of nineteenth-century education in India and I have endeavoured to give my approach a human interest rather than to content myself with a dreary catalogue of events—with what someone has called a mere 'charnel-house of facts'.

It is true, of course, that I have recorded facts in plenty—indeed, I have taken pains to ensure that these are stated with accuracy; if I have allowed any errors to creep in I must accept sole responsibility. On the other hand, I must admit that my method of presentation suffers from certain drawbacks. I fully realize, for instance, that there is considerable overlapping; this is particularly noticeable in the accounts of the lives and achievements of those great educational pioneers, Ram Mohun Roy, David Hare and Alexander Duff, and, to a lesser degree, in the sketches of Munro and Elphinstone, whose careers touched at many points. But it is difficult to see how, in a book of this sort, covering

[1] H. Sharp, *Selections from Educational Records, I, 1781-1839* (1920), p. iii.

the short space of little more than a hundred years, overlapping could be altogether avoided; I may justify this statement by pointing out that Duff had established his fame as an educationist before Macaulay arrived in India, that he did not finally return to Scotland until ten years after Thomason's death, and that he lived until 1878 to hear of Sir Syed Ahmed Khan's successful efforts to promote education among the Muslim community. If repetition has been unavoidable, I have tried to reduce it to a minimum and I have been careful to associate with each of the eminent men with whom I have dealt those events which are most closely connected with his name. Thus, for instance, credit for the foundation of the Hindu College belongs to David Hare rather than to Ram Mohun Roy, and so the story of the early days of this famous institution is included in the study of Hare; again, Wood's Dispatch is dealt with in the study of Alexander Duff, because he played an influential part in the events which led up to the issue of this great educational charter, though his most distinctive contribution to educational advancement—the establishment of the 'educational mission'—had been made some twenty-five years earlier. When it seemed necessary, or desirable, to refer in different contexts to the same event, I have endeavoured to change the emphasis so as to make clear the part played by the individuals concerned.

Secondly, as each of the following short studies aims at being more or less self-contained, I have laid myself open to the charge of sketchiness. There is, however, a thread of connexion running right through and, taken together, these studies embrace almost everything of importance in the history of Indian education in the last century. No apology seems necessary for the inclusion of so many biographical and personal details, for education—from whatever angle it be approached—must take account of the human factor; to write of Elphinstone or Sir Syed Ahmed Khan as if their lives had been devoted solely to educational reform would be untrue and misleading. Besides, omission of personal detail would rob this book of that human interest which is intended to be its chief characteristic.

From the point of view of the serious student, another objection may be raised on the score that I have relied almost entirely on what I may call 'original sources' which are extremely rare.

No one regrets more than I do that so many of the books mentioned
in the bibliographical lists and in the footnotes have long been out of
print and are hard to procure, even in well-equipped libraries.
This drawback, however, is counterbalanced by the fact that I have
been able to avoid the repetition of mistakes which recur with
monotonous regularity in other, and more ambitious, works.
Also, as some of my judgements on the past differ from those
which are commonly accepted, it seemed necessary that this book
should be well documented and that I should give references to
the authorities on whom I have placed most reliance. It is hoped
that the bibliographies and footnotes (together with an index and
a short chronological table) will provide the reader with all he
needs and, perhaps, incite some scholar to make a further and
more complete study of the period.

I wish to make it clear that I have purposely omitted to make
any mention of standard works of reference such as the
Encyclopaedia Britannica, *Dictionary of National Biography*,
Imperial Gazetteer of India and the like; I have also avoided, as
far as possible, reference to articles which have appeared in learned
journals. I must, however, acknowledge my indebtedness to the
following: (1) A. L. Covernton's 'The Educational Policy of
Mountstuart Elphinstone' (*Journal of the Bombay Branch of the
Royal Asiatic Society—New Series Vol. II, No. 1—1926*); (2)
H. G. Rawlinson's 'Sir Saiyid Ahmed Khan' (*Islamic Culture,
Vol. IV, No. 3—1930*): and (3) Percival Spear's 'Bentinck and
Education' (*The Cambridge Historical Journal, Vol. VI, No.
1—1938*). It may also be well to point out that the greater part
of this book was written before the outbreak of the War and that,
therefore, I have been able to draw only sparingly on books
published in the last six or seven years; of these by far the most
important is *Modern India and the West* (1941), edited by the
late L. S. S. O'Malley, which is a masterly study of the interactions
of two great civilizations written by experts—Indian and European.
I am particularly indebted to this authoritative work not merely
on account of its intrinsic merits but because it served to confirm
me in certain conclusions which I had already reached independently—in some matters on evidence rather different from that on
which Mr O'Malley and his collaborators rely.

As regards the spelling of Indian names and words, I have not attempted to follow any uniform system. Generally speaking, I have adopted the spelling most commonly used in current English; hence, *Punjab* is preferred to *Panjab*, *Bihar* to *Behar*, *Mohammedan* to *Muhammadan*, etc. In quotations, however, the original spelling is retained and this accounts for some apparent inconsistencies, e.g. *Hindoo* for the normal *Hindu*. The only exception is *tahsildari*, which is so spelt throughout, and the reason for this exception is that this word is sometimes spelt in different ways in the same document or in a series of related documents. Again, *Ram Mohun Roy* has been accepted, not because it is correct but because it appears to be most commonly used in English and was adopted by Miss Collett in her standard biography. Similarly, *Syed Ahmed Khan* has been preferred to other variants,[1] mainly because it was used by Col. Graham in his life of the great Muslim reformer. Regarding Indian words which have been taken over into English, the usual anglicized form has been accepted—*pundit* instead of *pandit*, *suttee* instead of *sati*, *Mogul* instead of *Mughal*, are a few examples. Where either of two alternatives seemed permissible, I decided the issue by personal choice: *Brahman* is more correct than *Brahmin* and *Rajah*, if not more correct than *Raja*, has the sanction of long usage—and appears more dignified!

In conclusion, I wish to express my thanks to the staff of the Oxford University Press for their sound advice and for the unfailing help which they willingly afforded me.

H.V.H.

BOMBAY
February 1946

[1] On the title-page of the Syed's *Review on Dr Hunter's Indian Musalmans* (1872) the author's name is given as Syed *Ahmad* Khan.

CONTENTS

ILLUSTRATIONS

CORRIGENDA

Page 16, line 30. *For* the *read* that
 ,, 37, footnote 1. *Before* Marshman *read* See
 ,, 54, line 3. *For* cause *read* course
 ,, 58, line 33. *For* Raja *read* Rajah
 ,, 154, line 30. *For* 1882 *read* 1883

CHARLES GRANT

CHARLES GRANT, 1746-1823

FOUNDER OF ENGLISH EDUCATION

THE foundations of the system of English education which exists
in India today were laid in the eighteenth century, not by British
administrators but by missionaries and private individuals. It is
true that some of the latter were officers of the East India Company,
but their educational activities were the outcome of personal bene-
ficence rather than part of their official duties; it is also true that
the Government did occasionally manifest a slight interest in educational schemes which aimed at supplementing the work done by
indigenous schools and sometimes they even sanctioned financial
assistance to such schemes as were calculated to conciliate the people
or to provide recruits for the public services. On the whole,
however, the most important of the early efforts to promote the
educational interests of the people emanated from missionaries.
Their original aim was to employ education, not as an end in
itself, but as a means to conversion and, very naturally, they
decided from the very beginning that teaching, as well as preaching, should be through the medium of the vernaculars. At times
enthusiasm for propagating the Gospel outran discretion, and some
of the early missionaries earned the displeasure of the civil authorities. Their desire to banish ignorance, however, led 'to single-
minded and whole-hearted efforts in the cause of education in and
for itself',[1] and their educational work, especially on the collegiate
side, gradually became almost entirely divorced from their
proselytizing activities. William Archer points out[2] that Western
enlightenment has come to the East in such close association with
Christianity that it is impossible to distinguish between the one
influence and the other, but it is equally true that 'a long list of
honoured names testifies to the solid educational work which
missionaries have accomplished in India'.[3]

The first Protestant missionaries in the field were the Danish,
headed by Ziegenbalg, who arrived in Tranquebar in 1706 and
immediately started to learn Tamil and Portuguese. Within a

[1] H. R. James, *Education and Statesmanship in India* (1917), p. 19.
[2] W. Archer, *India and the Future* (1917), p. 263.
[3] H. Sharp, *Selections from Educational Records* (1920), I, p. 6.

few years parts of the New Testament were translated into vernacular languages and a few schools had been established. His great successors were Schultz and Schwartz, the latter of whom arrived in India in 1750 and laboured in the south for almost half a century (*d.* 1798). Among the many and great services which he rendered to the country of his adoption, not the least was the establishment of schools in various important centres, including Tanjore, Trichinopoly and Madras. Indeed, it was the success of these mission schools which inspired John Sullivan, who represented the Madras Government at the court of Tanjore, to prepare a scheme for the founding of Government schools in every province for the instruction of Indians through the medium of English. This project was warmly supported by Schwartz himself and, with his assistance, Sullivan, acting on his own responsibility, started a few schools in the south. He then represented the matter to the Board of Directors and pointed out that his object was to break down the prejudice which existed against British rule. Not content with expressing their approval or granting formal sanction, the Directors contributed 250 pagodas to each of the schools which existed in 1787 and promised similar aid to any other institution which might be opened for the purpose of enlightening the minds of the people and of impressing on them ' sentiments of esteem and respect for the British nation, by acquainting them with the leading features of our Government so favourable to the rights and happiness of mankind'.[1] Dr Thomas considers that this is the first project for the education of Indians which can in any way be ascribed to Government, and that 'its chief importance lay in the fact that it was the means of attracting the attention of the Government, both in India and at home, to what soon became a plain duty'.[2]

In spite of difficulties, these schools appear to have had some success and it is interesting to note that, besides Tamil, the curriculum included Bible teaching as well as English. The reluctance of the Directors to patronize Christianity possibly led to the discontinuance of Government support and to the gradual disappearance[3] of the English schools founded by Sullivan of Tanjore. The

[1] Sharp, ibid., p. 4.

[2] F. W. Thomas, *British Education in India* (1891), p. 20.

[3] For further details see Frank Penny, *The Church in Madras* (1904), I, pp. 518 ff.

fact remains, however, that this was the first attempt, though one which was destined to early failure, to establish a Western school system. In the meantime, the influence of Schwartz had spread far beyond the Madras Presidency, and among those to whom his life and work were an inspiration the name of Charles Grant is by far the most distinguished. In spite of the services which he rendered to the East India Company he has been almost entirely forgotten and few people realize that he has a better claim than anyone else to be regarded as the real founder of Western education in India. As early as 1879 Dr George Smith[1] came to the conclusion, not altogether extravagant, that 'Charles Grant had, in 1792 sketched in detail . . . a scheme of tolerant English and Vernacular Education, of such far-sighted ability and benevolence that all subsequent progress to the present hour is only a commentary upon his suggestions'; in the Report of the Calcutta University Commission[2] it is stated that his advocacy of English education in 1792 'may be called the beginning of the whole movement', and James[3] considers that he was 'the man who first saw the possibility of the enlightenment which has since become in India a reality'. These casual references are not sufficient testimony to the importance of Grant as a pioneer of English education and, with the exception of Syed Mahmood, historians have been inclined to underestimate the significance of his *Observations*.

Charles was the eldest son of Alexander Grant, a Highlander belonging to the Urquhart branch of the clan of that name. He was born in 1746 on the shores of Loch Ness, a few weeks before the battle of Culloden in which his father was severely wounded. It is related[4] that Alexander Grant accompanied by some thirty friends went to the christening of his little son and participated in a very picturesque ceremony: 'They named him Charles after Charles Edward Stuart; and, drawing their swords, they crossed and clashed them over the baby's cradle, thus enlisting him under the banner of the Prince.' For several months after the decisive defeat of the Jacobites the father had to remain in hiding, and when he returned to his home early in the follow-

[1] G. Smith, *Life of Alexander Duff* (1879), I, p. 97.
[2] *Calcutta University Commission* (1919), I, p. 32.
[3] op. cit., p. 17.
[4] H. Morris, *Life of Charles Grant* (1904), p. 2.

ing year, he found that his property had been ruined by depred-
ations. In spite of strenuous exertions he was unable to retrieve
his fortunes, and nine years later he accepted a commission in one
of the Highland regiments which were raised to reinforce the army
in America. He distinguished himself at the siege of Havana,
which fell to the Spaniards in 1762, but died shortly afterwards as
the result of fever brought on by exposure.

In the meantime, his wife, a woman of strong character and
extreme piety, had been left with five young children and with
very scanty means. Several relatives came to her assistance,
particularly John, Alexander's younger brother, who held an
appointment in the Excise Department which brought him in only
£30 a year. The young Charles went to live with an uncle and
was sent to a school at Elgin, which was one of the best of its
kind in the north of Scotland. On the death of his mother in
1758 his uncle was forced to apprentice him as a clerk to William
Forsyth, a leading merchant and shipowner of Cromarty. For
more than four years he remained in Forsyth's office until, in
1763, he obtained a clerkship in a cousin's mercantile house in
London. His early training and his natural aptitude for figures
served him in good stead and he was rapidly promoted to the
responsible position of head clerk. He appears to have been fairly
comfortably off and was soon able to help his uncle and younger
brothers. His ambition, however, was to go abroad and he had
thoughts of seeking his fortune in America. Luckily, he made
such a good impression on his employers that his cousin suggested
that he should go to Calcutta, where he had considerable influence
and business interests, and in 1767 Charles, aged 21, set his face
towards the East. When he arrived in Calcutta it so happened
that Richard Becher,[1] who held a high position in the Company's
service, was on the look-out for a capable assistant to manage
his private business—civilians being allowed to trade on their own
account—and he was glad of the opportunity of being able to
employ the young Highlander, whom he had previously met in
London and of whose character and ability he had formed a high

---

[1] Related to Anne Becher, mother of Thackeray the novelist. Sir William
Hunter is of opinion that he may have suggested, at least partially, *Col.
Newcome*, vide *The Thackerays in India* (1897); also, H. G. Rawlinson, *The
Reminiscences of Augusta Becher* (1930).

opinion. Charles Grant soon found himself at the head of Becher's private affairs, but within a year Bengal was desolated by one of the most terrible famines (1769-70) ever known in India. Becher was an upright and kindly official who devoted all his energies to the alleviation of distress in Murshidabad. Grant threw himself so vigorously into the work of famine relief that he had a serious breakdown in health. Indeed, he was forbidden by his doctor to remain in India for another hot weather and reluctantly returned to England in 1771.

The voyage home and the invigorating climate of his own country soon restored him to normal health. Having married and been appointed to a writership in the Company's service he returned to Calcutta in 1773. He quickly made his mark as an able and conscientious official and in the following year was appointed Secretary to the Board of Trade—a new department for commercial and revenue affairs created by Warren Hastings. The young civilian appears to have been more than well pleased with his worldly success and, for a time, he led a life of extravagance and folly of which he was afterwards ashamed. He enjoyed to the full the gaiety of the social life of Calcutta which is so graphically described in the pages of the *Memoirs of William Hickey*—assuredly an Anglo-Indian classic. As a result, he found himself deeply involved in debt and was forced to curtail his hospitality and to cut down expenditure. In 1775 his brother John, for whose education he had provided and who had come out to India in search of employment, died suddenly, and in the following year his two little daughters died of small-pox within a few days of each other. These domestic afflictions had an immediate effect on the ambitious young Secretary, who regarded them as divine punishments for his past ungodly life. Henceforth he lived as a sincere and devout Christian, whose chief consolations were the reading of noble books and the company of pious friends. At this period began his lifelong friendship with John Shore—afterwards Lord Teignmouth—and William Chambers, a learned judge and intimate friend of Frederick Schwartz. Grant himself never met the great Danish missionary, but he was so impressed by what he had heard about his evangelical and social work in the south that he corresponded with him concerning a scheme to promote Christianity in Bengal.

In spite of the fact that he had incurred heavy debts and that the commercial ventures in which he had become lawfully engaged had proved unsuccessful, he never yielded to the temptation which few of his colleagues were able to resist—the making of money by dishonest means. A temporary loan from his brother Robert, who was now in the employment of the Nawab of Oudh, and a more simple and economical style of living helped him to tide over a difficult period. He threw himself more whole-heartedly than ever into his official work, and his efficiency soon attracted the notice of the higher authorities. In 1780 he was specially selected for the very responsible post of Commercial Resident at Malda, where the Company controlled a flourishing silk factory. For six years he remained head of one of the most fertile districts in Bengal, and these years were probably the happiest of his whole life—certainly the happiest of his career in India. One daughter and two sons were born at Malda. The elder son, Charles, eventually became Secretary of State and was raised to the peerage as Lord Glenelg; the younger, Robert, became Governor of Bombay (1835), but is probably better known as the writer of several well-known hymns; he was also the author of *A Sketch of the History of the East India Company* (1813).

At Malda, Grant was not only the administrative head of a large district but was also the owner of an indigo factory at Gumalti, which prospered exceedingly. Indeed, his private means were accumulating so rapidly that he became alarmed and conscience-stricken. In consequence, when Lord Cornwallis, who had determined to stamp out the peculation and dishonesty which were a disgrace to the Service, asked for his official accounts to be sent to Calcutta for audit, Grant requested that his private accounts should also be subjected to the most careful scrutiny. The Governor-General was more than satisfied with Grant's integrity and declared that he was the only member of the Service who did not deserve to be prosecuted for peculation. Indeed, Cornwallis was so impressed that he promoted the Commercial Resident to be Member of the Board of Trade. In spite of his arduous and responsible official duties, Grant took a very prominent part in various philanthropic movements, particularly those which aimed at the spread of Christianity which, according to Dr Smith,[1] was

---

[1] G. Smith, *Twelve Indian Statesmen* (1898), p. 13.

then almost dead even 'among the baptized residents of Calcutta'. This manifestation of evangelical zeal was nothing new, for in Malda he had founded a mission for the benefit of the workers in his indigo factory and others in the neighbourhood of Gumalti. Unfortunately, the engagement as head of the mission of Dr Thomas, a ship's surgeon, was not a success; he was not suited to the life of a missionary, and owing to his unstable ways and foolish speculations Grant had to dispense with his services. The mission scheme, which had cost the Commercial Resident over £1,000, had to be abandoned.

Shortly after his arrival in Calcutta Grant learned that Kiernander, a Danish missionary, who had built at his own expense an imposing church, had (through his own generosity and the folly of his son) become bankrupt and that, to defray his debts, the 'House of Prayer' was to be put up for sale. Grant generously came forward and paid £1,000 to rescue the church, which was handed over to Chambers, the Rev. David Brown and himself in trust for the S.P.C.K. Even before his transfer to Calcutta he had been associated with Chambers and Brown in the preparation of 'A Proposal for Establishing a Protestant Mission in Bengal and Behar', in which it 'was urged that the people of India had a claim on the British Government, and that it was the duty of Englishmen to impart to them the civil and religious privileges which they themselves enjoyed'.[1] It was proposed that eight young clergymen—one for each Division of the Province— should be sent out from England to start schools, found churches and translate the Scriptures. Influential persons, including the Archbishop of Canterbury and Frederick Schwartz, were approached, but the Directors expressed their unwillingness to countenance any such scheme and so it had to be dropped. Although not fruitful of any immediate results, this project was not an entire failure and to it may be attributed the establishment of the Church Missionary Society (1799), of which Grant was a founder and original member.

In the meantime Grant was beginning to feel the strain of overwork and an enervating climate, and his wife's health was causing him much anxiety. He realized that it was his duty to take his family home, but at the personal request of Lord Corn-

[1] H. Morris, *Heroes of Our Indian Empire* (1908), p. 23.

wallis he delayed his departure longer than he had originally intended. Eventually he sailed for England in July 1790 and the Governor-General wrote to Henry Dundas, President of the Board of Control, that his loss to the Commercial Department was irreparable. 'I need not repeat', he continued, 'how much I am personally obliged to him, or how much the East India Company and his country are indebted to his zealous services and superior abilities. I beg you for my sake to receive him with all possible kindness, and I should recommend you for your own to converse with him frequently upon every part of the business of this country.'[1] It is obvious that had he remained in India a little longer it would have been to his personal advantage, but he rightly considered that his obligations to his family were more important than his own advancement in the public service. Besides, he had acquired a competence which was more than sufficient for the education of his children and the maintenance of a quiet and simple home.

Having visited his relatives in Scotland, he settled down in Bloomsbury. In 1794 he moved to Clapham and became the intimate friend of Wilberforce, Thornton and other members of the 'Clapham Sect'. Some years previously he had corresponded with Wilberforce regarding his scheme for a mission in Bengal and there is ample evidence that Grant's enthusiasm for the evangelization of India made a deep impression on the Emancipator. The retired civilian had spent the greater part of the year 1792 in writing a remarkable pamphlet, to which he gave the clumsy title of *Observations on the State of Society among the Asiatic Subjects of Great Britain, particularly with respect to Morals; and the Means of Improving It*. This remained in manuscript for a considerable time and was shown only to a few intimate friends. In the following year the question of the renewal of the Company's Charter came up for consideration and Wilberforce strongly supported the inclusion of the 'pious clauses', which appear to have been drafted by Grant. He was particularly anxious that in the new Charter provision should be made for sending out missionaries and schoolmasters to India, but the opposition proved too strong and the 'pious clauses' were eventually rejected. Thereupon, Grant decided to seek election to the Board and he became a Director in 1797. In the same year, having completed the revision

[1] ibid., p. 27.

of his *Observations*, he modestly laid them before the Board 'as one of those many papers of business with which the records of your Governments have been furnished by the observations and experience of men whose time and thought have been chiefly employed in the concerns of active life'. (Introductory letter to the Honourable the Court of Directors.)   So little notice was taken of this document that 'it soon lay forgotten in the dusty archives of the Company'.[1] In 1813, however, when the battle over the Company's Charter broke out again, Parliament ordered Grant's essay to be printed and there can be little doubt that it was largely instrumental in convincing advanced opinion, both inside and outside Parliament, of the Government's duty to make some provision for the enlightenment of the people of India.

Meanwhile, Grant had thrown all his energies into his work at the India House. He soon became, in the words of Sir John Kaye,[2] 'not a Director, but the Direction', or, to quote Sir James Stephen,[3] 'the real ruler of the rulers of the East'.   In 1805 he was elected Chairman of the Honourable Board of Directors, an office which he also held in 1809 and 1815. He became Member of Parliament for Inverness borough in 1802, and represented the county from 1804 to 1818.   In the House of Commons he spoke with first-hand knowledge, if not with eloquence, on Indian topics such as Wellesley's policy, the deposition of the Nawab of the Carnatic, the Vellore mutiny and the freedom of the press. He was also mainly responsible for the establishment of the East India Company's college at Haileybury (1805).   The subject nearest to his heart, however, was the evangelization of India and he interested himself particularly in the work of various religious societies.   After an active public life lasting for more than 50 years, he retired from Parliament in 1818 and enjoyed a well-earned rest until his death in 1823.

This very bald summary of his career does nothing like justice to the memory of one of the noblest and ablest statesmen, who, as a servant of the Company, a chairman of its Board of Directors, and a Member of Parliament, laboured incessantly for the good of India.   He helped to mitigate the horrors of one of the greatest

---

[1] J. Richter, *A History of Missions in India* (1908), p. 146.

[2] J. W. Kaye, *The Administration of the East India Company* (1853), p. 632.

[3] Sir James Stephen, *Essays in Ecclesiastical Biography* (1849), II, p. 334.

famines on record, and, in an age of corruption, he set an example
of financial honesty which has few parallels. He befriended
missionaries such as Kiernander in Calcutta and Carey in Serampore, he sent out to India evangelical chaplains and helped to
found the Church Missionary and the Bible Societies. He fought
together with Wilberforce and Thornton for the freedom of the
African slave,[1] and from him Wilberforce derived the impulse
and the enthusiasm which won the first battles for religious
toleration in the Company's Charters of 1793 and 1813. His
Observations is a remarkable treatise on the social and moral
conditions of eighteenth-century India, but, like its author, has
been almost, if not entirely, forgotten. Merely as an educational
document it is of first-rate importance, and its historical position and
novel proposals entitle it to more careful consideration than
historians of Indian education have usually given to one of the
most valuable records of its time.

The treatise, which is divided into four chapters, opens with
the following words: 'Whatever difference of opinion may have
prevailed respecting the past conduct of the English in the East,
all parties will concur in one sentiment, that we ought to study
the happiness of the vast body of subjects which we have acquired
there. Upon this proposition, taken as a truth of the highest
certainty, the following observations are founded.' Grant's
sincerity is beyond question; and even those who may be inclined
to disagree with much that follows, must admit that the pamphlet
is written with the sole object of promoting the happiness and
prosperity of India.

The first chapter is a brief, and not very satisfactory, review of
the administration of the East India Company. In the second
chapter he paints a very lurid picture of the dreadful moral
conditions of Indian life, and gives reasons for his conviction that
Indians 'exhibit human nature in a very degraded, humiliating
state and are at once objects of dis-esteem and commiseration'. To
the Hindus he attributes a long list of vices, including lying and
perjury, avarice and cunning, cruelty and disloyalty, and many
others. The Mohammedans are described as proud and treacherous,
bigoted and superstitious, blood-thirsty, and sensual. 'Upon the
whole', he concludes, 'we cannot help recognising in the people

[1] R. Coupland, *Wilberforce–A Narrative* (1923), passim.

of Hindoostan, a race of men lamentably degenerate and base, retaining but a feeble sense of moral obligation . . . governed by their malevolent and licentious passions . . . and sunk in misery by their vices.' Grant's estimate of the morals of the Indians of his day is no more trustworthy than Miss Mayo's distorted view of modern India,[1] and he certainly was not justified in making such a sweeping condemnation of the moral tone of a whole people.

In his defence, however, certain allowances must be made: in the first place, there is ample testimony that, following on the break-up of the Mogul empire, India went through a period of lawlessness and anarchy which was marked by a moral and social degradation unparalleled in her long history; secondly, Grant was influenced by the evangelical and humanitarian movements of his time, and his object was to arouse the sympathies of generous-minded Englishmen and to induce Parliament and the Directors to improve and uplift an ignorant and unfortunate people; he was actuated by the highest and most philanthropic motives, and wrote 'not to excite detestation, but to engage compassion, and make it apparent that, what speculation may have ascribed to physical and unchangeable causes, springs from moral sources capable of correction'.

In the third chapter he argues that the causes of the demoralization which he has described may be attributed to the prevalence of degraded forms of religion and the influence of unscrupulous priests. It is the last chapter, however, which forms the most important section of this remarkable pamphlet. Herein Grant anticipates with uncanny foresight many of the great educational —and not a few of the political—reforms which have since been introduced. In the course of less than 40 pages he points out the remedies which should be adopted to relieve the deplorable social and moral conditions which hamper the progress and prosperity of a people whose best interests he has at heart. The conclusion at which he eventually arrives may be stated in a few words: evils which are due to ignorance and superstition can most easily be eradicated by the promotion of knowledge—by the establishment of a sound system of education; to quote his own words, 'the true cure of darkness is the introduction of light'.

Taking this as his text he goes on to consider the best method

[1] Katherine Mayo, *Mother India* (1927).

of spreading enlightenment, whether through the medium of the vernaculars or of English. He examines this problem with the thoroughness of an expert, and, although he is reluctant 'to pass an exclusive decision', he mentions various reasons which incline him to give the preference to English. He argues that the English have long been settled in India and that the people have already acquired considerable familiarity with their language; that, as the Mohammedans employed Persian, so should the English employ their own language in the affairs of the Government—a policy which would be welcomed by Indians themselves as a means of bringing them into closer contact with their new rulers; that the Government should patronize English education by starting *free* schools in various important centres which would attract 'multitudes, especially of the young'; that within a short time Indians themselves would be qualified to teach English, and, therefore, a knowledge of the language would quickly be disseminated; that suitable school books could easily be *printed* and made available in large and ever-increasing numbers. He willingly concedes that instruction through the vernaculars would have certain obvious advantages, but the poverty of 'the languages of the country', the dearth of suitable material for textbooks, the difficulty of printing strange scripts, and the scarcity of qualified teachers seemed to him to be serious, if not insurmountable, obstacles. However desirable in theory instruction through the vernaculars might be, he claims that it would be ineffectual in practice. Convinced as he is that the arguments in favour of English are overwhelming, he is ready to concede that vernacular education would be preferable to no education at all. His main contention is that knowledge must be imparted, and he is careful to emphasize that 'the *principle* of communicating our light and the *channel* or *mode* of communication were two distinct things; that the admission of the former did not depend on the choice which might be made of the latter'. Although 'the channel of the English language has been preferred, being deemed most ample and effectual', he considers that 'the channel of the country languages though less spacious, less clear, less calculated to express the light of our opinions, our arts and sciences' is the only other means by which ignorance can be banished from the land. For reasons which will presently appear, Grant did not consider the possibility of employing the classical languages for educational purposes.

Having proved to his own satisfaction that education must be imparted to the people of India and that English was by far the most suitable medium of instruction, Grant points out the advantages which must inevitably follow. English literature would be a key which would open to Indians a world of new ideas; a knowledge of natural and mechanical science would help them to build up their manufactures and improve the arts of life; the use of machinery would revolutionize old-fashioned methods of agriculture and increase the wealth and comforts of the peasants; and, above all, Christianity would banish idolatry and superstition and bring happiness and good-will to millions of wretched and priest-ridden people. It is no exaggeration to say that Grant considered that the most precious gift which England could bestow on India was a knowledge of the Christian religion, 'completely contained in the inestimable volume of Scripture'. He believed, as fervently as the most zealous missionary, that Christianity was the end of all education and the only adequate means of promoting the well-being and happiness of mankind. 'Do we, then', he pleads, 'wish to correct, to raise, to sweeten the social state of our Indian subjects? Would we, at little cost, impart to them a boon, far, far more valuable than all the advantages we have derived from them? The Gospel brings this within our power. Of the effects which it would produce in civil society we may, in the words of Bishop Horne, say that "in superiors it would be equity and moderation, courtesy and affability, benignity and condescension; in inferiors, sincerity and fidelity, respect and diligence; in subjects, loyalty, submission, obedience, quietness, peace, patience and cheerfulness; in all men, upon all occasions, a readiness to assist, relieve and comfort one another—whatsoever, in a word, that is pure, lovely, and good". And is this the religion we hesitate to communicate to those whose welfare it is alike our duty and our interest to consult?'

In many respects Grant foresaw, with remarkable insight, the course which educational development in India was to take, but his confident expectation that Indians had only to hear the Gospel message to embrace Christianity has not been realized. The edifice which has been raised on the foundations which he helped to lay would be as disappointing to Grant as to Schwartz, Carey or Duff. The policy of religious neutrality, which was adopted by the Government in Grant's lifetime and which is still followed, has resulted in a purely secular educational system for India. In the opinion of some, this in itself is an excellent thing, while others consider that education divorced from religion is not only inherently defective, but is a dangerous social experiment. However this may be, Grant is the forerunner of Duff, Wilson and other notable missionaries who have influenced in no small measure the development of education in India, but who accepted, as an obvious and fundamental principle, the postulate that English education and Christianity were complementary, if not identical.

It is true that his proposals for educational advancement are in many respects extreme and that they go far beyond anything contemplated by subsequent reformers such as Ram Mohun Roy, Duff or even Macaulay. Grant appears to have looked forward to the day when English would take the place of the vernaculars as the common language of the people and when Christianity would supplant Hinduism, Mohammedanism and other indigenous forms of religion. His ultimate aim seems to have been the establishment of a universal system of education, and so he did not give any serious consideration to the claims of the classical languages—Sanskrit and Arabic—which Hastings and others were anxious to encourage in order to conciliate the higher classes and to attract young men of good position to the ranks of Government service. On the other hand, he failed to realize the possibility of developing the vernaculars, which was the policy advocated, even during his own lifetime, by missionaries and social reformers. It seemed to him very obvious that modern English education would confer great benefits on India but, like many people of his day, he did not conceive it possible that increased knowledge could fail to bring about the conversion to Christianity of the followers of other faiths. Grant's argument that the spread of education would eventually better the financial interests of the Company did not appeal to the Court of Directors, who regarded his scheme for English education as fantastic and his proposals to spread Christianity in India as positively dangerous.

When, in 1793, the question of the renewal of the Company's Charter came up for decision and it became known that Wilberforce was going to propose the inclusion of a clause to the effect that it was the peculiar and bounden duty of the British legislature to promote the interest and happiness of the inhabitants of India, their advancement in useful knowledge and their religious and moral improvement, the Directors became alarmed and hastened to consult a number of prominent Anglo-Indians, who had passed the best part of their lives in India.   They were hastily summoned to Leadenhall Street and the various arguments which they advanced against the inclusion of 'the pious clauses' made a considerable impression on the anxious and bewildered Directors.[1] Mr Lushington, who had come home with a large fortune, argued that the proposal to send out missionaries and schoolmasters, whom he styled 'adventurers', was so dangerous that it was calculated to upset the peace and security of India; Mr Henchman said that only the very dregs of society—men who cared not what religion they accepted, provided it served their passing interests—would be converted and that, therefore, Christianity would be brought into contempt; Mr Randle Jackson expressed the extraordinary view that the secession of the American Colonies was due to the fact that England had been foolish enough to establish schools and colleges in different provinces and he warned the Directors 'to avoid and steer clear of the rock we had split on in America'. Lastly, Mr Prinsep urged that the whole scheme was 'idle, absurd and impracticable'.   It did not take much persuasion to convince the Directors[2] that 'the Hindus had as good a system of faith and of morals as most people' and they readily accepted the almost unanimous opinion of officials in India 'that it would be madness to attempt their conversion or to give them any more learning or any other description of learning than what they already possessed'. As regards Mohammedans it was believed that no more should be done than to 'endeavour to conciliate their confidence and to mitigate their vindictive spirit'.   It is not surprising that the Directors passed a resolution condemning the clause and those who were Members of Parliament were asked to appear in the House and vote against it.

When the Bill came up for its final reading Wilberforce moved

---

[1] For fuller details see (a) Kaye, *Christianity in India* (1859) ; (b) Marshman, *Life and Times of Carey, Marshman and Ward* (1859), I ; (c) Mayhew, *Christianity and the Government of India* (1929).

[2] H. Sharp, *Educational Records* (1920), p. 17; also, Kaye, *Administration of the East India Company*, p. 635.

that the Court of Directors should be empowered to nominate and send out to India from time to time a sufficient number of skilled and suitable missionaries and schoolmasters to spread secular knowledge and true religion in India. Dundas paid a compliment to Wilberforce, whose humanity and principles he admired, but said he had difficulties respecting the motion he had brought before the House and doubted whether any plan for conversion would yield fruitful results. Fox urged that all schemes of proselytism were wrong in themselves and productive in most cases of mischief, while the Bishop of St David's questioned the right of any people to send their religion to any other nation! It soon became obvious that the opposition was very strong; and when Dundas gave an assurance that he would call for further information and 'on some future occasion' give the whole matter the consideration which its importance deserved, the clause was reluctantly withdrawn. The triumph of the Directors was a great disappointment to Grant, who had sat through the debate in the Gallery, and to Wilberforce, who wrote in his Journal that Dundas had proved himself 'false and double' and that 'the Bishops, as a body, had given him no support'.

Disappointment, however, did not give way to despair. Grant set himself to work with redoubled energy to bring to fulfilment the consuming passion of his life. He revised his *Observations* and added a powerful note refuting the objections which had recently been advanced against the 'pious clauses'. He found no difficulty in disposing of such specious arguments as (1) that his scheme was idle, visionary or absurd; (2) that an insurmountable obstacle was the fanatical adherence of Hindus to their own religious beliefs and their deep-rooted attachment to age-long customs; (3) the Brahman priests, acting in self-interest, would prevent the introduction of new ideas and ways of life. He made light of objections such as the negligible success which missionaries in the East had so far attained, the official view that the happiness and prosperity of India depended entirely on the enactment and administration of a good system of laws, and the contention that the religion in which a people are born is the one which suits them best. A more formidable objection than any of these was examined in detail—the argument that it would be politically dangerous to introduce English education and the Christian religion. Stated in its 'strongest and amplest terms', says Grant, it may be thus expressed: 'If the English language, if English opinions, and improvements, are introduced in our Asiatic possessions, into Bengal, for example; if Christianity, especially, is introduced in that quarter; and if, together with these changes, many Englishmen colonise there, will not the people learn to desire English liberty and the English form of Government, a share in the legislation of their own country, and commissions in the army maintained in that country?   Will not the army thence become, in time, wholly provincial, officered by natives of India, without attachment to the Sovereign State?   Will not the people at last come to think it a hardship to be subject, and to pay tribute, to a foreign country?   And finally, will they not cast off that subjection, and assert their independence?'

This is the only objection which he considers to have any weight, but he argues that the principle of keeping the people of India for ever in darkness and error, lest English commercial interests should suffer, can be shown to be not only morally inadmissible but, also, contrary to all just policy. He contends that the transfer of military and administrative appointments and the establishment of a free political constitution do not necessarily depend upon the acceptance of Christianity; that there is no analogy to be drawn between recent happenings in the American Colonies and the probable course of events in India; that we should follow the example of the Romans, who civilized and improved the nations they subdued, rather than the example of the Mohammedans, Portuguese, Dutch and French, who produced no change in the character of a people whose welfare they never had at heart. He urges that it would be odious and immoral, owing to unfounded apprehensions of danger to British rule, wilfully to keep India in ignorance, and endeavours to convince his readers that the enlightenment of India will bring with it higher standards of living and increased wealth, with the result that the expansion of British commerce and the attachment of Asiatic subjects must inevitably ensue. He concludes with these remarkable words: 'In success would lie safety, not our danger. Our danger must lie in pursuing, from ungenerous ends, a course contracted and illiberal; but in following an opposite course, in communicating light, knowledge, and improvement, we shall obey the dictates of duty, of philanthropy, and of policy; we shall take the most rational means to remove inherent, great disorders, to attach the Hindoo people to ourselves, to ensure the safety of our possessions, to enhance continually their value to us, to raise a fair and durable monument to the glory of this country, and to increase the happiness of the human race.' It is difficult to realize that these words were written nearly a century and a half ago. Grant's fervour made a deep impression on Wilberforce and other members of the 'Clapham Sect', but the Directors had yet to be convinced that his scheme was practicable and that it would insure an extension of trade and, therefore, increased profits. In order to strengthen his position he agreed to offer himself as a candidate for the Company's Directorate and was elected without opposition; a few years later he extended his influence by becoming a member of Parliament.

In spite of his arduous work in Leadenhall Street and at Westminster, he identified himself with various schemes for the promotion of missionary enterprise and took a prominent part in the foundation of the Church Missionary Society (1799) and the British and Foreign Bible Society (1804). All this time he continued to fight shoulder to shoulder with Wilberforce in his campaign against slavery. The abolition of the Slave Trade (1807) is generally regarded as one of the most striking expressions of the enlightened spirit of the age. To Grant and other members of the 'Clapham Sect' it was particularly significant in that it marked the emergence of a new attitude towards backward peoples—a recognition by the British public that ruthless exploitation would no longer be tolerated. Equally important, from Grant's point of view, was the growing interest in the education of the masses. The efforts of Bell and Lancaster to grapple with this problem attracted considerable attention, and the establishment of the British and Foreign Schools Society (1805) and of the National Society (1811) did much to arouse enthusiasm for the spread of education among the poor. Of the many and varied humanitarian and philanthropic movements of the day, the agitation for the abolition of slavery, the rise of the great missionary societies and the beginnings of popular education received so much warm-hearted public support that Grant became optimistic about the ultimate success of his endeavours to win religious toleration and enlightenment for India. Religious leaders, both Anglican and Non-conformist, responded to his call, and before the question of the renewal of the Company's Charter came up again for discussion (1813) nearly 900 petitions on behalf of the missionaries had been placed on the table of the House of Commons. The awakening of the national conscience had manifested itself in many directions, and it was clear to Wilberforce and Grant that it was the desire of the people of England to alleviate the miseries of their fellow men abroad as well as at home.

Hardly less significant were certain events which were taking place in India about this time. Acting on Grant's advice, Carey sought refuge (1800) under the Danish flag at Serampore and, in association with his gifted colleagues Marshman and Ward, opened schools for Indian and Anglo-Indian children which grew rapidly in numbers and popularity. Schwartz's schools continued to flourish in the south, where there was also a marked extension of missionary enterprise. In 1811 Lord Minto wrote a memorable Minute[1] on the lamentable decay of learning among both Hindus and Mohammedans, and his proposal to incur additional expenditure on the promotion of education doubtless gave the Board of Directors much food for anxious thought. Indeed, it is far from unlikely that this Minute suggested an easy way out of the difficult situation in which they found themselves in less than two years' time: instead of spending money on English education—the dream of a visionary—or on the promotion of Christianity—a dangerous experiment—why not (they probably argued) conciliate Indian opinion and attract efficient recruits to the public services by accepting the Governor-General's more or less sensible proposals? These, incidentally, were based on the recommendations of Cole-brooke, who was himself a profound Sanskrit scholar and President of the Asiatic Society of Bengal from 1807 to 1814.

Encouraged by the change of feeling at home and of hopeful news from India, Wilberforce and Grant had every reason for perseverance. The opposition had not been idle, and retired Indian officials were enlisted to enlarge upon the dangers of 'the most wild, extravagant, expensive and unjustifiable scheme that was ever suggested by the most visionary speculator'. The mutiny at Vellore (1806) gave the secular party a convenient handle, and

[1] Sharp, op. cit., pp. 19-21.

the blame for this unfortunate episode was attributed to missionary activity and not to the stupid orders of the commander-in-chief about dress and sectarian marks.[1] Sydney Smith[2] entered into the fray and his articles in the *Edinburgh Review* held up to ridicule the enthusiasm of 'itinerant tinkers', 'consecrated cobblers' and 'visionary anabaptists'. His flippant treatment of missionary zeal gave considerable offence to Anglicans as well as to Nonconformists, and called forth a reply from Southey in one of the earliest issues of the *Quarterly* (1809). The future laureate exploded, in a cold but closely reasoned article, the suggestion of a fanatical uprising in India and showed that within a few years the Serampore missionaries—those low-born and low-bred mechanics—had done more to spread a knowledge of Christianity in the East than had been 'accomplished, or even attempted by all the world's princes and potentates and all its universities and establishments into the bargain'. How far Southey's championship was inspired by mere hatred of Sydney Smith or how far it was the product of genuine piety is, as Mr Mayhew[3] points out, not very easy to determine. It is quite clear, however, that the periodical press as a whole did not lend much support to the missionary cause; its opposition may have fortified the Directors and secularists in their obstinacy, and it certainly served as a warning to the evangelical leaders, who made most careful preparations for the debate on Indian policy which began in the House of Commons in March 1813. Wilberforce was the life and soul of the missionary party and his right-hand man was Grant.

It is unnecessary to follow in detail the lively proceedings which marked the passage through the House of Commons of the bill for the renewal of the Charter. The Directors had determined to resist any innovation, whether commercial, political or religious. They petitioned Parliament for leave to bring forward witnesses to support their claims that the changes contemplated by the Ministry would result in bankruptcy and would demolish the

[1] Vincent H. Smith, *Oxford History of India* (1919), p. 610.

[2] Sydney Smith, *Essays Social and Political* (Ward Lock & Co).

[3] A. Mayhew, op. cit. (1929), p. 95. It is interesting to note that another man of letters, John Foster ('the essayist') came to Southey's support. His best known work, *Essay on the Evils of Popular Ignorance* (1819), is a plea for national education.

whole fabric of government. After some discussion it was agreed that fuller information on the subject of India would be acceptable to all parties and the House resolved itself into a Committee to hear evidence. 'The records of that Committee present an entertaining picture of petitions from evangelical unions and counter petitions from mercantile associations, of heterogeneous witnesses, ex-Governors-General, missionaries, military heroes and collectors of Bogglywallah, herded together in the waiting-room.'[1] In the debates which followed the extremely able, but somewhat truculent speeches of Marsh and Prendergast proved no match for the fervour and eloquence of Wilberforce and Wellesley. Eventually Parliament approved the following important changes in the new Charter: (1) the abolition of the Company's monopoly in Indian trade, which was thrown open to all and sundry; (2) the setting up of an ecclesiastical establishment consisting of one bishop and three archdeacons—to meet the spiritual needs of Europeans in India; (3) the granting of licences to missionaries and others to reside and work in British teritories; (4) the allotment of a small grant for public instruction. Subject to these, and a few less important provisions, the Charter was renewed for a further period of twenty years.

In Parliament Wilberforce was the chief spokesman of the missionary party and his was the name which commanded the greatest respect throughout the country. Of the righteousness of his cause he had no doubt; indeed, he was of opinion that the Directors' 'distinct partiality for paganism' was, after the Slave Trade, 'England's greatest national sin'. 'This is indeed a cause', runs an entry in his Diary, 'for which it is worth while being a public man.' As leader of his party he displayed marked ability and tact, and his speeches on 'the pious clauses' made a profound impression on the House. A less spectacular, but hardly a less important, part was played by Grant, who was the most influential and best informed of the members of his small 'Privy Council', which also included Thornton, Stephen and Babington.

Grant did not take any considerable part in the debates on the 'pious clauses' and the explanation is quite simple. As a member of the Board of Directors and as a private Member of Parliament his position was extremely awkward. Further, although in many

[1] A. Mayhew, op. cit., p. 99.

respects he was a man of liberal and enlightened views, he considered that the abolition of the Company's monopoly in Indian trade
was certain to bring disaster to India no less than England.   For
philanthropic, as well as patriotic, motives he defended with
firmness and courtesy the commercial privileges of the Company.
During the discussions and debates on this subject he was not once
absent from the House and he spoke no less than sixteen times.
If he was mistaken—as assuredly he was—he erred in very
distinguished company, which included such able administrators
as Munro, Malcolm and Wellesley, and members of the 'Clapham
Sect' such as Thornton and Teignmouth, men whose advocacy
was entirely disinterested, who had no axe to grind, no private
interests at stake.   Notwithstanding their powerful opposition,
Parliament wisely and resolutely rejected the commercial claims of
the Directors and accepted the proposal of Lord Grenville to end
once and for all the Company's monopoly in Indian trade.

Nothing daunted by this setback, Grant turned his attention
to the subject of India's spiritual welfare, which he considered of
much more importance than questions of mere commercial policy.
It would have been difficult for him, as a private member, to oppose
in open Parliament his colleagues in the Directorate.   He was,
therefore, justified in leaving Wilberforce to pilot through the
Commons the resolutions which were calculated to further India's
moral advancement.   The first of these contained a proposal to
sanction the setting up of a small ecclesiastical establishment to
superintend the work of chaplains in the various settlements; Lord
Castlereagh declared that 'even for the sake of decency' some such
provision was necessary and no very serious opposition was
encountered.   Methodists and other Nonconformists supported the
resolution to give the Church of England an official footing in
India on the grounds that this was the first indication that a
Christian Government was no longer ashamed openly to acknowledge its adherence to its own faith.   Many of the Directors, however, seemed to think that the appointment of a bishop would be
regarded in India as a breach of their declared policy of strict
religious neutrality.   Lord Teignmouth probably caused a flutter
in ecclesiastical circles when he assured the House that the arrival
of a bishop in Calcutta ' would be viewed with perfect indifference'.
Wilberforce made it quite clear that the bishop was not to be made

in any way responsible for missionary activity and that his work would not have the slightest association with schemes for conversion. The ecclesiastical establishment was intended to be merely an outward and visible sign that a Christian Government 'intended to provide in a dignified manner for the more appropriate exercise of the religion it professed'. These assurances, coupled with the taunt that Christianity was the only religion which was not tolerated in India, left the opposition with very little to say and the first of the 'pious clauses' was passed without a division.

It may be added that the fears of the Directors soon proved to be groundless. In the following year, Dr Middleton, the first Indian bishop, arrived in Calcutta and 'there was no commotion, no excitement. . . . Offended Hinduism did not start up in arms; no indignant Mohammedan raised a cry of death to the infidel. . . . Everything went on according to wonted custom'.[1] Officials on the spot were relieved, and congratulated the authorities at home on their choice of a safe man. Middleton's subsequent episcopal career confirmed their sense of security. He was greatly impressed by the dignity and importance of his position, and had 'a decided taste for military salutes and struggled manfully for social precedence'.[2] The ceremonials belonging to his office were all the more warmly observed because the bishop made it quite plain that he would have nothing whatever to do with the making of converts. Missionaries and Nonconformist[3] clergymen appear to have irritated the bishop more than either Brahmans or prickly-heat, and on one occasion he talked of silencing altogether the missionary clergy. When news of the bishop's shortcomings reached England, Grant wrote out and gently reminded him of the supreme importance of missionary enterprise; he recalled the fruitful labours of 'the most excellent Schwartz', brought to his notice the regulation of King William (1698), which had never been repealed, that chaplains should instruct the heathen in the Protestant religion. The worthy prelate took not the slightest notice and did not even trouble to reply. It was little wonder that

[1] Kaye, op. cit., p. 290.

[2] ibid., p. 313; the author admits that he was not 'among the most ardent admirers' of Dr Middleton.

[3] vide J. Bryce, A Sketch of Native Education in India (1839), passim.

the worst apprehensions of the Directors were quickly allayed and that they reproached themselves for having conjured up in their fevered imaginations so many gloomy forebodings.

They had much more reason for alarm when it was proposed in Parliament that missionaries should be licensed to work in India. The second of the 'pious clauses' was in substance very similar to the resolution which had been rejected in 1793. It ran: 'That it is the opinion of this Committee that it is the duty of this country to promote the interest and happiness of the British Dominions in India, and such measures ought to be adopted as may tend to the introduction among them of useful knowledge and of religious and moral improvement. That in furtherance of the above objects sufficient facilities should be afforded by law to persons desirous of going to and remaining in India for the purpose of accomplishing these benevolent designs.' Grant and Wilberforce had learned by experience and disappointment, and when redrafting their resolution they were careful to omit any particular reference to missionaries (as apart from other philanthropists) and to avoid any suggestion of Government patronage or maintenance. The purport of the resolution was quite obvious and the chief interest in the debates on the renewal of the Charter centred round the proposal to extend religious toleration and to give missionaries free access to India. The strength of public opinion had already forced Parliament to extend to private merchants commercial privileges which had hitherto been the monopoly of the Company; they could hardly have consistently refused the grant of similar privileges to those who sought permission to work, not for material gain, but for the moral and spiritual welfare of a backward people. In spite of the very determined opposition of the 'die-hards', who argued that the misguided activities of 'apostates from the loom and the anvil' would endanger the security of the Empire, the second of the 'pious clauses' was passed by a comfortable majority. Henceforward, Christian workers were free to enter India and prosecute their legitimate labours without let or hindrance. They might preach, found churches, build schools—plant the seeds of Western civilization and advocate the principles of Christianity. These concessions 'were wrung from the Company after the most violent opposition and the most furious conflict'. As Marshman[1] points

[1] Marshman, op. cit., II, p. 45.

out, commerce had, for once, become 'the handmaid of religions' and the gates of India were thrown open to English goods and the truths of the Bible.

The last of the important changes in the new Charter was embodied in the section which sanctioned the annual expenditure —out of surplus revenues—of not less than one lakh of rupees for 'the revival and improvement of literature and the encouragement of the learned natives of India', and for 'the introduction and promotion of a knowledge of the sciences'. This clause marks an epoch in educational history, because it contains 'the first legislative admission of the right of education in India to participate in the public revenues'.[1] It is significant that at this time very few European countries recognized any governmental responsibility for education, which was largely controlled by the churches; in England itself the first government grant was not given until 1833 and then it was paid to two great religious societies which were mainly interested in the education of the poor. Again, the long and intimate association between religion and education made the Directors apprehensive, and the fear of propagandism seems to have been painfully present to their minds. Had not Grant himself in his *Observations* argued that a sound system of education must inevitably result in the overthrow of superstition and the acceptance of Christianity? They had every reason for anxiety and were quite justified in urging the cautious consideration of the issues involved. The educational resolution which was finally approved by Parliament was something in the nature of a compromise. It is very unlikely that the leaders of either party realized that they were laying the foundation of the grant-in-aid system, by which even missionary institutions were subsequently to benefit. It is quite certain that neither Grant nor Wilberforce foresaw that a resolution which derived its first impulse from religious fervour would ultimately prove to be the basis of a secular system of education for the whole of India.

The actual wording of the educational clause was extremely vague and, even now, it is difficult to say with certainty what were the real wishes of Parliament. It is clear, however, that the grant was intended for the promotion of *higher* education; the Directors, at any rate, were more interested in providing facilities

[1] Sharp, op. cit., p. 18. cf. Howell, op. cit., p. 13.

for the training of Indians for Government service than in
financing wild schemes for mass education, which no party in the
House would have regarded as a legitimate charge on public
revenues. It is equally certain that no one had the least intention
of giving financial assistance to the schools attached to temples and
mosques in the Indian towns and villages. It seems obvious that
the words 'the revival and encouragement of literature' and 'the
encouragement of the learned natives of India' indicated the
promotion of Oriental learning, which—as Lord Minto had
warned the Directors a year or two previously—had fallen into a
sad state of decay. On the other hand, the reference to 'the
promotion of a knowledge of the sciences' would appear to indicate
a desire to introduce and encourage Western learning. Grant, it
will be remembered, had stressed the benefits which would accrue
to India from the acquisition of modern scientific knowledge.
Lastly, the provision of a 'sum of not less than one lakh of rupees'
was so indefinite that it might mean anything. It was probably
accepted by the Directors on the assumption that it 'was not large
enough to produce any dangerously far-reaching results'.[1]
Wilberforce and Grant appear to have been content that Parliament
should endorse the principle embodied in this resolution—acceptance by the Government of responsibility for the enlightenment
of India—and education divorced from religion was to them
inconceivable. In the circumstances, the resolution was passed
without very much difficulty and on the moral and religious issues
which had caused such a stir the victory of the Evangelicals was
complete.

Some historians have held that the educational clause was
inserted by the opponents of missions. Marshman argues that the
grant was made for the promotion of Hindu learning and was
approved by the Directors only because it was to be paid out of any
surplus revenues which might remain over from ordinary
expenditure—'always a most improbable contingency'.[2] Richter's
reasoning is rather more subtle: 'by fostering oriental and occidental
science they hoped to create a reliable counterpoise, a protecting
backwater, against the threatened deluge of missionary enterprise'.[3]
The chief grounds for these specious arguments appear to be

[1] Mayhew, op. cit., p. 10.   [2] Marshman, op. cit., p. 51.
[3] Richter, op. cit., p. 152.

(1) that the clause was supported by the Earl of Buckinghamshire, who is supposed to have been influenced by a few retired officials whose enthusiam for Sanskrit was pronounced; (2) that the resolution was moved in the House by R. P. Smith (Sydney's brother 'Bobus'), who had formerly been Advocate-General in Bengal and whose antipathy to missionaries was well known. The truth of these facts is beyond any question, but the interpretations which have just been given are biased and wide of the mark; even if they were true the foundation of public instruction in India would still be due to Grant and Wilberforce.

Whatever may have been the wishes of Parliament—and Members seem to have had no very clear ideas on the subject of Indian education—the fact remains that this resolution marks the first and, therefore, a very important, step in the adoption of a generous educational policy. It is true that its exact meaning and intention formed the subject of a long and bitter controversy, that the Directors were not a little embarrassed over the disposal of the grant authorized by Parliament, that the pittance voted for the educational advancement of a vast country was misapplied. On the other hand, an impartial survey of the facts makes it quite clear that neither the intentions of the framers of the resolution, nor the wavering of the Directors at home, nor even the apathy of the officials in India, can in any way detract from the valuable services which Grant and Wilberforce rendered to the cause of Indian education. The latter may have played the more prominent and spectacular part in the House of Commons, but Grant, more than anyone else, is entitled to be regarded as the real founder of English education in India.

RAM MOHUN ROY, 1772–1833

THE FATHER OF MODERN INDIA

For every one who has heard of Charles Grant there are thousands who still venerate the memory of Ram Mohun Roy, the great Bengali reformer, the father of modern India. Judged by the most exacting standard he was, as Max Müller says, 'a truly great man, a man who did a truly great work, and whose name, if it is right to prophesy, will be remembered for ever as one of the great benefactors of mankind'.[1] He is, says Farquhar, 'the pioneer of all living advance, religious, social and educational, in the Hindu community during the nineteenth century'.[2] It is regrettable that a biography worthy of his character and achievements has yet to be written in English, and that so much doubt and uncertainty surround even the bare facts of his life.

He was born in Radhanagar, in the District of Hooghly, but the exact year of his birth is not known; some authorities give 1774—the date inscribed on his tomb—while others, including Miss Collett, consider that the evidence for 1772 is convincing. He belonged to an old and respected Brahman family which for many generations 'had given up spiritual exercises for worldly pursuits and aggrandisement' (his own words) and had had a long record of Government service under Mohammedan rule. His parents, however, were deeply religious and, in accordance with the orthodox custom of the day, he was given in marriage at a very tender age. His first bride soon died and his father married him to two other little girls. It is true that the future opponent of polygamy was not then in a position to form any judgement on these proceedings, but the fact remains that until 1824, when his second wife and the mother of his children died, he was a polygamist.

The story of his early life may be quickly told. Having acquired the rudiments of letters, probably at the local *patshala*, he was sent to Patna, one of the chief centres of Mohammedan

---

[1] Max Müller, *Biographical Essays* (1884), p. 29.

[2] J. N. Farquhar, *Modern Religious Movements in India* (1929), p. 29.

RAM MOHUN ROY

learning, where he acquired a sound knowledge of both Persian and Arabic. In those days Persian was still the language of administration, and a knowledge of Mohammedan culture was essential for anyone who aspired to the higher ranks of Government service. On his return home, when he was some sixteen years of age, his parents were amazed at his linguistic and other accomplishments, but shocked to find that his study of Sufi philosophy and of the Koran had undermined his faith in orthodox Hinduism. Unending religious controversy with his father caused much unhappiness and, to save his devout parents further pain, the argumentative but unyielding Ram Mohun decided to leave home. For three or four years he wandered about India studying the social customs and religious beliefs and practices of the people. The story that he penetrated into Tibet, and narrowly escaped death at the hands of some fanatical Buddhist priests, lacks confirmation. Eventually, a reconciliation was effected and he returned to his father's house. But Ram Mohun was more convinced than ever of the truth of the monotheistic doctrines which appealed to him so strongly, and the wrangling over religious issues was quickly renewed. We next hear of him in Benares, engrossed in the study of Sanskrit and seeking to find in certain of the Hindu scriptures confirmation of his own religious views. About the year 1796 he began to learn English, and this led to a close and critical study of the Bible. Not satisfied with the English translation, he subsequently acquired a working knowledge of Hebrew and Greek to enable him to read the Old and New Testaments in their original languages. It must be admitted that his intellectual gifts and his tenacious memory were remarkable; more remarkable still is the fact that as a comparatively young man he had made a first-hand acquaintance with the fundamental tenets of three of the great religions of the world and been influenced by the impact of three different cultures. The depth of his scholarship has been questioned, but none of his contemporaries was so versatile or so well equipped to work for the welfare of India and the betterment of mankind. Monier-Williams claims that he was 'perhaps the first earnest-minded investigator of the science of comparative religion',[1] but his chief claim to remem-

[1] N. Macnicol in his brochure on *Raja Ram Mohan Roy* (1928), p. 11, very rightly says that this is 'a statement which requires qualification'.

brance is the wholesome influence he exercised on various schemes
for the social and educational advancement of his country.

In 1803 his father died and Ram Mohun moved to Murshidabad, the former Mogul capital of Bengal. In the following year
he published a pamphlet, written in Persian with a preface in
Arabic, which caused no little stir in Hindu circles. It contains
a strong but unsystematic denunciation of idolatry, not merely in
Hinduism but in all religions, and is interesting only so far as
it shows the influence of Mohammedanism and philosophic deism
on the development of his religious thought. About this time he
joined the East India Company's service and worked under Mr
John Digby, who befriended him and helped him in his study
of English. He was a born linguist and in a few years was able
to speak and write English with ease and fluency. It is related
that close contact with Englishmen and acquaintance with their
literature broke down certain prejudices which he had formed in
early life and transformed him into a warm-hearted champion of
British rule. His industry and ability were conspicuous and he was
soon promoted to the responsible office of Diwan, which was then
the highest post in the Revenue Department open to Indians.
Meanwhile he continued in his leisure hours his study of the
Hindu, Mohammedan and Christian Scriptures, and often engaged
in lively debates with learned Brahmans on subjects such as
idolatry and widow-burning. In 1811 he witnessed the unwilling
self-sacrifice of his elder brother's unfortunate widow. The sight
of this terrible scene filled him with pity and indignation and, as
Andrews points out,[1] marked a 'turning-point in his religious life'.
He vowed that he would not rest until this atrocious custom were
rooted out and, largely through his influence, suttee was abolished
by Lord William Bentinck in 1829. Having served the Government for about ten years, he retired and settled in Calcutta (1814)
with the fixed object of devoting his time and energy to the
propagation of his religious views; to use his own words, 'he gave
up all worldly avocations and engaged in religious culture and the
investigation of truth'. He had saved enough money to live in
comfort, but there is no reason to believe that he had amassed a
fortune by dishonest means. Had he 'sold justice', as was suggested
as long ago as 1845, he would hardly have retained the confidence

[1] C. F. Andrews, *The Renaissance in India* (1912), p. 108.

of a Collector whose probity was above suspicion.[1] On the other hand, it is not unlikely that certain perquisites appertained to the office of Diwan which would not be tolerated in these days of better administration and more enlightened public opinion.

Freed from the trammels of official duty, Ram Mohun had ample leisure in which to undertake the work for which he had made a long and arduous preparation. Like Charles Grant, he had been forced to the conclusion that ignorance was the root cause of the bigotry, idolatry and superstition which were everywhere to be found. He had long been convinced that Hinduism had degenerated from its pristine purity and that the prevalence of certain doctrines and ceremonies proved conclusively that the majority of Hindus had little or no knowledge of the essential truths of their own religion. He began his work as a reformer by founding in 1814 the *Atmiya Sabha*, or Friendly Society, which lasted only a few years. Between 1816 and 1819 he published in Bengali and English portions of the Vedas and Upanishads which stressed the theistic aspects of Hinduism. These translations and a couple of pamphlets in defence of Hindu theism caused grave anxiety in the ranks of conservative and devout Brahmans; the author had to engage in controversial battles and to defend himself against charges of heresy. Meanwhile, he continued his studies and in 1820 he startled orthodox Christians as well as orthodox Hindus by publishing a very remarkable work called *The Precepts of Jesus, the Guide to Peace and Happiness*. His study of the Bible had led him to believe that the fundamental doctrines of Christianity were not only very similar to those set forth in the Vedas and Upanishads but 'were more conducive to moral principles and better adapted for the use of rational beings than any others which have come to my knowledge'. In the Preface he went so far as to say: 'This simple code of religion and morality is so admirably calculated to elevate men's ideas to high and liberal notions of one God . . . and is also so well fitted to regulate the conduct of the human race in the discharge of their various duties to God, to themselves and to society, that I cannot but hope the best effects from its promulgation in its present form.'

---

[1] 'There seems no reason to believe that the moderate wealth which he possessed was anything more than what had come to him by inheritance and which his own industry and ability had earned.'—N. Macnicol, *Raja Ram Mohan Roy* (1928), p. 9.

Orthodox Hinduism was naturally offended, but opposition came from a quarter from which it was least expected. The author had printed a series of extracts from the first three Gospels and, that there should be no doubt or ambiguity, he had recorded Christ's teaching in the very words of the Evangelists. He omitted any reference to miracles and he refused to acknowledge the divinity of Christ. It is not surprising that the Serampore missionaries, with whom he had been on the most friendly terms, regarded the *Precepts* as rank heresy. In the *Friend of India*, a journal issued from the Baptist Press, Dr Marshman referred with scorn to the puerile interpretation of the Gospels which had recently been published by an 'intelligent heathen'. Hurt at being called a heathen—even though an intelligent one—Ram Mohun began a controversy which caused a great deal of excitement. It resulted in the publication of three *Appeals to the Christian Public*, in which he claimed to be a believer in the one and only true living God and in which he argued that the doctrine of the Trinity was mere polytheism. He criticized with severity, though not with bitterness, the means employed by missionaries to win converts, and pointed out that their activities marked a departure from the promise of the British Government not to interfere with the religious beliefs of their subjects. He openly admitted that he acknowledged Christ as a great religious teacher and that 'by implication' he was labouring in the promulgation of Christianity but he claimed that he was justified in defending Christianity against a 'Christian perversion' of it. Dr Marshman and his colleagues, however, could not tolerate or forgive the rejection of the Trinity and the doctrine of Atonement. Finding they were getting rather the worse of the controversy, the missionaries refused to print the heretic's third *Appeal*; it is not improbable that they were warned that further publicity would be indiscreet and that they might incur, not for the first time, the displeasure of the Government. Subsequently, Dr Tyler,[1] a pugnacious surgeon in the Company's service, offered to debate with Ram Mohun Roy the 'damnable heresy of Unitari-

---

[1] Dr Tyler's qualifications for entering upon a controversy with 'the Erasmus of India' may be gauged by his assertion that the Hindu Scriptures had no 'higher antiquity than the entry of the Musalmans into India' and by his belief that the lives of Krishna and Buddha were merely corruptions of the life of Christ. S. D. Collett, *Life and Letters of Raja Ram Mohun Roy* (edition of 1913), p. 81.

anism' (which, like Hindu idolatry, he said, 'proceeded from the devil') and signed one of his more fiery effusions 'Your inveterate and determined foe in the Lord'. This controversy caused a good deal of amusement and the correspondence was issued as a pamphlet in 1820.

The publication of Ram Mohun's interpretations of Hindu and Christian theology had very unforeseen consequences. In the first place one of the Serampore missionaries, the Reverend William Adam, who was engaged on a translation of the Gospels into Bengali in collaboration with Ram Mohun himself, was so convinced by the arguments in favour of monotheism that he renounced his belief in the Trinity. He was often humorously referred to as 'the second fallen Adam'. His secession was a blow to the missionary party, but it led to the formation of the Calcutta Unitarian Committee in 1821. The object of the Society was not proselytism but the removal of 'ignorance and superstition by education, rational discussion and the publication of books', both in English and Bengali. In the following year the Committee opened an Anglo-Hindu school, which was controlled and largely financed by Ram Mohun himself. This, however, was not his first contribution to the educational advancement of his country.

In 1814, the year in which Ram Mohun settled in Calcutta, the Court of Directors issued their first Educational Dispatch.[1] This is an interesting document and shows very clearly that they were not a little embarrassed over the expenditure of the grant which had been forced on them by Parliament. They begin with the startling announcement that the question of the establishment of colleges need not arise for the simple reason that Hindus 'of caste and reputation would not submit to their subordination and discipline'; they might, however, submit 'to the practice long established among them of giving instruction in their own homes' and welcome 'the stimulus of honorary marks of distinction', not to mention 'grants of pecuniary assistance'. A little further on, and with little regard for consistency, the Directors order inquiries to be made concerning the 'branches of literature and science' taught at 'the ancient establishments' of Benares. In later paragraphs, reference is made to 'the many excellent systems of ethics' and to the 'treatises on Astronomy and Mathematics,

---

[1] H. Sharp, *Selections from Educational Records* (1920), I, pp. 22-4.

including Geometry and Algebra' written in Sanskrit. It would seem, therefore, that they had chiefly in mind the encouragement of higher Oriental learning—literary and scientific. In the body of the Dispatch they speak 'with particular satisfaction' of the useful work of Indian village teachers, from which it would appear that the claims of the vernaculars had not been entirely overlooked. No reference is made, however, to English education or to the requirements of the Mohammedan population. The authorities in India were asked to report on the various issues raised in the Dispatch and warned that they were not finally to adopt any scheme for the advancement of education until it had been duly approved and sanctioned. This warning against undue haste was hardly necessary, not because officials in India were apathetic but because more urgent matters were then engaging their attention. The war with Nepal (1814–16) was followed by campaigns against the Pindaris and the Maratha War (1817–19). In spite of his preoccupation with military operations, which were a great strain on the finances of his Government, Lord Moira,[1] the new Governor-General, penned a most important Minute[2] (1815) on judicial administration in which he described the degraded moral and intellectual condition of the country and discussed the best means of spending Government grants on public education. He speaks with appreciation of the services rendered to the country by 'the humble but valuable class of village schoolmasters' and strongly urges the improvement and expansion of elementary education among Hindus and Mohammedans. He regrets 'the general disregard of established institutions which appears to have marked the steps of the British Government hitherto', and opposes 'the immediate encouragement of the superior descriptions of science by any bounty to the existing native Colleges' where there no longer remain 'any embers capable of being fanned into life'. He is particularly scathing about the state of learning in the 'University of Benares' (concerning which the Directors had asked for information) and gives it as his considered opinion that any money set apart for the advancement of education 'would be much more expediently applied in the improvement of schools, than in gifts to seminaries of higher degree'. He concludes with these memorable words: 'To be the source of blessings to the immense

---

[1] Later Lord Hastings.   [2] Sharp, op. cit., pp. 24 ff.

population of India is an ambition worthy of our country. In proportion as we have found intellect neglected and sterile here, the obligation is the stronger on us to cultivate it. The field is noble: may we till it worthily!' This Minute can hardly have been palatable to the Board of Directors and it was followed by a direct application for permission to encourage schools rather than higher Oriental institutions, which had hitherto enjoyed the monopoly of Government support. Lord Moira, it may be added, also wrote a private letter to Charles Grant 'to enquire whether the Court could not be persuaded to give support to schools formed on right principles rather than to Hindu universities'.[1] Grant replied that, although opposition to schemes for the moral and intellectual improvement of India was beginning to weaken, he did not think the time had yet arrived when he could urge, with any hope of success, the substitution proposed by the Governor-General.

It is significant that at the time when Lord Moira advocated the policy of what we should now call 'mass education', there was an insistent demand in Calcutta for more and better schools, both vernacular and English. In the foundation of elementary schools the missionaries were particularly active and their lead was being followed by private individuals, European and Indian. In 1814 the Rev. Robert May, a Nonconformist missionary, opened his first school in Chinsura; in the following year he had 16 schools and nearly 1,000 pupils, and in 1818 his schools numbered 36 and contained some 3,000 pupils, including Mohammedans as well as Hindus. Again, in 1816 Captain Stewart, under the auspices of the Church Missionary Society, opened two schools in Burdwan, which in 1818 increased to 10 with over 1,000 pupils. Lastly, the Serampore missionaries had established a number of schools in the neighbourhood of Calcutta, and in 1820 these numbered not less than 20 with an enrolment of over 800 boys. In 1816 Dr Marshman published an important pamphlet entitled *Hints Relative to Native Schools; together with the Outline of an Institution for their Extension and Management*; this created a profound impression in India and attracted considerable attention even in England.[2] Leading Indians in Calcutta, headed by Ram Mohun Roy and Dwarkanath Tagore, warmly supported the

---

[1] J. C. Marshman, *The Life and Times of Carey, Marshman and Ward* (1859), II, p. 118.

[2] Marshman, op. cit., II, p. 119.

missionaries in their campaign against ignorance, and it is recorded
that the former offered Eustace Carey, nephew of the great Dr
William Carey, a plot of land for the establishment of a school in
Calcutta itself.   More surprising is the fact that the Governor-
General, who had more than once befriended the Serampore
missionaries and had been impressed by the scheme outlined in
Dr Marshman's *Hints*, persuaded the Directors to sanction a grant
of Rs. 600 a month to May's schools and this was raised to Rs. 800
in 1818.   Small grants were also made to a few up-country schools,
including a Mohammedan school near Cuttack and a Hindu
school in Benares.   Howell regards these grants as the earliest
instances of the application of what was subsequently called the
'grant-in-aid' system.[1]

   Not less important than the efforts of the missionaries to foster
primary education was the foundation of the Calcutta School
Book Society (1817) and of the Calcutta School Society (1818).
The object of the former was to prepare and publish cheap books
suitable for use in elementary schools, and the Society received
from the Government in 1821 a donation of Rs. 7,000 and a
monthly grant of Rs. 500.   The Calcutta School Society was
inaugurated under the presidency of the Governor-General himself
'for the distinct execution of three principal objects': (1) for the
establishment and support of a limited number of regular schools;
(2) for aiding and improving the indigenous schools of the country,
and (3) for the education of a select number of pupils in English.[2]
In 1821 the Society controlled 115 vernacular schools containing
nearly 4,000 pupils, and in 1823 the Government sanctioned an
allowance of Rs. 500 per mensem on condition that 'prudent and
considerate attention' were paid to the religious opinions of the
pupils.   This grant, says Howell, marks 'the first recognition on
the part of the home Government of the claims of education for
the masses'.[3]   Within ten years of the insertion of the educational
clause in the Charter of 1813, great strides had been taken in the
direction of establishing a far-reaching scheme of primary education;
and the efforts of the individuals and societies concerned had

[1] A. Howell, *Education in British India prior to 1854* (1872), p. 7.
[2] C. Lushington, *Religious, Benevolent and Charitable Institutions* (1824),
p. 168.
[3] Howell, op. cit., p. 23.

received the financial support of the Board of Directors and the patronage of a Governor-General who had boldly declared (in an address delivered to the students of the College of Fort William) that 'the strength of the Indian Government would not be based on the ignorance but on the enlightenment of the people'.[1]

In spite of this promising start, the success of the various efforts to extend elementary education was short-lived. The educational activities of the missionaries were passively opposed by the Mohammedans who, for the most part, held · themselves sullenly aloof, and were actively opposed by orthodox Hindus, who were unable to rid their minds of the fears of proselytism. It is related that on the day following the baptism of Carey's first convert not a single pupil attended one of the Serampore elementary schools; in Burdwan a Hindu parent, rather than entrust the education of his child to a missionary, left him out at night to be devoured by jackals![2] In spite of the support of enlightened men such as Ram Mohun Roy, those who had the best interests of the people at heart found it extremely difficult to make much headway against the suspicion and prejudices of an ignorant populace. It is true that opposition to missionary enterprise did impel some orthodox Hindus to start new schools and to reopen old ones, but these appear to have enjoyed a more ephemeral success than those against which they strove to compete. Not only was there a reluctance to make use of printed books, but slender financial resources and the dearth of efficient teachers made failure inevitable. The chief reason for the rapid decline in the popularity of elementary education remains to be noted; it was not so much due to shortage of money, paucity of funds or fear of conversion, as to the urgent and insistent demand on the part of Indians themselves for English education. The growing opportunities for employment in Government service and in commercial firms and the increasing desire for closer contact with the new rulers, including an acquaintance with their literature and civilization, created in the minds of progressive Indians a determination to learn English; and in this the missionaries, no less than private individuals, saw possibilities for the future. It soon became apparent that the schools which taught English

[1] Marshman, op. cit., II, p. 156.
[2] J. Long (Editor), *Adam's Reports on Vernacular Education in Bengal and Behar* (1868), p. 4.

continued to prosper, while elementary vernacular schools steadily declined.   Indeed, primary schools came to be regarded as mere feeders for English schools and mass education ceased to be esteemed in and for itself.   In Calcutta several private schools[1] had sprung up before 1820 with the avowed object of imparting a sound knowledge of English; they were founded to meet a popular demand and were patronized by many well-to-do Hindu families. Some of them appear to have been thoroughly efficient and not a few turned out to be successful financial ventures.   The wave of enthusiasm for English education which spread over Calcutta and other Indian cities in the first quarter of the nineteenth century is a matter of plain historical fact, the importance of which no student of the period can afford to ignore.   Indeed, there are good grounds for believing that the demand of Indians for English education was a more important factor in the development of educational policy than the desire of the Government to find suitably qualified recruits for the public service or the efforts of the missionaries to employ education as a means of conversion.

In the forefront of this movement for the spread of English education stood Ram Mohun Roy.   He was the leader of a small but influential group of ardent reformers, who realized that changing social and political conditions made it imperative that India should emerge from her cultural isolation and come into closer contact with Western thought and civilization.   The unique position which he occupied in the life of the metropolis gave his advocacy of the 'new learning' an influence which carried much weight.   In spite of his religious controversies and heterodox views, he remained on terms of intimacy with prominent Hindus and Mohammedans, and he retained the friendship and respect of a number of missionaries and officials.   As a result of the extension of English education, he saw the vision of a new India freed from the fetters of conservatism and convention, and every effort to make this dream a reality had his warmest approval and support.   He himself was by no means blind to the beauties of Sanskrit literature or to the profundity of Hindu philosophy; he realized, however, that higher Oriental learning had always been confined to

[1] See W. H. Carey, *The Good Old Days of Honorable John Company*, I, (1906) and B. N. Law, *Promotion of Learning in India by Early European Settlers* (1915).

a privileged class, that it had ceased to have any direct bearing on modern problems and that it was an unsuitable weapon with which to combat the ignorance and superstition of the masses. By his own efforts he had made himself familiar with much of the best that Western literature and thought had to offer, and he felt that the time was ripe for the absorption by young India of those liberal ideas which were the basis of England's power and progress. It seemed to him that the spread of English education must inevitably result in the raising of the moral, social and political life of his backward and degenerate countrymen. It is little wonder that he identified himself with almost every scheme that was set on foot for the promotion of education of a modern and practical type.

When David Hare conceived the idea of starting an institution to communicate a knowledge of Western literature and science to the rising generation, he enlisted the support of the great Hindu reformer. At the time, Ram Mohun had thoughts of founding a seminary for the study of the higher and purer doctrines of Hinduism. Hare's enthusiasm and practical common sense could not be withstood, and Ram Mohun not only postponed the establishment of his own Academy but joined hands with the rationalist watchmaker in founding the Vidyalaya, or Home of Learning, 'for the tuition of the sons of respectable Hindoos'.[1] Together they laid their plans, issued circulars, gathered subscriptions and sought the patronage of prominent Hindus and high officials, including Sir Edward Hyde East, the Chief Justice. A public meeting was called and it was unanimously resolved that 'an institution for the teaching of English to the higher classes' should be started and a Managing Committee, composed of Indians and Europeans, was appointed to carry the scheme into effect. In this way began the Hindu, or Anglo-Indian, College—'the very first English seminary in Bengal, or even in India, as far as I know', wrote Dr Duff.[2] The association of Ram Mohun Roy with the promoters alienated several orthodox Hindus, who threatened to withdraw their support and to boycott the proposed college. One influential Brahman informed the Chief Justice that

[1] Quotation from the original prospectus, which is given in full in J. C. Mittra's *Biographical Sketch of David Hare* (1877), Appendix A.

[2] Howell, op. cit., p. 10; Sharp, op. cit., p. 78.

even the acceptance of a subscription from Ram Mohun would offend Hindu sentiment because 'he has chosen to separate himself from us and to attack our religion'.[1] Fearing that further participation in the affairs of the college would endanger the success of a project which had met with unparalleled public support, Ram Mohun willingly renounced his connexion and modestly withdrew into the background. Opposition was overcome and the Hindu College of Calcutta was opened in 1817 to impart a liberal education in which the most important place was assigned to English. Two things are noteworthy about the foundation of this famous institution: (1) although chief credit for the inception of the project belongs to David Hare, the foundation of the college was only made possible by the generosity of the public, and it remains to this day as a visible expression of the desire of the more enlightened citizens of the period for adequate facilities for English education; (2) although Ram Mohun considered it his duty to sever his connexion with David Hare and his colleagues, he was one of the original founders of an institution which subsequently developed into the Presidency College of Calcutta and still maintains pride of place among the collegiate institutions of India.

If the atmosphere of the Hindu College was from the start secularist and rationalistic, Bengal 'had not long to wait for an antidote'.[2] The Baptist missionaries founded the Serampore College[3] in 1818, and nine years later this institution was incorporated by Royal Charter, granted by the King of Denmark, with power to confer degrees; it is thus the first instance of the foundation of a modern university in India. In 1820 Bishop's College was opened in Calcutta in honour of Bishop Middleton. These institutions, though sectarian in origin, show that the missionaries were anxious to meet the demand for higher English education. They had already established primary and secondary schools, but these were not sufficient to meet the needs of a public which clamoured for something more than a knowledge of the mere rudiments of English.[4]

[1] B. D. Basu, *Education in India under the Rule of the East India Company* (n.d.), p. 40.

[2] *Calcutta University Commission Report (1917-19)*, (1919), I, p. 33.

[3] G. Howells and A. C. Underwood, *The Story of Serampore and its College* (1918).

[4] H. R. James, *Education and Statesmanship in India* (1917), pp. 18 ff.

Strangely enough, the Government appear to have been unaware of the trend of public opinion or, perhaps, reluctant to pander to what was considered to be a passing, but dangerous, agitation. In 1823 a Committee of Public Instruction was set up to take over the whole management of state education, including the expenditure of public funds. It was composed of ten senior Bengal Civilians, most of whom had distinguished themselves at the College of Fort William and were enthusiastic members of the Asiatic Society. This probably explains why it was that, from the beginning the Committee were biased in favour of Oriental learning, which they endeavoured to encourage in order to win the confidence of the more educated and influential classes and to avoid any suspicion of proselytism. The inadequacy of the funds at their disposal made it impossible for them to render any substantial aid to the promotion of mass education, but in fairness it must be stated that the improvement of the vernaculars, so that they should ultimately become suitable media of instruction, was an aim which was steadily kept in view.

One of the very first measures of the newly appointed Committee was to sanction the completion of the Sanskrit College in Calcutta, which had been approved and liberally endowed by the Government in 1821. When this decision was made known Ram Mohun took the bold and almost unprecedented step of addressing a letter of protest to the Governor-General himself.[1] He informed Lord Amherst, who had succeeded Lord Hastings, that the establishment of a college to impart such knowledge as had been current in India for two thousand years 'with the addition of vain and empty subtleties since produced by speculative men' would be a retrograde step. He urged the need for instruction in modern science and mathematics, and pointed out the futility of loading 'the minds of youths with grammatical niceties and metaphysical distinctions of little or no practical use to the possessors or to society'. He argued that 'if it had been intended to keep the British nation in ignorance of real knowledge, the Baconian philosophy would not have been allowed to displace the system of the schoolmen, which was best calculated to perpetuate ignorance. In the same manner the Sanskrit system of education would be the best calculated to keep this country in darkness, if

[1] Sharp, op. cit., p. 99.

such had been the policy of the British Legislature. But as the improvement of the native population is the object of Government it will consequently promote a more liberal and enlightened policy of instruction'. This letter is remarkable not merely because it was written by one who was himself an accomplished Sanskrit scholar, but because it affords irrefutable proof that advanced public opinion was dissatisfied with the attitude of the Committee of Public Instruction towards the educational needs of the people. In spite of its 'good English, good sense and forcible arguments' which impressed Bishop Heber,[1] the memorial remained unanswered. The reasons why the Committee decided to ignore Ram Mohun Roy's letter make interesting reading though, it must be confessed, they are not very convincing. Mr Harington, Chairman, wrote 'it is entitled to no reply, as it has disingenuously assumed a character to which it has not pretensions. The application to Government against the cultivation of Hindu literature, and in favour of the substitution of European tuition, is made professedly on the part and in the name of the natives of India. But it bears the signature of one individual alone, whose opinions are well known to be hostile to those entertained by almost all his countrymen. The letter of Ram Mohun Roy does not, therefore, express the opinion of any portion of the natives of India, and its assertion to that effect is a dereliction of truth, which cancels the claim of its author to respectful consideration'.[2] This defence of official high-handedness confirmed the Committee in their self-complacency and steps were taken to expedite the opening of the Sanskrit College 'for the revival and improvement of Literature and the encouragement of the learned natives of India'. The letter, however, was not entirely ineffective: it was the first serious criticism of the Government's policy of encouraging Oriental learning, which had been more or less steadily pursued since the time of Warren Hastings, and it started a long and bitter controversy between the 'Anglicists' and 'Orientalists' which paralysed the efficiency of the Committee of Public Instruction for ten years and required the eloquence of Macaulay and the firmness of Bentinck to settle—in favour of the

---

[1] R. Heber, *Narrative of a Journey through the Upper Provinces of India* (1828), III, p. 360.

[2] Quoted by U. N. Ball, *Ram Mohun Roy* (1933), p. 163.

system which Ram Mohun Roy had so forcibly advocated. 'It is one of the most unintelligible facts', says Howell,[1] 'in the history of English education in India, that at the very time when the natives themselves were crying out for instruction in European literature and science and were protesting against the prevailing Orientalism, a body of Englishmen appointed to initiate a system of education for the country was found to insist upon the retention of Oriental learning to the exclusion of European learning.'

In 1824 the Court of Directors sent out a Dispatch,[2] believed to have been drafted by James Mill, dealing with certain reforms which had been proposed for existing Oriental seminaries and the establishment of the new Sanskrit College. It was so strongly worded that it would have shaken the faith in Orientalism of any body of men less obstinate and prejudiced than those who composed the Committee of Public Instruction. It recommends the promotion and extension of *useful* education and regrets that the plans for Oriental seminaries were 'originally and fundamentally erroneous'. As regards the sciences, it states, 'it is worse than a waste of time to teach them in the state in which they are found in the Oriental books', and it adds that Oriental literature contained 'a great deal of what was frivolous, not a little of what was purely mischievous and a small remainder, indeed, in which utility was in any way concerned'. Following on Ram Mohun Roy's vigorous protest, this onslaught might have been expected to awaken the Committee to a sense of their responsibilities towards the people and to have stirred them to energetic action. In their reply,[3] however, they counselled caution and warned the Directors of the danger of offending the susceptibilities of learned pundits and maulvis. They even expatiated on the merits of Oriental poetry and philosophy, though the Dispatch had emphatically stated that 'poetry is not useful and we suspect that there is little in Hindoo or Mahomedan literature that is', and 'it has never been thought necessary to establish Colleges for the cultivation of poetry'. They tried to justify their position by urging the necessity of going 'with the tide of popular prejudice' which held that 'European science and literature were not worth the trouble of attainment'—a plea which

[1] Howell, op. cit., p. 18.   [2] Sharp, op. cit., pp. 91-3.
[3] Sharp, op. cit., pp. 93 ff.

can hardly have impressed the Directors in London and which certainly was not supported by events which were actually taking place in Calcutta. Having answered to their own satisfaction the questions raised by a tiresome Board of Directors, the Committee embarked on a comprehensive scheme for the publication of Sanskrit and Arabic books and made liberal grants to a new Hindu college at Agra and a new Mohammedan college at Delhi. It was not until 1829 that a separate institution was founded in Delhi for the cultivation of Western learning and this was a result of the 'urgent solicitation of the authorities of that place'.[1] It is true that the forcible language of the Directors about the importance of *useful* knowledge did not go entirely unheeded, for the Committee came to the assistance of the Vidyalaya (Hindu College) in 1824 and, subsequently, sanctioned the opening of English classes in the Oriental colleges in Calcutta, Agra and Delhi; a few Anglo-Vernacular schools continued to receive financial support, but the efforts to promote modern education were grudging and hesitant and the Committee's faith in Orientalism remained, if not as firmly fixed as ever, at least strong enough to retard the progress of English education.

In 1830 their policy of masterly inactivity received another shock. Dr Alexander Duff arrived in Calcutta and within a few months made himself thoroughly acquainted with local conditions. Acting against the express orders of his Committee in Scotland and against the advice of several missionaries on the spot, he decided to start a college in Calcutta in which not only English but the Bible should be compulsory subjects. 'Having listened to the young Scotsman's statement of his view', says Duff's biographer,[2] 'Ram Mohun Roy expressed general approval. All true education, the reformer emphatically declared, ought to be religious, since the object was not merely to give information, but to develop and regulate all powers of the mind, the emotions and the workings of the conscience. Though not a Christian by profession he had read and studied the Bible and declared that, as a book of religious and moral instruction, it was unequalled.' As was anticipated, he had to face strongly organized hostility and it was chiefly through the intervention of Ram Mohun Roy that he was able to secure suitable premises and it was Ram Mohun who was

[1] C. E. Trevelyan, *The Education of the People of India* (1838), p. 4.
[2] G. Smith, *The Life of Alexander Duff* (1879), I, p. 171.

instrumental in finding for him his first pupils.[1]   The Hindu reformer doubtless remembered the help and the comfort which he had received from some of Duff's fellow-countrymen in the days when he had to face persecution on account of his scathing condemnation of certain Hindu practices and beliefs; which, he tells us, 'raised such a feeling against me that I was at last deserted by every person except two or three Scottish friends to whom and to the nation to which they belong I shall ever remain grateful'.[2] Although unwilling to subscribe to every article of the Westminster Confession of Faith, he became a regular member of St Andrew's Church and it was he who suggested to Dr Bryce—the first chaplain sent out to Calcutta by the Church of Scotland—that India was a suitable sphere for Presbyterian missionary effort. It is a strange coincidence that the cultured Indian theist, who had scorned the overtures of a well-meaning but tactless Anglican bishop[3] and of devout but narrow-minded Baptists, should have welcomed the advent of Presbyterian missionaries and had a share in the origination of Duff's great educational work.   This began in an atmosphere of uneasiness, and trouble was foreseen when the earnest but impetuous young missionary announced his intention of making Bible classes compulsory.   Again, Ram Mohun came to the rescue and pointed out that a study of the Bible could not possibly do any harm and need not necessarily undermine the faith of devout Hindus.   Within a short time the success of the College was assured, and Duff was unable to find room for the hordes of applicants who sought admission.   Here is another

[1] There is no truth whatever in the statement that Ram Mohun Roy's alliance with Duff implied that he was 'ashamed to patronize' the Hindu College whose 'anti-Christian success' he deplored. (Smith, I, p. 145; also p. 39.)

[2] 'Autobiographical Sketch,' which originally appeared (1833) in the *Athenaeum* and the *Literary Gazette*.   Reprinted in Mary Carpenter's *Last Days in England of Ram Mohun Roy* (1866).

[3] Bishop Middleton had tried in a well-meaning but tactless way to persuade Ram Mohun to accept Christianity.   He pictured the grand career which a change in faith would open out and added that 'he would be honoured in life and lamented in death—honoured in England as well as in India. His name would descend to posterity as that of the modern apostle of India'. (Collett, op. cit., p. 70).   This way of putting forward the claims of Christianity offended, even disgusted, an earnest seeker after truth and Ram Mohun never met the bishop again.

proof, if one were needed, that at this time there existed an 'insatiable hunger for a knowledge of English amongst the younger generation of the better classes in Calcutta'.[1]   Even the daily recital of the Lord's Prayer, followed by a Bible lesson, was not a deterrent to the hundreds of Indian parents who desired that, above all else, their sons should enjoy the benefit of a sound English education.   The unexpected success of Duff's hazardous enterprise, coupled with the growing popularity of the Anglo-Indian College, forced the Committee to realize what had been obvious to others for some years past—that, with or without official patronage and support, English education was bound to prosper.

It is significant that in their Report for 1831 they speak with enthusiasm of the academic attainments of the students of the Hindu College, which, they said, had always been one of the chief objects of their attention: 'a command of the English language and a familiarity with its literature and science have been acquired to an extent rarely equalled by any schools in Europe. A taste for English has been widely disseminated, and independent schools, conducted by young men reared in the Vidyalaya, are springing up in every direction'.[2]   In the same year Duff held a public examination of his pupils, to which prominent residents of Calcutta were invited, and the progress which had been made in a twelvemonth was so remarkable that it became the talk of the whole city. It is as clear as noonday that the establishment of English education in Bengal was mainly due to the efforts of such far-sighted men as Ram Mohun Roy, Hare and Duff, and not—as has often been claimed—to the policy of an alien and unsympathetic Government. The Committee of Public Instruction were reluctant to take any action which would give the impression that a foreign system of education was being forced on an unwilling people or that any attempt was being made to interfere with deep-rooted religious convictions, and this is the obvious explanation of their cautious attitude towards a movement which at first seemed to them to be dangerous and was regarded by others as unpatriotic.

Duff's College was opened in July 1830 and before the end of the year Ram Mohun Roy set sail for Europe—an almost

[1] J. Richter, *A History of Missions in India* (1908), p. 178.

[2] Syed Mahmood, *A History of English Education in India* (1895), p. 35.

unheard-of thing for a Brahman in those days even to contemplate.[1]
He had long been anxious to visit England in order to obtain 'by
personal observation a more thorough insight into its manners,
customs, religion and political institution', and he welcomed the
invitation of the Emperor of Delhi, who still maintained a nominal
suzerainty and who conferred on him the title of Rajah, to proceed
to London with a petition to the British Government for the
redress of certain grievances.   The various schemes for the
amelioration of his country to which he had devoted his energy
and attention were either completed, or were well on the way to
completion.   The Brahmo Samaj (1828) was firmly established
and permanently housed in a building for the use of 'all sorts and
descriptions of people without distinction who shall behave and
conduct themselves in an orderly, sober, religious and devout
manner for the worship and adoration of the Eternal, Unsearchable
and Immutable Being who is the Author and Preserver of the
Universe'.[2]   Sacrifice and idolatry (even the use of carving, paint-
ing, picture, portrait or the likeness of anything) were prohibited
and only such forms of worship were allowed as would foster
'the contemplation of the Author and Preserver of the Universe'
and promote 'charity, morality, piety, benevolence and the
strengthening of the bonds of union between men of all religious
persuasions and creeds'.   Secondly, suttee had at last been abolished
(1829) and made a most serious criminal offence.   Lastly the
Hindu College, which had been taken over by the Government
in 1824, was in a flourishing condition, Duff's college had been
successfully launched, and the claims of English education were
on the eve of official recognition.   He felt that he could well
afford to absent himself for a while from the scene of his arduous
labours.

His fame as a scholar and a reformer had preceded him and
his reception in England was more cordial and magnificent than

---

[1] The first high-caste Hindu to visit England is said to have been Ganesh
Das, a native of Delhi. On his return (about 1774) he was baptized by
Kiernander and took the name Robert, after his sponsor, Sir Robert Chambers.
He became Persian Translator to the Supreme Court. (vide Richter, op. cit.,
p. 130.)

[2] This and the following quotations are from the original Trust Deed, of
which extracts are given by Farquhar (op. cit., p. 35); the full text is given in
The English Works of Ram Mohun Roy (1906).

he or anyone else could have anticipated. He was presented
by the Chairman of the Board of Control (Charles Grant, the
younger) to King William IV, at whose coronation he was
assigned a place among the ambassadors representing the great
European powers, and was introduced into the House of Lords
by the Duke of Cumberland. The Directors of the East
India Company gave a banquet in his honour, at which the
Chairman paid a warm tribute to the many and great services
which the enlightened Hindu had rendered to his country. Everywhere he was received with the deference due to a very
distinguished visitor and hardly any social function was complete
without his presence. The Dowager Duchess of Cork, a noted
lion-hunter, 'early marked him down for her prey',[1] and this
partially accounts for Dr Bryce's unsympathetic verdict that he
fell into the hands of 'utterly unworthy companions' and wasted
away 'his little hour as the lion of the metropolis'.[2] He met on
equal terms members of the nobility and leaders of both the great
political parties and he enjoyed the friendship and respect of some
of the most eminent literary and scientific men of the day. His
dignified presence, obvious sincerity and sound judgement impressed everyone with whom he came into contact, and Englishmen
were amazed at the Hindu philosopher's intimate knowledge of
the Bible and his lively interest in the great political and social
questions which were then agitating the public mind. He
frequently attended the House of Commons and no one was
a more enthusiastic supporter of the Reform Bill, the Bill for the
Abolition of Slavery and the Factory Act—measures which enhanced his admiration for the British people and strengthened his
determination to promote, by every means in his power, the
amelioration of his own country.

Amidst the throng of social engagements and the pressure of
literary and other work, India was never very far from his
thoughts. If he had come to England as the accredited ambassador
of the Emperor of Delhi, he came also as the living representative
of the peoples of India. He was the first great Hindu to venture
across the seas and he was spontaneously acknowledged in the

---

[1] Sophia D. Collett, *Life and Letters of Raja Ram Mohun Roy* (Sarkar's
edition of 1913), p. 183.

[2] J. Bryce, *A Sketch of Native Education in India* (1839), p. 59.

heart of the Empire as the visible and personal embodiment of Indian piety and culture. His visit to England was not a trifling episode in the reformer's busy and eventful life 'nor a mere appendix or postscript to a career already complete'. It made Englishmen aware, as they had never been aware before, of their responsibilities and obligations towards their distant subjects, and it made them realize that Indians could assimilate and appreciate the culture of the West. 'As he had interpreted England to India, so now he interpreted India to England',[1] says Miss Collett, and no one of his day or generation was more eminently fitted for the performance of either task. His views on great social and religious issues were treated with the utmost respect and on the subject of India they were particularly influential.

The active part which he had taken in the campaign against suttee won the unstinted admiration of a humanitarian age, and Ram Mohun Roy had the satisfaction of being present in Parliament when the appeal against its abolition was summarily dismissed. Some years previously he had assured Lord William Bentinck that this inhuman rite was 'nowhere enjoined by the religion of the Hindus as an imperative duty', and this assurance had emboldened the Governor-General to take a risk which more than one of his predecessors had considered too dangerous. Even Ram Mohun Roy himself, when he learned that it had been decided to make the observance of the rite a criminal offence amounting to culpable homicide, considered that the time was not yet ripe for such a drastic step and he endeavoured to persuade Bentinck to proceed more cautiously. Contrary to expectations the new Regulation caused no disaffection in the army and gave rise to no civil disturbance. In Calcutta, conservative Hindus worked up an agitation for the withdrawal of the prohibition and presented a monster petition in which more than a hundred pundits supported the view that suttee was a religious duty sanctioned by Scripture and honoured by immemorial custom; it was also urged that the action of the Governor-General was at variance with the declared policy of the Court of Directors (1808)[2] to refrain from any interference with the religious practices of the people. Counter-

---

[1] Collett, op. cit., p. 175.

[2] Extracts given by Sharp, op. cit., p. 4; quoted in full by J. W. Kaye, *Christianity in India* (1859).

petitions were submitted by Christians and by Ram Mohun Roy's party, and Bentinck steadfastly refused to alter a decision at which he had arrived after much anxious thought. He intimated, however, that should there be any genuine conviction that the recent Regulation was contrary to the enactments of the Imperial Parliament he would be happy to forward an appeal to the King in Council. Thereupon the orthodox party petitioned Parliament against an unwarranted interference with their religious rights and liberties. Before leaving India Ram Mohun Roy, who staunchly supported the measure which he had at first considered premature, drew up another counter-petition which he undertook to present personally to the authorities in England. Lord Wellesley was also present in the House of Commons when the Hindu reformer heard the announcement that Parliament (1833) were pleased to ratify and confirm the Regulation which had been framed by a humane and courageous Governor-General, solely for the sake of the happiness and welfare of the people concerned. The final triumph of a cause to which Ram Mohun Roy had devoted himself without intermission for more than twenty years considerably enhanced the reputation which he had already established in England and, in the opinion of many competent judges, marks the culmination of his humanitarian work for India. 'These services', says Edward Thompson, 'were a fitting crown to the brave life of the great Indian.'[1] There is little doubt that he shares equally with Lord William Bentinck the chief credit for the suppression of a cruel practice which had long been a disgrace to Indian civilization and which, in spite of the predictions of pessimists, was suddenly and finally put down 'without the slightest tumult, without even a national sigh'.[2]

Less spectacular, but not less important, were the services which he rendered to India when the question of the renewal of the Company's Charter came up for consideration. We know that even before he left India he had entertained the hope that he would be able to urge the necessity of certain administrative reforms: in a letter of introduction to Lord Brougham, William Roscoe wrote, 'amongst the many and important motives which induced him to leave his country . . . he is induced to hope he may be of some assistance in promoting the cause of the natives

[1] Edward Thompson, *Suttee* (1928), p. 81.   [2] Marshman, op. cit., II, p. 418.

of India in the great debate which must ere long take place here, respecting the Charter of the East India Company'.[1] The authorities in Leadenhall Street and in Westminster were equally anxious to profit by his unrivalled knowledge of Indian affairs and he welcomed the opportunity of being able to express his views on matters of the greatest political importance. He submitted to the Select Committee of the House of Commons written evidence on the Revenue and Judicial systems of India, together with shorter notes on the Indian Peasantry and on the Settlement of India by Europeans. It is unfortunate that historians have tended to overlook these documents and that, in consequence, few people realize that Ram Mohun Roy was in no small degree responsible for certain provisions of an Act which had very important bearings on the development of Indian educational policy.

The Charter of 1833 is usually dismissed with a bald statement to the effect that it deprived the Company of its remaining commercial interests and turned it into a political organization, or governing agency. It is significant, however, that the Chairman of the Board of Control, the younger Charles Grant, afterwards Lord Glenelg, was careful to point out in the House of Commons that the Bill aimed at 'securing the good government and promoting the religious and moral improvement of the people of India'. This comprehensive, but vague, statement did not cause the slightest uneasiness and no one rose to accuse the Government of legislating for the conversion of Indians to Christianity. There was no repetition of the heated controversies which the insertion of the 'pious clauses' had aroused twenty years earlier, although certain sections in the new Charter went far beyond anything which Wilberforce had ventured to propose; in the substance, if not in the wording, of some of these it is not fanciful to trace the influence of Ram Mohun Roy, whose evidence contained some very far-reaching suggestions. Among other things he strongly recommended (1) the substitution of English for Persian as the language of the courts, (2) the codification of the Criminal and Civil Law, and (3) the appointment of Indians to posts of trust and responsibility. The first of these proposals was not accepted, but it is interesting to note that the chief argument which Ram Mohun Roy advanced in its favour was that it would stimulate

---

[1] Collett, op. cit., p. 184.

the study of English. The question appears to have been discussed as early as 1829 and in 1837 a Resolution was passed authorizing the use of the vernaculars as the language of the Courts—a change which was approved by the Directors in the following year. In 1844 the policy of making English the language of all official business was foreshadowed by Lord Hardinge and this reform, which was mainly of an administrative nature, gave a great impetus to English education, as Ram Mohun Roy had clearly foreseen it would do. The second recommendation was accepted and the Supreme Council was reinforced by the addition of a Law Member. Macaulay was the first person to hold this post and he initiated the work which subsequently resulted in the drawing up of the Penal Code and the Codes of Criminal Procedure. He also became Chairman of the Committee of Public Instruction and his famous Minute of 1835 turned the defeat of the Orientalists into an absolute rout. It is a curious coincidence that Ram Mohun Roy was indirectly connected with the appointment of two of the greatest of the early protagonists of English education in India—Duff and Macaulay.

Unquestionably, the most important clause in the new Charter was Section 87 which stated that no Indian, by reason of his colour, caste or creed should be 'disabled from holding any place, office or employment under the Company', language which Vincent Smith[1] considers even more emphatic than that used in Queen Victoria's Proclamation of 1858. Ram Mohun Roy had urged the recruitment of Indians to the public service partly for reasons of economy, but mainly because this reform would win over the confidence and support of 'those respectable families which were disaffected towards the British Government' and who 'considered it derogatory to accept of the trifling public situations' which had been thrown open to Indians. He also argued that the employment of Indians 'would improve the conditions of the inhabitants and stimulate them with an ambition to deserve the confidence of the Government'. The cumulative effect of these arguments appears to have carried much weight and no serious objection was raised against the proposal to appoint suitably qualified Indians to responsible posts.[2] It is not suggested that

[1] *The Oxford History of India* (1919), p. 669.
[2] A. Mayhew, *The Education of India* (1926), p. 13.

Ram Mohun Roy was the only person who advocated this change; it was supported by several official witnesses, including Holt Mackenzie, Charles Lushington and A. D. Campbell, and in the debates which followed it transpired that the appointment of Indians to responsible posts. was seriously contemplated. Further, it was made clear that the object of this important innovation was not merely to keep down the cost of the administration, for it was argued that the appointment of Indians in the service of the state would stimulate modern education and, thereby, elevate the moral and intellectual conditions of the people at large. Ram Mohun Roy was the only person who was in a position to put the case from the Indian point of view and there is no reason to question the claim of Dr Carpenter that his wise and judicious recommendations 'were highly valued by our Government' .and that they aided in the formation of a 'new system by which the well-being of our vast dependencies in India must be so greatly affected'.[1] It is unlikely that many realized as clearly as the Hindu reformer what were the educational implications of the new Charter Act, but it soon became obvious that it embodied an administrative reform which necessitated a change in educational policy and made it desirable that higher education should be imparted mainly, if not exclusively, through the medium of English. From this time onwards the popularity of English education increased very rapidly and the Committee of Public Instruction were soon forced to withdraw their support of Oriental learning and to devote all the funds at their disposal to the encouragement of English education. The withdrawal of the Company's monopoly in the China trade seems almost insignificant in comparison with the momentous administrative reform which was sanctioned by the India Act of 1833 and which had been urged by Ram Mohun Roy in the interests of the British Government and the Indian people. Few of those who remember his memorial to Lord Amherst, or his share in the foundation of two great Calcutta colleges, realize the part he played in the framing of a Charter which gave English education in India a permanent official footing. It might even be argued that his last, and least known, contribution to the educational progress of his country was his

---

[1] Mary Carpenter, op. cit., pp. 90-1.

greatest, for it heralded the final triumph of a policy which, for more than a hundred years, has had an incalculable influence on the cause of India's social and political history.

Strange to say, the new Charter Act aroused little interest in England, either inside or outside Parliament, but it was enthusiastically received in India. It was passed in August, but before the end of the year Ram Mohun Roy died suddenly in Bristol, where he had gone to visit some friends. On his tomb it is recorded that 'his unwearied labours to promote the social, moral and physical condition of the people of India, his earnest efforts to suppress idolatry and the rite of Suttee, and his constant zealous advocacy of whatever tended to advance the glory of God and the welfare of man, live in the grateful remembrance of his countrymen'. A simpler, but perhaps a nobler inscription would have been his favourite quotation from the Persian poet, Safi: 'The true way of serving God is to do good to man.' Even to this day his grave, in the secluded cemetery of Arno's Vale, is regarded by Indian visitors of every class and creed as a place of pious pilgrimage.

Ram Mohun Roy is chiefly remembered as a great religious reformer and there is no denying that the impulse which drove him to strive for the progress and enlightenment of his countrymen was essentially religious. On the other hand, he clearly realized that any attempt to develop higher moral and religious ideals in a community without, at the same time, trying to improve the ordinary conditions of life was a fruitless, if not an impossible, task. In education he saw ready to hand a weapon which could be used to fight against the abuses and corruptions which disfigured Indian social life and, as an inevitable result of the spread of modern knowledge, he foresaw the dawn of a brighter future for his unhappy country. The learning which, even in India's darkest days, had been fostered and kept alive by zealous pundits was too theoretical, vague and remote to touch the lives of the people; he felt that the liberalizing influence of Western ideas would not only invigorate and quicken the lore of the pundits but would also have far-reaching social and political consequences. He himself said, in justification of his educational policy, that 'the Indian was instinctively a philosopher and a mystic and that he greatly needed the scientific point of view and accurate training

of the West'.[1] He was perhaps the first of his race to realize that
Indian culture had grown sick and weary and that scientific teaching
was exactly the tonic which its infirmities called for. No one was
more strongly convinced that 'English education would contribute to Oriental culture just those complementary qualities
which it lacked'.[2] Most assuredly he did not advocate the
wholesale substitution of European for Indian learning, nor did
he favour a complete breakaway from the ancient cultural heritage
of his race. He aimed at a synthesis, or correlation, which would
preserve what was best in the old learning and assimilate what
was best in the new and thus bring the East and the West more
closely together. As Lord Ronaldshay has finely said, Ram
Mohun Roy (together with a few other men of vision) saw 'the
need of a new synthesis of the best that Europe and Asia had to
give and strove, consequently, to weave into the tapestry of Indian
life such threads from the spindles of the West, without bringing
about a complete alteration in the pattern upon the Indian loom'.[3]
In a unique way the Hindu reformer was, 'the mediator of his
people, harmonizing in his own person . . . the conflicting
tendencies of immemorial tradition and of inevitable enlightenment'.[4] For this reason alone Ram Mohun Roy stands out as a
majestic, even a prophetic, figure in the annals of modern Indian
education.

It is unfortunate that many of his critics have failed to grasp
the real significance of the reformer's contribution towards Indian
educational advancement. He has been accused of aiming at the
'westernization' and, therefore, the denationalization of his country;
he has been made to share the blame for the excesses of young
collegians whom English education—not fully assimilated—had
estranged from the culture and traditions of their fathers; he has
been held partially responsible for the introduction of a system
of education which all but excluded everything Indian; it has
even been laid to his charge that he looked forward to the day
when Christianity would be universally accepted in the land
of his birth. Such criticisms are very wide of the mark and show

[1] W. J. McKee, *New Schools for Young India* (1930), p. 17.
[2] ibid.
[3] Earl of Ronaldshay, *The Heart of Aryavarta* (1925), p. 48.
[4] Collett, op. cit., p. 238.

that Ram Mohun Roy's message to his own age, and to succeeding generations, has been grossly misunderstood. His own acquaintance with Western literature and thought did not cut him adrift from his own people nor make him despise his own country and its great traditions; it made him love his country more deeply than ever and anxious to share with others the enlightenment which he himself had received. Although he opposed the opening of the Sanskrit College he did not underestimate the cultural and historical value of the classical languages; indeed, he founded an institution of his own for the higher study of Sanskrit and he supported the Government's policy of granting stipends to pundits. Again, he realized the importance of the vernacular languages of the country and he looked forward to the time when, refined and enriched by English influence, they would become not merely suitable media of instruction, but adequate vehicles for the expression of literary and scientific thought. He himself revealed the latent possibilities of his own mother-tongue and his is the first important name in the history of Bengali literature. Further, he himself deplored the reprehensible conduct of many of the students of the Hindu College, whose religious beliefs had been undermined by secular education, and he was disappointed that religious tolerance, of which his own life-was a very striking example, had made such little headway.

Lastly, though he saw the need for the application of science to the problems of modern life, he was firmly convinced that the best education must be moral—even religious. On examination it seemed to him that the fundamental doctrines of all the great religious systems were identical in that they were theistic, and he appears to have cherished the hope that out of the clash of warring creeds there would emerge what Monier-Williams calls 'a kind of eclectic Catholicism', which could be unreservedly accepted by all as satisfying man's reason and the cravings of the human heart. Unfortunately, he has left no clear and consistent expression of his deepest religious beliefs and these have been interpreted, and misinterpreted, in different ways. One thing, however, is certain; although a better Christian than many professed believers, he himself never embraced Christianity nor wavered in his acceptance of the essential doctrines of 'pure' Hinduism. It is true that many of his contemporaries looked with suspicion on the two

great institutions—one secularist and the other Christian—which
he had helped to found for the promotion of English education;
it may even be conceded that, to begin with, there was some
justification for the popular outcry that 'Hinduism is in danger'.
These admissions, however, cannot be regarded as adequate
grounds for the belief that Ram Mohun Roy had any intention of
eradicating Hinduism and substituting Christianity in its place.

Those critics are on safer ground who claim that the two famous
colleges with which his name is so closely associated were founded
primarily for the sons of better-class parents. Ram Mohun Roy
made no secret of the fact that he believed that the movement for
the enlightenment of India could make little progress unless it
had the support of the higher classes. He himself rebelled against
the time-worn and cramping restrictions of caste, which he foresaw
would be swept away by the advance of modern knowledge, but
he saw little prospect of the success of any educational scheme
designed solely, or even mainly, for the children of the lower
classes. Ignorant parents were not likely to appreciate the value
of any sort of education and the upper classes regarded the poorer
and more unfortunate members of the community with open
contempt. Besides, in the early years of the last century few
persons in any country considered that it was necessary, or even
desirable, to provide popular education for the masses. Ram
Mohun Roy was, like other great men, the creature of his own
age and he thought that he had no alternative but to enlist the
sympathy of well-to-do families on behalf of educational schemes
which would primarily benefit their own children. It is true that
he did support various efforts to expand primary education, but
most of the elementary schools of his time were feeders for central,
or secondary, schools and were attended, almost exclusively, by
children belonging to high-caste families. In many respects Ram
Mohun Roy was far in advance of his age, but in so far as he
believed that education must begin at the top and spread down-
wards, he was in agreement with the prevalent opinion of his
day. With many others he considered that culture and useful
knowledge would inevitably 'filter' down from above and, gradually
at first and then more rapidly, would reach the masses. Subsequent
history has shown that those who pinned their faith to the
filtration theory were too optimistic; but it is not difficult to see

why the earlier educational reformers made their first appeal to the intelligentsia. In one respect, however, Ram Mohun Roy was far ahead of his contemporaries, for he was almost alone in his advocacy of female education, which had been encouraged by Hindus in olden times but had long fallen into abeyance. Outside missionary circles, the suggestion was regarded as fantastic and little was done until many years after his death to promote and extend the education of girls. But the women of India owe much to the chivalrous reformer who fought for the abolition of suttee and polygamy and who advocated widow-remarriage and female education. Had others been able to take the same broad-minded and generous view of the status of women, social reform in the nineteenth century would have made more rapid progress and many of the evils which called forth his scathing condemnation would have been more speedily alleviated.

Perhaps enough has been said to indicate the importance of Ram Mohun Roy in the history of modern Indian education. During the British period, no single individual identified himself so closely with so many different movements for the enlightenment of India and no one person exercised a more healthy or widespread influence. He co-operated with missionaries and secularists who founded colleges to bring India into line with modern thought; he supported movements for the provision of primary and secondary schools for the teaching of Bengali and English; and, as a protest against the iniquitous treatment of women, he championed the cause of female education. In Calcutta, at a time when young India was thirsting for modern knowledge, he raised his powerful voice against the retrograde policy of encouraging Oriental learning, and in London he made recommendations to the British Parliament which involved a sudden and complete change in the Government's educational policy. His moral earnestness and untiring energy, his boldness of imagination and firm grasp of first principles mark out Raja Ram Mohun Roy not merely as a great educational reformer but as a nation-builder whom any country would be proud to number among her most illustrious sons. That he turned to the West for inspiration is no reflection on his patriotism; rather it shows the strength of his devotion to truth and the breadth of vision which entitle him to be called 'the Prophet of the Indian Renaissance'.

DAVID HARE

DAVID HARE, 1775-1842

SECULARIST AND PHILANTHROPIST

LITTLE or nothing is known of the early life of David Hare, the secularist watchmaker, who for more than a quarter of a century was an active and zealous advocate of English education in Calcutta. He was born in 1775 and arrived in India in 1800; having, within the short space of fifteen years, amassed a moderate fortune, he then made over his business to a relative called Grey. This change of hands prompted one of the newspapers of the day to remind its readers of the well-known tendency of 'old hair' to turn 'grey'. Instead of returning to England to live in ease and luxury, Hare decided to stay on in the country of his adoption and to devote the remainder of his life to the education and moral improvement of the people of Bengal. With this object in view he studied the Bengali language and identified himself very closely with the people—particularly the leading members of the Hindu community, who came to regard him almost as one of themselves.

There is no lack of contemporary evidence that he was a man of the highest moral character; in spite of·the fact that he was unable to accept the dogmas of religion, 'he was compelled by his heart' to lead an essentially Christian life. According to Dr Duff, he was 'an ordinary illiterate man',[1] and one of the Serampore missionaries, in· an obituary notice which appeared in *The Friend of India*,[2] marvelled that one who was himself 'without any refinement of education, without intellectual endowments' should have been able to accomplish so much to promote the education and improve the morals of the rising generation. Kerr, on the other hand, has left it on record that 'he must have received a good plain education. He was a man generally well informed. He spoke well—that is, simply and to the point. He wrote a good certificate, or letter. He had read some of our best authors. He might have passed for a well-educated man, but for the simplicity and sincerity which were natural to him and which

---

[1] G. Smith, *The Life of Alexander Duff* (1879), I, p. 100.
[2] Quoted by P. C. Mittra, *A Biographical Sketch of David Hare* (1877), p. 78.

raised him above the pedantry of learning. With his usual love of paradox he set himself down as an uneducated man friendly to education'.[1] If he was not a scholar, he was a man of broad human sympathy and sound common sense, and there is little doubt that he gauged correctly the trend of enlightened public opinion and formed a just estimate of the educational needs of the people of Bengal. In reply to an address, presented by grateful admirers in 1830, Hare said that on his arrival in Calcutta 'he saw that India was teeming with productions of all kinds, that her resources were inexhaustible, that her people were intelligent and industrious and possessed of capabilities, if not superior, at least equal, to those of the other civilised inhabitants of the world, and that centuries of mis-rule and oppression had completely destroyed her own learning and philosophy, and buried this land in almost total darkness. To improve her condition, nothing appeared to him more essential than a dissemination of European learning and science among her people'.[2] Like Charles Grant and Ram Mohun Roy, he regarded the spread of modern knowledge as the surest and quickest means of promoting the social uplift, material progress and political advancement of a backward country. In order to bring about these desirable ends he planned a system of education embracing a mastery of the mother-tongue and a knowledge of English—without the addition of Christian teaching. Within a few months of his retirement he seized an unexpected opportunity of putting into practice a plan which had long occupied his thoughts.

He happened one evening to be present when some prominent Hindus were discussing ways and means of subverting idolatry. Ram Mohun Roy was anxious that an association should be formed to encourage the study of the higher and purer doctrines of Hinduism, but Hare ventured to suggest that the establishment of an English school, or college, would materially serve their purpose. This proposal was enthusiastically received but, to Hare's disappointment, nothing was done to carry it into effect. He, therefore, had the matter brought to the notice of the Chief Justice,

[1] J. Kerr, *A Review of Public Instruction in the Bengal Presidency from 1835 to 1851*, 2 vols. (1853); a good account of the Hindu College is given on pp. 1–43.

[2] Mittra, op. cit., p. 35

who was greatly impressed by Hare's desire to promote the welfare of the people. Having satisfied himself that a number of prominent Hindus welcomed the proposal to start an English college, Sir Edward Hyde East presided over several preliminary meetings which were held in his own house to work out details of the scheme. Meantime, Hare was quietly but actively engaged in collecting subscriptions and in impressing upon Hindu parents the cultural and utilitarian value of an English education. When the success of the project seemed assured an unexpected difficulty arose: a number of orthodox Hindus, who resented Ram Mohun Roy's association with the proposed college, threatened to withdraw their support. Thereupon, Hare persuaded the Hindu reformer to sever his connexion with the scheme and thus regained the goodwill and co-operation of the orthodox party. A few months later, on 20 January 1817, the college was formally opened with the Governor-General as Patron, the Chief Justice as President and Mr Harington (who had assisted in the framing of the rules) as Vice-President;[1] the management was entrusted to a Committee of representative Indians and Europeans. In this way began what was not merely the first English college, but 'the first experiment in the direction of a purely and avowedly secular education that India had seen'.[2] David Hare, who shunned publicity, claimed no credit for the establishment of this famous institution, but the testimony of Duff, Kerr, and Dwarkanath Tagore and the early records of the Committee of Public Instruction make it clear that he was the life and soul of a movement which marks the beginning of a new era in Indian education.

As a member of the Committee, Hare used to visit the College almost every day and he took a lively interest in the work of the staff and the progress of the pupils. He appears to have known each individual boy and to have welcomed every opportunity of

[1] Shortly afterwards pressure was brought to bear on these highly placed officials and they were forced to resign; it had been represented to the Governor-General that their active participation in the management of the Vidyalaya might be wrongly construed as an indirect attempt on the part of the Government to make converts to Christianity. So solid, however, were the foundations of the college that 'when some of its supports were violently and prematurely removed it still stood erect and unshaken'.—J. Sargent, *Life of the Rev. T. T. Thomason* (1834), p. 234.

[2] A. Mayhew, *Christianity and the Government of India* (1929), p. 167.

making the acquaintance of parents. When anyone was absent
he used to go to his home and in cases of sickness he used to
provide medicine and recommend treatment. His joviality and
sympathy endeared him to pupils and parents alike and the early
success of the Hindu College owed a great deal to his personal
guidance, not to mention his liberal financial support. In spite
of the fact that no fees were charged, the number of pupils enrolled
at the beginning was small, not exceeding twenty. Hare continued
his propagandist work and persuaded many orthodox Hindu
parents, who were prejudiced against English education, to entrust
the education of their sons to his own personal supervision. By
degrees the attendance improved and in five or six years reached
sixty or seventy. Unfortunately, however, financial mismanage-
ment led to friction between the Indian and European members of
the Committee and most of the latter resigned; to make matters
worse, the bank in which the college funds were deposited went
into liquidation. The Committee were at a loss what to do but
Hare saved the situation, firstly by persuading the Government to
come to the assistance of the college and then by inducing the
Committee to accept the conditions on which assistance was
offered.

In 1823 the newly appointed Committee of Public Instruction
resolved to open a Sanskrit College in Calcutta, to take the place
of the colleges which the Government had promised to establish
at Nadia and Tirhut. Their original intention was to confine
instruction to Sanskrit and they were embarrassed when they
learned that a gift of 'extensive philosophical apparatus' (including
a 'complete whirling table' and other strange novelties) had been
made by the British India Society and sent out by the Directors
to Calcutta for use in the new college.[1] On receipt of the application from the Hindu College for financial support, it was decided
to revise the plans for the Sanskrit College and to provide
additional accommodation so that both institutions could be housed
in the same building. The main object of this resolution, adopted
on the recommendation of Dr Wilson, was to enable common
teaching in science to be given to the students of both colleges
and so meet the wishes of the Government and the Directors who
were anxious 'to introduce European science as far as practicable'.[2]

[1] H. Sharp, *Selections from Educational Records*, I, p. 80.   [2] ibid., p. 86.

The Committee were also of opinion that 'the union of Hindu and European learning being thus quietly effected in one case, it will hereafter be comparatively easy to carry the combination into other departments, and the improved cultivation of science and literature may be thus successfully and extensively promoted'.[1] This scheme was approved by the Government, who also agreed to make a substantial grant to the Hindu College on condition that it was allowed, through the Committee of Public Instruction, to exercise a reasonable measure of control. The suggestion of Government interference called forth a protest from a Committee faced with bankruptcy, but it was finally settled that Dr H. H. Wilson, Secretary of the Committee of Public Instruction, should be appointed visitor and that his supervision should be limited to the expenditure of the funds contributed by the Government. Dr Smith suggests that Wilson was selected because he was the 'least Christian of all the oriental party'[2]—a needlessly perverse judgement, which is characteristic of the author. Duff himself, in his evidence before the Select Committee of the House of Commons (1853),[3] had no hesitation in saying that Wilson was appointed because, as a great Sanskrit scholar 'his influence was deservedly great' and he generously added that, 'as an honourable man', he infused new life into the institution and made many inprovements. At any rate, Hare's foresight and tactful handling of a delicate situation not only prevented the college from having to close down, but 'first brought Government into active participation in the cause of English education'.[4]

In 1824 the foundation stone of the new building was laid, on a plot of land handed over to the Government by Hare himself, and in 1827 the original Hindu College began work under the same roof as the new Sanskrit College. Hare, who remained a member of the Managing Committee, continued his intimate association with the institution he had saved from collapse, and Wilson, who became Vice-President, proved an able and sympathetic administrator. Under the superintendence of these two gifted men the Hindu College quickly developed from what was little more than a small and struggling school, with a modest curriculum, into a collegiate institution designed to impart a

[1] ibid., p. 87.   [2] Smith, op. cit., p. 186.   [3] ibid., p. 101.
[4] ibid.

sound education in English and covering a wide variety of subjects. Liberal Government grants, annual and special, placed the College on a firm financial basis; donations to the extent of about a lakh of rupees were made for the foundation of scholarships; for the first time in its history it was housed in a suitable building and provided with facilities for the teaching of science and with a well-equipped library; distinguished scholars were appointed to the staff and high academic standards were reached and maintained; in spite of the odious innovation of charging fees the number of students shot up rapidly to over 400. The annual examinations which were held in public—sometimes in Government House in the presence of the Governor-General himself—afforded reliable testimony, to sympathizers and scoffers alike, that English education in Calcutta was making wonderful progress.

The early records of this famous college are by far the most interesting things[1] in the early history of Western education in Bengal. Its success was due to a number of causes which combined to give it a place in the intellectual life of Bengal such as no other collegiate institution in the land has ever held. References have already been made to the growing and insistent demand for English education which, in spite of the opposition of conservative opinion and apparent official indifference, had become almost inconveniently vocal in the days of Lord Hastings; this demand was intensified by the decision of the Directors to encourage 'useful learning', by which they obviously meant learning which would fit Indians for employment in the public service. This policy had been strongly urged by Elphinstone in Bombay and by Munro in Madras and was endorsed by the Directors in their Dispatch of 5 September 1827, which impressed upon the Governor-General the necessity of keeping *utility* steadily in view and pointed out that 'the first object of improved education should be to prepare a body of individuals for discharging public duties'.[2] In their next important educational Dispatch, issued three years later, emphasis was again laid upon the desirability of appointing Indians to posts of 'higher trust and responsibility', and a guarded reference was made to the possibility of gradually introducing English as the language of official business. These Dispatches are

[1] J. Ghosh, *Higher Education in Bengal under British Rule* (1926), pp. 55 ff.
[2] A. Howell, *Education in British India prior to 1854* (1872), p. 18.

of great importance because they are among the first indications of a change of policy in favour of English, rather than Oriental, learning.

In spite of instructions from London and in spite of the growth and popularity of the colleges founded by Hare and Duff, the Committee of Public Instruction were reluctant to make any sudden or sweeping innovation. In their Report for 1831,[1] however, they did call attention to the success of the Hindu College, which had 'surpassed expectation', and added that schools conducted by young men who had been educated at this institution 'were springing up in every direction'. These symptoms of modernity were, perhaps, somewhat disturbing and the members of the Committee of Public Instruction had some justification for believing that, outside Calcutta and a few other large centres, there were no openings for young men with a knowledge of English and that in smaller civil stations such knowledge would be almost useless in the transaction of public business. Further, they remained firmly convinced that the encouragement of English on the scale contemplated by the Directors would offend influential Hindus and Mohammedans, particularly pundits and maulvis, who appreciated very warmly the patronage and support which the Government had long extended to Oriental learning. Finally, events soon showed that the extension of modern secular education would have dangerous religious and social repercussions which might well be disastrous. The Committee have been blamed for their unsympathetic and reactionary policy and, doubtless, they were slow to read the signs of the times, out of touch with enlightened public opinion and unduly apprehensive of the results of the spread of modern knowledge. On the other hand, the progressive or Anglicist party, who eventually carried the day, were equally at fault. Had an early compromise been reached between extreme Orientalism and extreme Anglicism,[2] education would probably have developed along sane and normal lines such as would have had the approval and support of the leaders of both conservative and progressive public opinion.

In the same Report (1831) the Committee of Public Instruction

[1] Syed Mahmood, *A History of English Education in India* (1895), p. 35.
[2] Smith (op. cit., I, p. 186) aptly calls the extremists on either side 'Anglo-maniacs' and 'Oriento-maniacs'.

sounded a mild note of warning: they not only spoke with satisfaction of the progress in English made by the students of the Hindu College, but they went on to point out that 'the moral effect has been equally remarkable and an impatience of the restrictions of Hinduism and a disregard for its ceremonies are openly avowed by many young men of respectable birth and talents and entertained by many more who outwardly conform to the practices of their countrymen'.[1]   Reformers such as Ram Mohun Roy had, from the very beginning, foreseen that modern education was bound to react upon traditional beliefs and practices, but they could hardly have anticipated that this reaction would manifest itself in conduct which would cause such widespread offence and merited disapproval.   Hare, who made no secret of his rationalistic views, has been held responsible for the wave of irreligion which spread from the Hindu College and quickly overtook the whole student community of Bengal.

This sudden outburst, however, cannot fairly be attributed to the influence of any one individual—not even to that of the talented Anglo-Indian philosopher-poet, Derozio, who acquired a remarkable place in the estimation of Calcutta students.   He and others certainly did give an impetus to the secularist movement which began in an age of transition, when India found herself between two worlds—one dead and the other not yet born.   The splendour of her ancient social and religious institutions had grown dim, her art, literature, and learning had lost their vitality and the land was buried in almost complete ignorance.   Many turned to the past for help and guidance and, finding none, they lost hope and courage; some bolder spirits fixed their gaze ahead and sought in the more virile civilization of the West a solution of the problems which baffled their elders.   The light which flowed in from across the seas revealed, in all their grim ugliness, the defects and corruptions of a feeble and exhausted civilization.   The inevitable result was that young men broke away in disgust from the cramping restrictions which fettered liberty of thought and action and embraced the new learning with almost religious fervour. 'Westernism', to quote Lord Ronaldshay,[2] 'became the fashion of

---

[1] C. E. Trevelyan, *On the Education of the People of India* (1838), p. 8; Syed Mahmood, op. cit., p. 35.

[2] Earl of Ronaldshay, *The Heart of Aryavarta* (1925), p. 45.

the day and Westernism demanded of its votaries that they should cry down the civilization of their own country. . . . The ancient learning was despised; ancient custom was thrown aside; ancient religion was decried as an outworn superstition'. When students in the Hindu College found that every day opened to them 'a succession of new and strange phenomena in the unsettled realm of history, science and philosophy, they were suddenly thrown adrift from the moorings and anchorages of old creeds and thrown upon the wide sea of speculation and extravagance. It was no wonder that social and moral obligation began to share the fate of religious beliefs and that the whole community was in alarm at the spread of new ideas'.[1] Little wonder, indeed, that young men, having broken away from the bondage of ancient taboos, should have been guilty of abusing their new liberty and reluctant to submit themselves to the discipline which a more liberal moral code and a wider intellectual outlook demanded. On the other hand, when every allowance has been made for the impetuosity of youth, it must be admitted that the reforming zeal of many of the Hindu College students was carried to such extremes that people of all shades of opinion—progressive no less than conservative—had reason to complain.

One may, perhaps, sympathize with the tendency to question traditional beliefs, to condemn idolatrous practices, to revolt against the restrictions of caste, but it is difficult to excuse indulgence in vices which became popular simply because they were wrongly supposed to be typically English. Among Hindus the cow is regarded as particularly sacred and nothing is more offensive to orthodox believers than beef-eating. Many of the students of the Hindu College adopted out of mere bravado a meat diet and one young stalwart justified his newly acquired taste by saying that 'beef-eaters were never bullied'.[2] We read also of a dinner party at which a number of students, not content with eating beef, threw the remnants into the garden of a neighbouring Brahman. It is idle to pretend that this was in the nature of a college 'rag'; it was little short of sacrilege — a blasphemous and unforgivable insult to an innocent and devout Hindu. Again, the drinking of wine was regarded with abhorrence by Hindus as well as Moham- medans, but when it was discovered that 'an intelligent and highly

[1] A. Howell, op. cit., p. 10.   [2] A. Mayhew, op. cit., p. 167.

civilized race like the English were fond of it',[1] the ancient prejudice was contemptuously abandoned. All right thinking people deplored these excesses of misguided young men who, in the words of a contemporary, 'were cutting their way through beef and ham and wading to Liberalism through tumblers of beer'.[2] Even the college authorities became alarmed and disciplinary measures had to be taken against the worst offenders.

Lax discipline, however, was not the root cause of the trouble; this lay much deeper and may be traced to the educational ideals which inspired reformers in an age of intellectual awakening and moral instability. No one would deny that the college authorities had a genuine admiration for Western learning and a generous faith in the capacity of the Bengali mind to assimilate modern ideas; at the same time, it must be said that they failed to realize that Western civilization had grown up slowly in its own natural environment and that it could not suddenly be transplanted intact to a foreign soil. Further, a living culture not only has its roots in the past, but reflects the thoughts and ideals of the present. The new learning which was being imported from abroad and disseminated from the Hindu College had no relation either to India's past history or to her present problems. Ardent, but well-meaning, reformers were mistaken in thinking that modern knowledge would rapidly transform young Bengalis into young Englishmen and they failed to see that an 'educated aristocracy', ignorant and contemptuous of India's history and traditions and unsympathetic towards the beliefs and outlook of the masses of the Indian people, might do more harm than good. In short, they made the capital mistake of trying to supplant Eastern by Western culture, whereas they should have aimed at a synthesis or fusion of what was best in each.

Again, the education imparted at the Hindu College was narrow, not merely because it was entirely secular nor even because it aimed solely at the cultivation of the intellect; too much importance was attached to literary studies and, in spite of the 'extensive philosophical apparatus', nothing was done to inculcate the scientific spirit which had long been dormant in India. The

---

[1] J. Ghosh, op. cit., p. 79 ; cf. Ronaldshay, op. cit.. p. 47.
[2] *Bengal Obituary* (1851), p. 104; cf. Mittra, op. cit., Appendix B, p. xxviii.

uncritical study of English authors, not always chosen with discrimination, had an upsetting effect on the impressionable Bengali mind and, in the last resort, the excesses of reckless students may safely be attributed to a system of education devised by enthusiastic, but short-sighted, amateurs. The warmth and sincerity with which the college staff communicated the new know-ledge made an instant appeal to young men who looked forward to successful careers as the reward of ambition and intelligence, enterprise and application. Men like Derozio and, later, Richardson, were held in the highest esteem and regarded as almost infallible guides. Even Dr Duff never gained a greater ascendancy over the students of Calcutta than the youthful Professor Derozio, who (in the words of his biographer) 'did more than any man to arouse, quicken and impel the thought of young India'.[1] He used to impress upon his students that they should think things out for themselves and he encouraged free discussion on all subjects—social, moral and religious. As a result, many of them began to question the most cherished convictions of their elders and to heap ridicule upon ceremonies which the orthodox performed with the utmost reverence. Conservative parents were horrified when they discovered that their sons not only defied caste restrictions but partook of prohibited food and dined with all and sundry. Popular opinion was not far wrong in regarding Derozio as the head and source of offence and an agitation for his removal was started, and quickly gained ground. The Managing Committee were in a quandary: a sudden fall in numbers made them realize the danger which threatened the college and they feared the withdrawal of Government support; on the other hand, Derozio's competence was unquestioned and his popularity among students immense. Pressure was brought to bear on a number of parents, who took their sons away and sent them to Duff's college, and eventually feeling ran so high that the Committee were forced to take action.

They met in solemn conclave to consider three allegations which had been brought against Derozio, but he was not informed what the charges were nor was he given an opportunity to speak in his own defence. In spite of the efforts of Hare and Wilson,

---

[1] Quoted by J. Ghosh, op. cit., p. 77.

who appreciated his exceptional ability and force of character, it was resolved to dispense with the services of the most scholarly and inspiring teacher the college had ever had. This decision was conveyed to him in a private letter from Dr Wilson and, to save himself the mortification of receiving notice of dismissal, Derozio immediately tendered his resignation. This was accepted and then he learned—for the first time—that he had been accused of denying the existence of God, of advocating filial disobedience and of holding that 'marriage between brothers and sisters was innocent and allowable'. His reply[1] to Dr Wilson is not merely an indignant denial but a dignified confession of faith. He began by emphasizing that he had never, in the hearing of any living being, denied the existence of God, but confessed that he had discussed the doubts which philosophers had raised on this momentous issue. He insisted that it had been his duty to examine the arguments which Hume and others had advanced against theism rather than to turn his students into 'pert and ignorant dogmatists by permitting them to know what could be said only on one side of a grave issue'. This admission explains why parents of an older generation, unacquainted with the spirit of free inquiry which characterizes Western thought, regarded him as an atheist, and once he was branded as an atheist they were ready to believe anything that might be said against him.

The other allegations were entirely baseless and, in spite of the occasional excesses and tactless conduct of some of the Hindu College students, there is good reason for believing that Derozio exercised a healthy influence on the younger generation both inside and outside the College. Indeed his biographer claims that 'the moral teaching of Derozio was as high and pure as his own life was blameless',[2] while an Indian contemporary has left it on record that, although he was outspoken in his condemnation of idolatry and superstition, he raised the moral standards of his students to such an extent that 'their conduct was exemplary and gained the applause of the outside world'.[3] The subsequent careers of a few meat-eaters and drunkards is no proof that Derozio's influence was not on the

---

[1] Mittra, op. cit., pp. 22-7.

[2] T. Edwards, *Henry Derozio, the Eurasian Poet* (1884), p. 36.

[3] F. B. Bradley-Birt (Editor), *Poems of Henry Louis Vivian Derozio* (1923), p. xxxiv.

side of virtuous living. The truth of the matter is that the anti-religious feeling which startled a priest-ridden community was 'the inevitable result of pouring new wine into old bottles' and, 'there is no doubt it went to the heads of young Bengal'.[1] Clearly Derozio was made a scapegoat in order to appease the forces of bigotry and intolerance. He felt that he had been shamefully treated, but sought in journalism an outlet for his energy and independent view. He founded and edited *The East Indian*, the first paper to champion the cause of the Anglo-Indian community. He, also, contributed to various other papers which the keen intellectual awakening of the day had called into existence, and he continued to interest himself in everything which concerned the advancement of modern education. His sudden and untimely death in his twenty-third year cut short what promised to be a brilliant career and deprived India of one whose courageous leadership she could ill afford to lose. Dr Smith, in his biography of Duff,[2] grudgingly admits that he was a 'Eurasian of some genius and much conceit', a biased and unsympathetic verdict. There is little doubt that he was a scholar of exceptional ability and, still less, that he was a born teacher whose enthusiasm had a remarkable influence upon his students. Dr Mill, Principal of Bishop's College, considered that his exposition and criticism of Kant showed great philosophical insight and originality of thought.[3] Unfortunately, this was never published and his slender volumes of verse have not helped to enhance his reputation. They were extravagantly praised in his own day but, in spite of formal beauty of language, metrical felicity and luxuriant imagery, they have failed to stand the test of time. They are interesting mainly as the precocious output of a sensitive and overwrought youth and hold out a promise which a longer span of years might have brought to fulfilment. As a poet he is deservedly forgotten, but as a teacher who encouraged moral and intellectual integrity, who cultivated a taste for what was best in literature and admirable in

[1] Ronaldshay, op. cit., pp. 18 and 45.
[2] G. Smith, op. cit., I, p. 143.
[3] Edwards, op. cit., p. 13. This appreciation is all the more valuable because Mill was a very distinguished Scholar and Fellow of Trinity College, Cambridge. (See H. Whitehead, *Indian Problems in Religion, Education, Politics* (1924), p. 177.)

conduct, his memory is still revered by many who do not belong to the community of which he was an enlightened member.

With the departure of Derozio the agitation against the Hindu College died down and, notwithstanding the rival attraction of Duff's institution, its popularity and attendance increased. No change in policy, however, was introduced and the college continued to impart, in a purely secular atmosphere, a modern education on Western lines. In 1836 D. L. Richardson,[1] on the recommendation of Macaulay, was appointed Professor of English and, later, he became Principal. Like Derozio, he had earned a reputation as a minor poet and versatile journalist, and his success as a teacher was hardly less pronounced than that of his youthful predecessor. Without losing the confidence or respect of parents, he exercised a great influence over students and he gave a great impetus to the study of English.

Indeed, so modern did the curriculum become that the classical languages were crowded out altogether. Young men who seized every opportunity to denounce Hindu religion and culture were not likely to be attracted towards the study of Sanskrit, and at an early stage the teaching of the 'language of the gods' was discontinued. In 1841 the Persian classes were abolished, with the result that the curriculum became exclusively modern. The total neglect of Oriental classical learning was a serious blunder, but circumstances compelled Hare and his colleagues to take a step which, although it may have been expedient, was extremely short-sighted. Lord William Bentinck's decision to employ an ever-increasing number of qualified young Indians, trained under European supervision, in posts of responsibility, and the discontinuance of Persian (1837) as the language of public business made the demand for English education more pressing than ever. In

---

[1] David Lester Richardson (1801-65) was invalided as a Major from the Bengal Army (1833). He subsequently devoted himself to educational work and literary pursuits. He was successively Principal of the Hindu, Krishnagar and Hooghly Colleges, but his appointment as Principal of the Presidency College (1859) was disallowed by the Secretary of State. Among his many published works are *Sonnets and Other Poems*, *Literary Leaves* and *Literary Recreations*. Scholar, essayist and poet, he was regarded as the most eminent Professor of English in India. Macaulay is reported to have said to him, 'I may forget everything about India, but your reading of Shakespeare—never'. *Vide* K. Zachariah, *History of Hooghly College, 1836-1936* (1936).

Duff's college the study of classical literature had never received encouragement and, even at Serampore, the Baptist missionaries found it necessary to modify their curriculum and, as early as 1836, they decided to give that attention to the cultivation of English which they had previously given to the study of Sanskrit. In each of these three colleges, however, great emphasis was laid upon the importance of the vernaculars and Hare, who had himself studied Bengali and found it deficient in modern learning, realized as clearly as the missionaries that it would be educationally unsound to neglect the mother-tongue—the spoken language of the vast majority of the people. Indeed, it is quite true to say that the importance which the Hindu College attached to modern languages, Bengali as well as English, was the first serious blow aimed at Oriental classical learning which, ever since the time of Warren Hastings, had been liberally patronized by the Government.

Throughout these eventful years Hare continued to guide the destinies of the Hindu College. His optimism and perseverance were an inspiration to his colleagues on the Committee and, despite his modest and retiring disposition, his influence carried the greatest weight. He remained steadfast in his conviction that the spread of modern knowledge was India's most urgent need and his policy of 'uncompromising modernism' was steadily pursued. No one welcomed more warmly Macaulay's Minute, while Bentinck's Resolution (1835), which followed hard upon its heels and authorized the expenditure of Government funds on English education *alone*, put the seal of official approval on the policy Hare had consistently advocated for well-nigh twenty years. In coming to a decision which marked a complete break with the past, neither Bentinck nor Macaulay was unmindful of the phenomenal growth of the English colleges in Calcutta, nor were they unaware of the prominent part which Hare had played in promoting the intellectual and moral advancement of the people of Bengal. In their Report for 1835 the Committee of Public Instruction recommended that Hare's 'invaluable and disinterested services to the Hindu College and to the cause of education generally' should receive some fitting recognition from the Government; they pointed out that there need be no fear of creating an awkward precedent, because few others would ever be found to bestow years of unremitting labour on such a noble cause 'without any expectation of reward except what is to be derived from the gratification of benevolent feeling'.[1] A few years later, in recognition of his services to the cause of education, Hare, whose charitable activities had made serious inroads on his bank balance, was appointed a Commissioner of the Court of Small Causes. His official duties, however, did not prevent him from devoting a great part of his time to the affairs of the Hindu College, the Medical College and the School Society's School, each of which he visited almost daily.

Concerning his association with the two latter institutions a few words must now be said. In 1833, Lord William Bentinck, shocked at the deplorable state of medical education which was then mainly given through the medium of Hindustani at the Medical Institution (1822), appointed a Committee to report on the subject. It had been suggested that medical education might well be imparted through English, but Dr Tyler, who was Superintendent of the Institution and an accomplished Orientalist, considered that such a step would be utterly impracticable. Duff, however, succeeded in persuading his colleagues on the Committee that scientific instruction in and through English should present no greater difficulties among Bengalis than among the Gaelic-speaking peoples of Scotland, Ireland and Wales. 'The battle which had been so well contested in the Education Committee was fought over again in this new field',[2] and the result was another victory for the advocates of modern learning. Deliberations were prolonged for more than a year and eventually the Committee unanimously resolved to recommend the establishment of a new college in which the various branches of medical science should be taught through English on the latest and most approved European lines. One of the last acts of Bentinck's administration was the opening of the new Medical College, the first of its kind in India, in 1837. Its success was immediate: a hospital was provided three years later and in 1841 a female hospital, with a midwifery ward, was added; within ten years the number of students increased from 60 to about 500. It had been feared that the ancient prejudice against handling dead bodies would debar high-caste Hindus from entering the medical profession. These fears were

[1] Mittra, op. cit., p. 42.   [2] Trevelyan, op. cit., p. 29.

quickly dispelled when Mahasudan Gupta, a student from Hare's college, performed the first dissection in the presence of an admiring class of young men who had thrown off the shackles of ancient prejudice. The scene was graphically described by Bethune[1] when he unveiled a portrait of Mahasudan Gupta, which remains one of the most cherished possessions of the Calcutta Medical College. His courageous example was quickly followed and from that time onwards, says Trevelyan,[2] Brahmans and other high-caste Hindus could be seen in the dissecting room 'handling the knife with even more than the indifference of European professional men'.

It would be ungenerous not to acknowledge the prominent part played by Duff in the founding of the Medical College, but it is surprising that his biographer says that, although David Hare 'seems to have been equally zealous', 'we have no record of his action'.[3] Had he consulted Peary Chand Mittra's little book he would have found that Dr Bramley, the first Principal, had left it on record that 'scarcely had the order from Government for the institution of the College appeared, before this gentleman [Hare] prompted by the dictates of his own benevolent spirit . . . immediately afforded me his influence in the furtherance of the ends it had in view. . . . Indeed, I may say, that without Mr Hare's influence any attempt to form a Hindu Medical Class would have been futile and I trust I bespeak the indulgence of the Committee in availing myself of this opportunity of recording publicly, though inadequately, how much the cause of medical education owes to that gentleman, as well as the extent of my deep obligation to him personally'.[4] Hare's contribution to the advancement of scientific medical knowledge does not rest on mere hearsay, as Dr Smith seems to imply. In 1837 he became Secretary of the Medical College and, when he resigned in 1841, he was appointed by the Government an Honorary Member of the Council 'in which situation he was usefully and actively employed till his decease'.[5] No further evidence is necessary to show that no one has a stronger claim to be regarded as one of the founders of European medical education in India and that no one was more closely

---

[1] J. A. Richey, *Selections from Educational Records*, II, *1840-1859* (1922), p. 313.   [2] Trevelyan, op. cit., p. 33.   [3] Smith, op. cit., I, p. 216.
[4] Mittra, op. cit., p. 132.   [5] ibid., p. 45.

associated with the administration of a college whose standards, according to Dr F. J. Mouat, quickly reached the level of those maintained at the various Colleges of Surgeons in Great Britain.

The importance of the two great collegiate institutions with which Hare's name is so closely associated is apt to create the impression that he was solely interested in the promotion of higher and professional education. This is far from being the case, for he devoted much of his time, and not a little of his money, to the advancement of elementary education for girls as well as boys. He became a member of the Calcutta School Book Society (1817) and paid an annual subscription of Rs. 100; he was one of the founders and European Secretary of the Calcutta School Society[1] which was started in the following year to improve indigenous schools, establish new elementary schools and provide English education for a select number of promising pupils and thus create a supply of qualified teachers. Among the new schools which were opened that at Arpooly was, at Hare's request, made over to his personal control.[2] A small grant for its upkeep was made by the Society, but, as no fees were charged, this was insufficient and the balance was willingly paid by Hare out of his own pocket. In spite of the fact that he decided to restrict admission to pupils whose parents were too poor to pay for the education of their children, this school was the most successful and most efficient of all the Society's institutions. In the Report for 1820 it is stated that Hare's school at Arpooly had 'not only the advantage of his personal superintendence' but was 'conducted at his own expense'.[3] A few years later, lack of funds compelled the Society to close down four of its five new schools, but the Arpooly school prospered to such an extent that an English department was added, to which the brightest pupils were promoted, and prepared for admission to the Hindu College. One of the early Reports of the Committee of the School Society mentions that 'the Society's scholars continue to rank among the brightest ornaments of the College' and Hare took a justifiable pride in the successes gained by the pupils of his own school. The English department, however, was not allowed to overshadow the vernacular, and even those who were promoted to the higher classes were obliged to continue their study of Bengali in the *patshala*.

---

[1] Mittra, op. cit., p. 48.   [2] ibid., p. 49.   [3] ibid., p. 52.

This practice was not only sound in itself but set an excellent example to the other schools in the neighbourhood. Hare's name became a household word in the city and an Indian gentleman is reported to have said that the interest which a 'temporary resident' showed in the welfare of the inhabitants of Calcutta put his own countrymen to shame.[1] If Hare paid the piper he also called the tune: he insisted on the use of suitable textbooks, introduced sound methods of teaching and discouraged corporal punishment. His sympathy and generosity won for him a host of friends and admirers and the Arpooly school soon became known as 'Hare's School'. He himself, with his usual dislike of publicity, deplored the fuss which was made over what he considered a trifling service to his fellows; but some years after his death the Government approved of the change of name and the Hare School still remains as a memorial to its benevolent founder.

Not even the progress of the Hindu College gave Hare more satisfaction than the gradual but steady growth and improvement of the vernacular education of boys. Shortly before his death he told a friend that, if he were spared for another ten years, he would live to see an equally striking expansion of female education. Primary education had long occupied his thoughts and in the first Report of the School Society (which he, as Secretary, probably penned himself) it was stated that 'adult and female education, the extension and improvement of the indigenous system and the education of a greater number of clever boys . . . are all objects of great importance to be vigorously pursued in the metropolis and its vicinity'.[2] As early as 1819 the Calcutta Female Juvenile Society was formed and in the following year it began work with a small class of eight pupils. In spite of slender resources, the difficulty of finding teachers and the prejudices of the people— particularly the better classes—the Society was maintaining in 1824 six schools with 160 girls. It also undertook the publication of Rajah Radhakant Deb's *Tract on Female Education*, a pamphlet which aimed at showing that, in the past, Hindus had encouraged the education of girls and that history afforded numerous examples of women whose learning and intellectual attainments were of a high order. The pioneer work of this Society deserves to be remembered,

[1] Mittra, op. cit., p. 50. [2] ibid., p. 52.

but more solid achievements stand to the credit of Miss Cooke
(afterwards Mrs Wilson),[1] who arrived in Calcutta in 1821 to
place her services at the disposal of the School Society. Several of
the Hindu members of the Committee objected strongly to the
engagement of a schoolmistress and it is doubtful whether the
financial resources of the Committee could have stood any additional strain. Miss Cooke, however, began work under the
auspices of the Church Missionary Society and in 1822 she had
established eight schools. She received the active help and
encouragement of the Marchioness of Hastings and in 1824 the
number of schools had increased to 24, containing over 400 girls.
In this year the management was entrusted to the Ladies Society
of Female Education, of which Lady Amherst consented to be
Patroness and of which David Hare was an enthusiastic member.

Progress, however, continued to be very slow and the Government were reluctant to participate in a movement against which
there was a strong prejudice—one which was not founded on
any direct precept of the Hindu faith, but rather on immemorial
custom and tradition. In 1849 Bethune, who had succeeded
Macaulay as Law Member and who became President of the
Council of Education, established the famous girls' school which
bears his name and in the following year Lord Dalhousie's Minute
indicated that the Government had at last abandoned its policy of
non-interference and resolved to encourage, openly and generously,
the cause of female education. It has been calculated[2] that in 1852,
ten years after Hare's death, the Government had made practically
no provision for female education, while the missionaries had
provided schools for over 13,000 girls. Even this small measure
of success was partially, at any rate, due to the efforts of far-
sighted and disinterested reformers, of whom Ram Mohun Roy,
Radhakant Deb, and David Hare were not the least noteworthy.

This is not the place in which to dilate upon the various other
services which Hare rendered to his adopted country. He stoutly
championed the liberty of the press, the introduction of trial by
jury, the use of English in the courts; he was an active member
of the Asiatic Society, the British India Society, and the Agricultural

---

[1] Richey, op. cit., pp. 35 ff.

[2] F. W. Thomas, *History and Prospects of British Education in India* (1891)
p. 53.

and Horticultural Society of India; above all, he was a liberal subscriber to every deserving charitable cause and seems to have valued money only in so far as it enabled him to help others. In the midst of his many benevolent activities he, like Derozio, was suddenly stricken down by cholera and died after a short illness (1842). To the end he retained his cheerfulness and courage: when he realized the gravity of his complaint he said to his servant 'Go and tell Mr Grey to prepare a coffin for me', and when the doctor tried to relieve his sufferings he asked to be left alone as 'he wanted to die peaceably'.[1] His death cast a gloom over the whole city and, in spite of a torrential downpour, thousands of sorrowful mourners attended one of the largest funerals ever seen in Calcutta. Hare's religious views had been so unorthodox that his dead body was denied the rites of Christian burial and his remains were laid in a grave in College Square, over which a monument was afterwards erected by a sad but grateful people. An Indian contemporary, who subsequently embraced Christianity, declared that he did not know what Hare's doctrine was 'but that his life was that of a veritable Christian'.[2] It was certainly 'rich in sympathy and in service and in the inspiration that comes from a lofty end steadily pursued';[3] it would be difficult to find in the pages of India's long history a more conspicuous example of disinterested benevolence. Even to this day the anniversary of his death is observed with sincere and sorrowful veneration, and the Presidency and Medical Colleges, the Hare School and the David Hare Training College perpetuate the memory of a benefactor whom India rightly claims as her own.

The fact that Hare was neither a Government official nor a Christian missionary gives him a unique place in the history of modern Indian education; indeed, it is a very remarkable thing that a private individual—without even the advantages of high social standing—should have been able to introduce, with the help of a few Indian reformers, a type of secular collegiate education which served as a model for the Government in his own lifetime and which, with few modifications, is still followed in every part of India. It was the success of Hare's venture which paved the way for the legislative measures which are associated with the names of various statesmen and administrators; also, had the Hindu

[1] Mittra, op. cit., p. 72.   [2] ibid., p. 116.   [3] Ghosh, op. cit., p. 59.

College proved a failure, as very nearly happened, Duff would have found it even more difficult than he did to carry through his daring educational experiment. In spite of. Hare's successful pioneer work, the credit for having introduced English education into India is usually given to Bentinck and Macaulay, and their enlightened policy has been extolled to the skies. Hare, on the other hand, has been belittled for no other reason, apparently, than that he was a rationalist. Assuming that the decision to introduce Western learning was a wise one (and even hostile critics admit that something may be said in its favour), Hare would seem to be entitled to not a little of the eulogy which has been heaped upon others. In the first place, he was mainly responsible for the foundation of the Hindu College and it was largely due to his influence that the Government were induced to identify themselves with the movement for the promotion of higher *secular* education; secondly, beyond the welfare and prosperity of the people, he had no ulterior motive, whereas Macaulay, Trevelyan and others who also were not missionaries, thought that Western enlightenment would destroy Hinduism and pave the way for the introduction of Christianity;[1] in other words, they looked on English education not merely as a cultural but as a proselytizing agency.

This inner conviction was not expressed in public utterances nor in official papers and, consequently, some might feel inclined to accuse those who shaped the Government's educational policy of hypocrisy or deceit;[2] but this would be unjust. Macaulay's belief that modern enlightenment would undermine Hinduism and bring in Christianity was, in his day, 'a reasonable guess',[3] and there is no doubt that those who shared his views thought

[1] The conventional view is that Macaulay was an orthodox Christian, and this has been accepted without question by historians of Indian education. Macaulay, however, was very reticent about his religious beliefs and several critics, not all of them ill-informed, have argued that he had no religious convictions whatever; *vide* Prof. C. F. Montague (Editor), *Critical and Historical Essays* (Standard Edition), I, p. xxv (1903), and E. E. Kellett, *Reconsiderations* (1928).

[2] A. H. Benton, *Indian Moral Instruction and Caste Problems* (1917), pp. 44-6.

[3] E. Thompson and G. T. Garratt, *Rise and Fulfilment of British Rule in India* (1934), p. 310.

they were playing a perfectly fair game. Unfortunately, Macaulay knew very little about the East and never managed to get into the right relationship with India; what Trevelyan calls 'the excrescences of Hinduism' stirred his indignation, but he had no conception of the value of Sanskrit literature nor of the depths of Hindu philosophy. He had not the least doubt that the introduction of English letters and modern science would usher in a new heaven and a new earth, and we may be perfectly sure that he never accused himself of duplicity and was never troubled by any qualms of conscience on the score of his educational proposals. To Hare, Hinduism was just as repugnant as it was to Macaulay or to Duff and he associated with it all the ills and abuses that he was anxious to redress; his aim, like theirs, was to employ modern education as a means of undermining an outworn creed which hampered the reconstruction of a 'decomposed society'. Where Hare differed from the others was in his belief that all religion was mere superstition and his open rejection of Christianity offended many of his own countrymen. His rationalism, however, won him the confidence and support of a large number of Indians, who were relieved to know that his educational scheme was not designed to make converts. The assurance that Hare had no concern with the salvation of souls, but that he was eager to make this a better and a happier world, is the main explanation of the early success of the Hindu College. To argue that his philanthropy was misguided simply because it was not Christian seems rather bigoted; to argue that his views were less liberal than those of Macaulay, is hardly fair to a reformer who honestly believed that he was acting in the best interests of those whose moral and material welfare he sought to promote. If Hare had not the intellectual attainments of men such as Duff and Macaulay, he had a larger heart and broader human sympathies.

It is well to remember, also, that David Hare had never any intention of formulating a scheme of higher education for a whole continent. His aim was more limited and more practical—to provide in Calcutta itself facilities for the training of higher class Hindus, which would fit them to take their places as the enlightened leaders of society. Until the Vidyalaya became the Presidency College (1854) admission was restricted to high-caste Hindu students and it was to the upper classes that Hare looked for

6

recruits who would carry out a comprehensive programme of social reform. His primary object was not to train a large number of subordinate officials, still less to form an educated aristocracy who would despise their own country and cut themselves off from all contact with the ignorant masses. He regarded education mainly as an instrument of social uplift, as a means of raising the standards of ordinary life and of making people more prosperous and contented. Further, he believed that those who had had the benefit of an English education would, through the medium of their own language, spread modern knowledge among the masses and in this way serve the community at large. It was on this account that he attached special importance to the study of Bengali and made it compulsory even in the highest college classes. For various reasons his expectations were not fulfilled: the caste system is not favourable to the working of 'filtration' and, particularly in the early days, few educated Indians showed any inclination to improve the lot of their more unfortunate countrymen; again, the increasing opportunities for Government service and for employment in mercantile or other offices were fatal to the success of the plans which many of the early reformers had in view. Even in Hare's own day there were signs that showed pretty clearly which way the wind was blowing and, as time went on, the utilitarian, or cash, value of an English education became paramount. When Hare applied to the Government for financial assistance for the Hindu College, he could not possibly have foreseen the course which events were to take. Even the publication of Bentinck's Resolution was little indication that higher education would shortly be confined, almost entirely, to the training of clerks and subordinate officials. Nor was this the intention of the Court of Directors: their early educational dispatches show very clearly that, over and above the needs of the public service, they had in mind the intellectual and moral improvement of the people and the development of the material prosperity of the country. These were the ideals which inspired Hare and his colleagues and they are deserving of wholehearted admiration. It is unfortunate that the system which grew up from small beginnings in one private college was made to serve narrower and more selfish ends, but for this unexpected development Hare cannot be held responsible.

It has been claimed that the education imparted at the Hindu College was, even from a purely secular point of view, inherently defective and that the failure of a system based on Hare's model was inevitable. There are good grounds for this line of attack and it is true that mistakes which were made at the beginning were perpetuated in later foundations. It was, for instance, a blunder to over-emphasize the importance of English literary studies, to exclude entirely the Oriental classics, and to make little or no provision for science. One must bear in mind, however, that the demand for a knowledge of English and for an acquaintance with European literature was as genuine as it was widespread and this had a tremendous influence on the early reformers when they came to frame courses of study; they themselves regarded English as a powerful civilizing agency and were proud to follow the example of the ancient Romans who made Latin the vehicle of imperial culture. Hare was not a highly educated man and so his contempt for Sanskrit, and his failure to realize the importance of the scientific spirit, can easily be understood. On the other hand, the English education which the Hindu College imparted to eager young Bengalis had, in spite of its narrowness, an immense influence for good. There is no gainsaying that it enlarged the boundaries of the Indian mind, that it weakened the hold of superstition, that it broke down the tyranny of social convention, that it developed certain manly qualities of character, that it gave birth to new hopes and aspirations, that it even helped to build up a sense of corporate life and national unity. These were solid gains which more than balanced the losses on the debit side. It is little wonder that the Government were greatly impressed by the many and fruitful results of Hare's experiment and decided to model their own collegiate institutions on the lines of the Vidyalaya.

Finally, Indians set great store by Western learning and the growth of English education during the last twenty-five years of Hare's life was little short of phenomenal. It is impossible to say with any accuracy when English was first taught in Calcutta, but it is convenient to regard the establishment of the Supreme Court in 1774 as the first real stimulus to the acquisition of the language of the new rulers. Up to the turn of the century, however, little progress had been made, although a number of 'venture' schools had sprung up to meet the growing demand. When Hare arrived English education was in its infancy; a little more than sixteen years later he founded an institution which gave modern learning a prestige it had never previously enjoyed. For a quarter of a century his intimate association with this 'home of learning' remained unbroken and in the year of his death the number of youths learning English in Calcutta alone was in the neighbourhood of 10,000. The secularist jeweller had played a prominent part in the campaign against ignorance and superstition; indeed, his contributions to India's educational advancement suffer little in comparison with those of his more eminent contemporaries. It is true that in certain respects his educational views were narrow, but there is ample evidence that many great historical movements have been originated by men who were able to see only one side of a question.

ALEXANDER DUFF

ALEXANDER DUFF, 1806-78

PIONEER OF MISSIONARY EDUCATION

I⊤ has been said that the history of English education in India could be told in the lives of three Scottish missionaries. This statement contains an element of truth, in that it emphasizes the fact that missionaries from Scotland have played a very prominent part in building up the present educational system. The names of Duff, Wilson and Miller—to name only a few—readily occur to the mind, and of these Dr Alexander Duff, a man of rare ability, tremendous energy and indomitable will, is by far the most important. Not only was he the first in the field, but he inaugurated a new method of missionary enterprise which has had notable educational results. He was, beyond all question, the founder of the modern Educational Mission, which, since its inception in 1830, has been well served by many devout and able men. He was not, however, the first missionary to engage in educational work, nor even the first to found a missionary college. Schwartz and many others before him had opened schools in various parts of the country and the Serampore trio had, in their Danish settlement, established a college which was raised by the King of Denmark to university status (1827) a few years before Duff set foot in India. It was he, however, who gave a new direction to higher education and made it the vehicle of spiritual culture; consequently, the establishment in Calcutta of the General Assembly's Institution—the prototype of the great missionary colleges in Bombay, Madras and other Indian cities— opens up a new chapter in educational history.

Alexander Duff was born in 1806 and was educated at Perth Grammar School and St Andrew's University. He had a very brilliant academic career and was inspired by one of his professors, the celebrated Dr Thomas Chalmers, to dedicate his life to missionary work. In 1829, shortly after his marriage, he was ordained and started on an eventful voyage to India, which lasted more than seven months and was interrupted by two shipwrecks. His Missionary Board had decided that education should be employed as a means of propagating Christianity and, except that he was instructed

to choose a centre in the interior rather than make Calcutta the
scene of his activities, Duff was given an entirely free hand.
Possibly the authorities at home thought that there would be more
scope for useful work in a place where missionary enterprise had
not yet penetrated, possibly they thought that competition with
other Protestant missionaries in the capital would damage the
common cause. However this may be, Duff had no definite plan
in mind when he arrived. He hastened to visit the various
missionary establishments in the city and neighbourhood and very
quickly came to the conclusion that he must disregard the one
injunction he had received. He saw that not only was there
room in Calcutta for an educational institution run on Christian
lines but that, in order to meet the demand for English education
and to combat the secularism of the Hindu College, such an
institution was a most urgent need. The older missionaries tried
to dissuade the impetuous young Highlander and assured him
that his foolhardy scheme would do more harm than good—
that it would 'deluge Calcutta with rogues and villains'.[1] The
aged Dr Carey, however, gave his warmest approval to the project
for a Christian college in Calcutta and, heartened by the blessing
of the most eminent living missionary, Duff decided to carry his
scheme into immediate effect.

The proposal to establish a Scottish College had been made
by Dr Bryce as early as 1824 and had been approved by the
General Assembly of the Church of Scotland in the following
year. Bryce, apparently on the strength of an essay on Christianity
in the East which was awarded the Buchanan Prize by the
University of Aberdeen, had been sent out to Calcutta in 1814
by the East India Company as their first Presbyterian Chaplain
in the newly created Ecclesiastical Establishment. He actually
travelled to India in the same boat as Dr Middleton, but the
relations between the Anglican Bishop and the Scottish Chaplain
were never very harmonious. Each, however, went to the scene
of his labours fully determined to confine his ministrations to his
own countrymen. Dr Middleton, in spite of the entreaties of
Thomason, Corrie and other 'evangelical' chaplains, always fought
shy of missionaries, but Dr Bryce, 'encouraged by the approbation

[1] J. N. Ogilvie, *The Apostles of India* (1915), p. 390.

of Ram Mohun Roy, presented to the General Assembly in 1824 the petition and memorial which first directed the attention of the Church of Scotland to India as a field for missionary exertions on the plan . . . to which this eminently gifted scholar, himself a Brahmin of high caste, had specially annexed his sanction'.[1] Dr George Smith considers that Bryce's 'plan for a "Scottish College" was dictated by sectarian hostility to the Bishop's College of his rival'[2] and that the 'secular ecclesiastic' (he had proved himself an efficient Superintendent of the Stationery Office) had chiefly in mind an institution for the instruction of clergymen in the languages of the country. He may have thought that a college of this type, under the superintendence of the minister of St Andrew's Church, would help to enhance his prestige and, possibly, irritate the Bishop whom he had already worsted in the squabble over the relative height of the steeples of the Anglican and Scottish churches. Whatever may be the truth of the matter, the college which Duff founded in 1830 was of a totally different type. His primary aim was not to prepare Indians for the ministry, still less to instruct in the vernacular new recruits to the mission field. As a leader of the church militant he planned a great spiritual campaign against Hinduism, the 'preparing of a mine and the setting of a train which shall one day explode and tear up the whole from its lowest depths'.[3] For Duff, education was to be the handmaid of religion, and instruction saturated with Christianity was to be used as an evangelical agency for the eradication of a firmly established system of superstitious belief and idolatrous practice. It is only fair to Dr Bryce to state that, whatever his original intentions may have been, he became a warm admirer of Dr Duff and prided himself that he had had some share in the establishment of a college which rivalled Bishop's College in the splendour of its structure and strove to outdo it in the range of its Christian usefulness.

Duff had not been long in Calcutta before he realized that the results of missionary effort had hitherto been disappointing. Everywhere congregations were small, primary schools poorly attended and converts limited to a few orphans and members of

[1] J. Bryce, *A Sketch of Native Education in India* (1839), p. 58.
[2] G. Smith, *The Life of Alexander Duff* (1879), I, p. 40.
[3] ibid., p. 109.

the lowest castes, who became financially dependent on the missions of their choice and were popularly known as 'rice Christians'. Missionaries themselves were becoming disheartened, and not a few must have begun to think that the Abbé Dubois[1] was not very far wrong when he said that it was impossible to convert true Hindus and useless to try. The apparent hopelessness of the situation did not discourage Duff, it merely spurred him to more energetic action. He saw very clearly that the methods which the missionaries had hitherto adopted were inadequate to the great task they had undertaken, that they were limited in range and efficiency; he was perhaps the first to realize that if any substantial measure of success were to be achieved efforts must be made to get into closer touch with the more influential classes of society. In order to attain this end, he decided to found a system of modern education which would ultimately embrace all the branches of knowledge ordinarily taught in the higher schools and colleges of Europe, but 'inseparable with the Christian faith and its doctrines, precepts and evidences, with a view to the practical regulation of life and conduct'.[2] In this way he determined to make Christianity 'not merely the foundation on which the whole superstructure of all useful knowledge was to be reared, but the animating spirit which was to pervade and hallow all'.[3] His main object was to appeal to Brahmans and other high-caste Hindus, who were the leaders of society and 'the sole possessors of knowledge and of an already developed intellectual life'.[4] From them would radiate, he confidently expected, a general knowledge of Christian doctrine and Christian views of life, which would not only become a matter of public interest but would enter into ghostly conflict with the spirit and ideals of Hinduism. He saw no reason to doubt that many young men, belonging to the best families, who were given the benefit of a religious education would become converted to Christianity and that some of them, at least, would enter the ministry. In a word, his scheme for higher Christian education was designed as an indirect attack on the stronghold of Hinduism and was intended to supplement, rather

---

[1] J. R. Dubois, *Description of the Character, Manners and Customs of the People of India* (1817); translated and edited by H. K. Beauchamp, 1897.

[2] Smith, op. cit., I, p. 110.   [3] ibid.

[4] J. Richter, *A History of Missions in India* (1908), p. 175.

than to supplant, the more direct efforts of the older missionaries. Duff realized that open-air preaching and the running of elementary schools must continue to occupy a prominent place in the mission field, but he decided that his own work would be more profitably pursued along different lines.

The policy of using higher education as a missionary instrument was not entirely new. Here, as in almost every other direction, the Serampore trio had given a lead; but the influence of their college was restricted owing to the fact that it was situated in Danish territory at what was, in those days, a considerable distance from Calcutta. Bishop's College had developed into a theological seminary and the Anglicans, always nervous of incurring the Government's displeasure, were mainly interested in the training of Indian pastors and in baptismal statistics. The Hindu College, although it aimed at the overthrow of Hinduism, was anything but a missionary establishment and did not seek to inculcate Christian or any other religious dogma. Secular education was, for Duff, a contradiction in terms and he resolved to establish an institution which would not only undermine false religion but also combat agnosticism. His plan was to attack each where each appeared to be strongest—among the ranks of the higher and educated classes. This policy, which marks a new departure in missionary endeavour, involved two momentous decisions. In the first place, if higher education was to be truly Christian, the Christian religion must be placed in the very forefront of his educational programme; secondly, instruction must be given through the medium of the English language. It is little wonder that experienced missionaries were alarmed and tried to prevent the latest recruit to their ranks from following such a revolutionary course.

Fortified by the blessing of Carey and the encouragement of Ram Mohun Roy, Duff made light of the fears and warnings of others. He himself believed in the literal inspiration of the Bible and it was unthinkable that this great repository of divine truth should be excluded from his programme or given a subordinate place in the curriculum. Rather than accept such a proposal he would have abandoned his scheme altogether. He, therefore, resolved to make it known to everybody that some portion of the Bible would be read and expounded in each class every day.

Although he regarded Christianity as the centre of all truth and the consummation of all knowledge, he was quite willing to make provision for useful knowledge, first in the elementary forms and later in the higher classes. In a speech, delivered in Edinburgh in 1835, he said 'if in India you only impart ordinary useful knowledge, you thereby demolish what by its people is regarded as sacred. A course of instruction that professes to convey truth of any kind thus becomes a species of religious education'.[1] Every subject, therefore, was to be approached from the religious standpoint and interpreted in the light of the Christian revelation, for it was the spirit in which education was imparted that mattered most and secular subjects, provided they were taught with sympathy and understanding, could be made the vehicles of divine knowledge. As Andrews puts it, 'his principle was this: English education is not a mere secular thing, but steeped in the Christian religion. English literature, English history, English philosophy carry with them of necessity Christian conceptions of life; for the atmosphere in which they have been produced has all along been Christian'.[2] In the nineteenth century many who had no pronounced sympathy with missionary enterprise regarded it as almost axiomatic that English education—even without any explicit Christian teaching—would not merely undermine Hinduism but would gradually win over converts to the Christian faith. History has found that these people 'greatly underestimated the power of resistance in that multiform religion. Hinduism is always changing and yet remains much the same. It has withstood the assaults of Buddhism and Islam; now it is preparing itself to swallow up Christianity'.[3] This is the verdict of a modern educational missionary, a verdict which would have shocked Alexander Duff but would not have shaken his conviction that every form of truth was a *preparatio evangelica*.

As regards the medium of instruction Duff had to choose between Bengali, Sanskrit and English. He fully appreciated the importance of the vernacular for missionary work and no sooner had he landed in Calcutta than he set himself to master Bengali— a language in which he never attained more than average pro-

---

[1] Smith, op. cit., I, p. 292.

[2] C. F. Andrews, *The Renaissance of India* (1912), p. 33.

[3] S. Neill, *Builders of the Indian Church* (1934), p. 113.

ficiency. He was soon driven to the conclusion that 'it was a poor language, like English before Chaucer, and had in it, either by translation or by original composition, no works embodying any subjects of study beyond the merest elements. As a native of the Highlands I vividly realized that the Gaelic, though powerful for lyric and other poetry and also for popular address, contained no works that could possibly meet the objects of higher and comprehensive learning. Hence those who sought that found it in English Colleges and returned to distribute the treasures of knowledge, acquired through English, among the Gaelic people'.[1] He himself was of Gaelic descent and bilingual; his own experience indicated that there need be no difficulty in combining the use of Bengali for ordinary everyday affairs with the use of English for purposes of learning and culture. The rejection of Bengali as a suitable medium for higher education did not imply that a study of the mother-tongue was to be neglected. Far from it; he gave every encouragement to the study of the vernacular and hoped that in time—perhaps within a generation or two—Bengali would be improved and refined to such an extent that it would become the medium of higher education. He looked forward to the day when cultured Bengalis, who had themselves enjoyed the benefit of an English education, would use their own language to spread modern knowledge among the masses of the people. For these reasons he did everything he could to promote vernacular education and, from the very beginning, he made Bengali an obligatory subject in all college classes. As time went on, however, the proper place of the vernaculars in the educational system of the country became obscured, and Duff's efforts to make them serve as the bases of all educational training were either ignored or forgotten.

As regards the claims of the Oriental classical languages, Duff was able to point to the moribund condition of the Sanskrit College and the Madrassa. In reply to those who argued that less opposition would be encountered if Sanskrit were made the medium of instruction, he could quote the opinion of Ram Mohun Roy that Sanskrit was the language of a small and jealous minority, that it was more difficult than English to master, and that it contained

---

[1] Smith, op. cit., p. 189.

no works dealing with modern learning. The greatest objection, however, was that the sacred language was inseparably linked with the errors of Hinduism and would, therefore, strengthen and consolidate those very beliefs which it was his main object to eradicate. As a means of conveying modern knowledge Sanskrit was plainly unsuitable; as a means of imparting a Christian education Sanskrit was well-nigh impossible.

English, on the other hand, although a highly developed language, was not particularly difficult; it embodied a great deal of useful knowledge which India sorely needed and, in the Bible, offered the noblest expression of divine truth. Duff had not been slow to perceive that the demand for English education, particularly among the better classes to whom he wished to make a strong appeal, was auspicious for the success of his plans. He had made the acquaintance of Ram Mohun Roy and other reformers and could see for himself that the Hindu College was the most popular, and the most efficient, educational institution in the city. He was quite willing to believe that many of those who clamoured for English education were actuated by worldly and selfish motives and that few sought to acquire Western knowledge for the sake of culture or enjoyment. He welcomed the demand for English, even though it were based on the ground of self-interest, because he was convinced that secular knowledge could be imbued with the spirit of true religion and brought into the closest alliance with Christianity. To those who argued that English was popular simply because it opened up the way to prosperous careers he replied that he would 'overstock the market' with educated Indians, and thus 'make it necessary for those who wished to obtain better positions to remain longer at school so as to obtain a higher degree of knowledge which would not only enlarge the intellect but regulate the morals and manners'.[1] To those who warned him that a smattering of English would increase the number of scoffers and ne'er-do-wells he retorted that the great truths of religion, enshrined in the noble language of the English Bible, would safeguard the morals of the young and gradually permeate down to the lowest strata of society. No argument could persuade him that there was any inherent weakness in his great

[1] ibid., pp. 123-4.

project to impart education, through the medium of English, as a means to a higher end—the formation of character and the salvation of the soul. His missionary friends doubted the wisdom, even the sanity, of such a revolutionary scheme and officials scented danger. Among Hindus some were amused, many were indifferent, while a few watched with some concern the preparations which were being made—with the help of the apostate, Ram Mohun Roy—to demolish the religion of their fathers.

Neither disapproval nor derision could deter the fearless young Scotsman. Ram Mohun Roy, for whose 'most valuable and efficient assistance'[1] Duff was ever grateful, persuaded some Brahmans to rent, on moderate terms, a suitable building, and induced a few personal friends, whose religious prejudices were not very strong, to send their sons to the new school. One morning Duff interviewed five little boys and explained through an interpreter—for he had not yet been two months in the country —what his aims were. In a day or two several others came to seek admission and 'on every successive morning there was a fresh succession of applicants, till classification and weeding out became necessary'.[2] Ram Mohun Roy attended the public opening on 13 July 1830, when Duff slowly and solemnly read the Lord's Prayer in Bengali and then asked his pupils to turn up a particular passage in the New Testament. There was a murmur of protest and a young Brahman said, 'This is the Christian Shastra. We are not Christians; how then can we read it?' Ram Mohun Roy hastened to explain that famous English Oriental scholars, like Dr H. H. Wilson, had studied the Hindu Shastras and had not become Hindus; that he himself had read the Koran again and again and still he had not become a Mohammedan; that he had also studied the whole Bible, but had not become a Christian. 'Why then do you fear to read it? Read and judge for yourself.'[3] There were no further interruptions and the fact that instruction was to be frankly and unashamedly Christian caused no falling off in attendance. Until he sailed for England Ram Mohun Roy visited the school almost every day for the Bible lesson and delighted in hearing the recitation of the Lord's Prayer, which he considered the most beautiful and comprehensive prayer to be found in any religion. Duff's alliance with the author of

[1] ibid., p. 132.   [2] ibid., p. 121.   [3] ibid., pp. 121-2.

The Precepts of Jesus pleased neither missionaries nor orthodox Hindus, but classes went on smoothly and, with the help of an Anglo-Indian lad and a few pundits, rapid progress was made in English and Bengali. Duff put all his energy into the work; he supervised every detail of the administration, planned future expansion, taught the rudiments of English for five or six hours a day and spent his leisure in the preparation of graduated Readers and other textbooks. At the end of a twelvemonth he announced that a public examination would be held under the chairmanship of Archdeacon Corrie. The proficiency that his pupils showed in ordinary school subjects and the readiness and accuracy with which they answered questions on the Bible were regarded as 'absolutely marvellous' and were given generous publicity in the press. 'This examination proved the turning point as far as popular appreciation was concerned. . . . Many prominent English residents became convinced believers in Duff's methods and the leaders of the Indian community changed their attitude so considerably that floods of applications poured into the institution, and so many visitors desired to see the school in working that a special day had to be set aside for them, to prevent discipline being ruined.'[1]

Duff, however, was far from content with the results which others considered almost miraculous, and he was determined to raise the General Assembly's Institution above the level of a 'mere school'. His firm conviction was that a few years of ordinary schooling would not be sufficient to open the minds of young boys to the errors of Hinduism and, therefore, he determined to induce as many as possible to remain with him till they reached the years of puberty and 'could attain that maturity of judgement which may render knowledge operative and impressions lasting'.[2] From the start his aim had been to make higher education a powerful evangelical instrument and the school was merely the foundation for the great superstructure which he intended to erect. With the assistance of the Rev. W. S. Mackay, an accomplished scholar and an inspiring teacher, the collegiate department was rapidly organized and developed and within a very short time the Christian college was in a position to challenge its older and secular rival, the Vidyalaya. It is true that Duff did not levy any

[1] W. Paton, *Alexander Duff* (1933), pp. 75-6.
[2] Smith, op. cit., I, p. 175.

fee[1] and that he did not restrict admission to pupils belonging to high-caste families; for all that, no one could have expected that the attendance at the new college would quickly outstrip that at the older institution with an established reputation. More surprising still was the fact that the English education given by the missionaries was recognized as in no way inferior—in some respects it was definitely superior—to that which was imparted at the Hindu College. The venerable Carey, now in the evening of his days, saw visions of the rise of a 'Christian Benares', while Hare, despite his anti-clerical leanings, generously acknowledged the contribution which the intrepid young missionary had made to the educational life of the capital.

Much as Duff disapproved of the secular atmosphere of the Hindu College, he was ready to regard it as an ally in the campaign against superstition and idolatry. 'We rejoiced', he wrote, 'when, in June, 1830, we fairly came in contact with a rising body of natives, who had learned to think and to discuss all subjects with unshackled freedom, though that freedom was ever apt to degenerate into licence in attempting to demolish all claims and pretensions of the Christian as well as of every other professedly revealed faith. We hailed the circumstance . . . as heralding the approach of an auspicious era—an era that introduced something *new* into the hitherto undisturbed reign of hoary and tyrranous antiquity.'[2] He regarded scepticism merely as a stage on the road from false to true religion, and determined to exploit the prevailing trend of thought and to turn it to higher ends. He was not, therefore, disconcerted when he discovered that the first reaction of his Hindu students to Christian teaching was a tendency to disbelieve in the doctrines of their own religion and to ridicule popular cults and ceremonies. Many of them behaved in precisely the same way as those who had been infected with 'the most virulent forms of Western rationalism' and come under the demoralizing influence of the atheistical Derozio. Strangely enough, Duff's biographer applauds the revolt of Duff's students, fortified

---

[1] 'The absence of fees counterbalanced the necessity of studying the sacred scriptures and dogmas of Christianity. Hazarding the chance of conversion, the Hindus flocked thither in considerable numbers.'—F. W. Thomas, *The History and Prospects of British Education in India* (1891), p. 28.

[2] Smith, op. cit., I, p. 145.

by Christian education, and condemns the misdemeanours of those who had studied at Hare's College 'false philosophy and impure literature'.[1]   There is no truth, however, in the reckless statement that 'the principal English text-books' used at the Vidyalaya were 'the more licentious plays of the Restoration',[2] although, among the books read outside class, Paine's *Age of Reason* enjoyed a temporary popularity and Paley's *Evidences* was ransacked to provide material for attacks on Christianity! It is idle to pretend that the conduct of some of Duff's students was less culpable than that of some of the 'advanced' young men from the Hindu College, or that it was any less offensive to orthodox believers.   Flushed with their victory in the matter of Derozio's dismissal, the conservative party—backed by the Dharma Sabha and one or two reactionary papers—turned their attention to the Scottish College and threatened to excommunicate those who allowed their sons to attend.   By this time, however, the public were growing more accustomed to the rationalistic outlook of the younger generation and the outcry 'Hinduism is in danger' did not excite the same uneasiness as in the past.   The agitation gradually subsided and the attendance at the college returned to normal.   Students continued to alarm their elders by their defiance of the restrictions of caste and attendance at lectures and debates on religious topics. A little later four converts were made, one, at least, of whom was a student of the Hindu College.   The great experiment of using higher education for evangelical purposes was beginning to justify itself; even if the number of converts was small they were representative of the best Bengali families.   Duff had every reason to feel well pleased with the firstfruits of his missionary labours; he had never expected that all who heard the Gospel message would openly accept Christianity and he found comfort in the text, 'Many are called but few are chosen'.   The tremor which swept through Hindu society he regarded as the rumbling of an approaching storm, which would sweep away an edifice whose foundations were 'built upon the sand'.   His zeal and perseverance were more than a match for the spasmodic opposition of agitators and alarmists.   His enthusiam and buoyancy made him a popular hero in the student world and his criticisms of Hindu life and manners, although often expressed in forcible language, caused no resent-

[1] ibid., p. 111.   [2] ibid., p. 144.

ment. In an incredibly short time he succeeded in building up a college which was recognized, even by those who had little or no sympathy with his ideals, as a tribute to his energy and ability. Had Duff not lived to render many other services to the cause of Indian education, the work which he accomplished during his first four years in Calcutta would be enough to stamp him as a very remarkable man. In his own field he was a pioneer and, though many have followed in his footsteps, none has achieved the same success and none has left such a permanent imprint on the educational system of the country. The first period of his Indian career, short though it was, 'eclipses any other period in his life; indeed, it might be truly said to eclipse all the other periods together'.[1]

In spite of a robust constitution, unceasing work and a trying climate told upon his health. Dysentery followed malaria and, very unwillingly, Duff was invalided home. On reaching his native land he was bitterly disappointed to find that the prevailing attitude towards foreign missions was one of complete indifference. With characteristic energy he set himself to dispel this unpardonable apathy and 'by the magic of his burning eloquence' the missionary spirit of Scotland was roused as never before: thousands of pounds were subscribed to provide suitable buildings for the College in Calcutta; the Scottish Ladies' Society was founded to promote female education in India; many notable recruits, including the Rev. J. Anderson, were drawn to the mission field. By his sermons and addresses Duff's fame as the great Apostle of Missions spread all over the land and the University of Aberdeen 'honoured itself and surprised the young divine' by conferring on him the degree of Doctor of Divinity. His reputation was further enhanced by the publication in 1839, shortly before his return to Calcutta, of *India and India Missions*.[2] As a defence of his educational policy, this book is still worth reading; it reveals, however, a lamentable ignorance of Hinduism.

Duff had been at home for only a few months when Macaulay wrote his historic Educational Minute (1835). With a dispatch unusual in official transactions Lord William Bentinck issued,

---

[1] Ogilvie, op. cit., p. 395; cf. Paton, op. cit., p. 234.

[2] Smith, op. cit., I, p. 306.

a few weeks later, his famous Resolution[1] which declared that in future 'all the funds appropriated for education would be best employed on English education alone'. The success of the Scottish College was one of the strongest practical arguments in favour of modern learning and Duff had repeatedly requested high officials (particularly Trevelyan, Macaulay's brother-in-law and leader of the Anglicist party in the Committee of Public Instruction) to urge the Government to adjust their educational policy to the requirements and wishes of the people. In a letter to Dr George Smith, written some forty years later, Trevelyan,[2] having eulogized 'the great and pregnant reforms which must always give Dr Duff a high place among the benefactors of mankind',[3] goes on to say that 'the indirect influence of his exertions upon the action of Government was at least equally important' and 'entered largely into the causes which brought about the Resolution'. Duff's own estimate of the importance of the belated decision of the authorities to abandon their patronage of 'vicious Orientalism' was thus expressed: 'We do not expect sudden or instantaneous changes, but we do look forward to a great ultimate revolution. We do regard Lord William Bentinck's Act as laying the foundation of a train of causes which may for a time operate so insensibly as to pass unnoticed by careless or casual observers, but not the less surely as concerns the great and momentous issue.'[4] On the other hand, he did not hesitate to point out that the new enactment fell far short of his own ideal, and in an important pamphlet, entitled *New Era of the English Language and English Literature in India*, he argued that it was satisfactory as far as it went, but that it did not go far enough: 'While we rejoice that true literature and science is to be substituted in place of what is demonstrably false, we cannot but lament that no provision has been made for

---

[1] C. E. Trevelyan (*Education of the People of India*, p.11) says that 'although homely in words it will be mighty in its effects long after we are mouldering in the dust'. By a curious coincidence, the Resolution was signed (in his official capacity as Secretary to Government) by H. T. Prinsep, who was leader of the defeated Orientalists and subsequently attacked the Government's policy.

[2] In his *Education of the People of India* (1838) Trevelyan paid a handsome tribute to Duff (p. 29).

[3] Smith, op. cit., I, p. 196.

[4] Ogilvie, op. cit., p. 395.

substituting the only true religion—Christianity—in place of the false religion which our literature and science will inevitably demolish. Our maxim has been, is now and ever will be this: *wherever, whenever and by whomsoever Christianity is sacrificed on the altar of worldly expediency, there and then must the supreme good of mankind lie bleeding at its base*.'[1] He felt that the weakness of a nominally Christian Government placed a still greater responsibility on the Church, and, in an address to the General Assembly (1837), Duff put the missionary case in these very striking words: 'Let us hail true literature and true science as our very best auxiliaries—whether in Scotland, or in India, or in any quarter of the habitable globe. But, in receiving these as friendly allies into our sacred territory, let us resolutely determine that they shall never, never be allowed to usurp the throne, and wield a tyrant's sceptre over it.'[2]

The immediate result of this important Resolution was the stoppage of the publication of Oriental books and the withdrawal of the support to the Madrassa and Sanskrit College. With the funds thus made available the Committee opened six new schools and added six more in the following year. The foundation of the new Medical College (1835) was an earnest of the Government's desire to patronize higher English education; that this policy had the support of public opinion is shown by the fact that, when the Hooghly College was founded in the following year, more than 1,200 names were enrolled within the first three days.[3] Such revolutionary changes created a stir and were condemned by the Asiatic Society as 'destructive, unjust, unpopular and impolitic'. H. T. Prinsep, leader of the defeated Orientalists, wrote a Minute[4] in which he criticized very severely the 'partisan policy' which had been advocated by Macaulay and sanctioned by the Governor-General—a policy which was 'inconsistent with past and with recent professions of the Government, as proclaiming a principle unfair and illiberal in itself and calculated to set against us those without whose co-operation we can do nothing to promote science and literature'. The Muslim residents of Calcutta implored the

---

[1] Smith, op. cit., I, p. 201.   [2] ibid., p. 361.
[3] Trevelyan, op. cit., p. 82.
[4] H. Sharp, *Selections from Educational Records*, I, (1920), pp. 134 ff.

Governor-General, in a petition signed by 30,000 persons,[1] to spare the Madrassa and to abstain from measures which were calculated not only to destroy the religious system of Islam but to convert Indians to the faith of their rulers. Lord William Bentinck, although unwilling to reverse his decision in favour of English education, replied that 'such motives never have and never can influence the counsels of Government'.[2] A few days later, in reply to a parting address from missionaries he was even more explicit when he said, 'the professed object of your lives is conversion. The fundamental principle of British rule—the compact to which Government stands pledged—is strict religious neutrality'.[3] It is interesting to note that in his private capacity Bentinck approved of missionary enterprise and was anxious to see the diffusion of Christianity throughout all countries. He had the greatest admiration for 'the inestimable Dr Duff' and believed that 'the offer of Christianity in the school of a humble, pious and learned missionary was without objection, for his labours, divested of all human power, caused no distrust'.[4] The great reformer in whom Bishop Wilson found 'a strange dislike for bishops' and 'a lamentable absence of church principles'[5] had no sooner left the shores of India than he sent Dr Marshman a cheque for £50 towards the Serampore Mission;[6] the man whose official position compelled him to reject an application for a Government grant to the Scottish College—on the ground that 'all interference and injudicious tampering' with the religious beliefs of pupils in institutions supported by the State must be 'positively forbidden'[7] —was ready to congratulate Duff on the 'unparalleled success' of his great educational experiment. Duff, in turn, paid more than one tribute to the 'British manliness and courage' of the Governor-

---

[1] H. H. Wilson, in an article on 'Education of the Natives of India' which appeared in the *Asiatic Journal* (Jan., 1836), says that the number was ' above 8,000 '.

[2] A. Howell, *Education in British India prior to 1854* (1872), p. 33.

[3] ibid., p. 34.

[4] Smith, op. cit., I, p. 260.

[5] A. Mayhew, *Christianity and the Government of India* (1929), p. 114.

[6] J. C. Marshman, *Life and Times of Carey, Marshman and Ward* (1859), II, p. 494.

[7] Bentinck's predecessor, Lord Amherst, had previously refused to sanction a Government grant to Bishop's College; *vide* Mayhew, op. cit., p. 164.

General who had welcomed him to India with 'genial Christian sympathy'.

Bentinck's timely assurances that the Government had no intention of departing from its position of 'strict religious neutrality' created a good impression, and the steps taken by the Committee of Public Instruction to promote English education were, on the whole, well received. Their work was made easier by the resignation of the more uncompromising Orientalists and among the new members who were appointed were two influential Hindus, Radhakant Deb and Russomoy Dutt. According to the interpretation of the new Committee the resolution which had caused such a ferment merely indicated that in higher education English was to be given preference over Sanskrit and Arabic. They went on to say, in their first Annual Report, 'we conceive the formation of a vernacular literature to be the ultimate object to which all our efforts must be directed. A teacher of the vernacular languages is already attached to several of our seminaries, and we look to this plan soon becoming general'.[1] Instead of improving the indigenous elementary schools, the Committee made a half-hearted attempt to encourage vernacular education by attaching elementary classes to secondary schools, and this brought to a head another controversy—that between the Anglicists and the Vernacularists. With very limited funds at their disposal the Committee were unable—even if they had been willing—to tackle energetically the problem of mass education. Their helplessness was brought home to them when they received a copy of the first of Adam's reports. He had been appointed by Lord William Bentinck early in 1835 (a couple of months before the Resolution on higher English education was issued) to make a survey of the indigenous schools in Bengal and Bihar.

Between 1835 and 1838 he submitted three elaborate reports[2] in which he estimated that there were about 100,000[3] indigenous

[1] Trevelyan, op. cit., pp. 22-4.

[2] Long's *Adam's Reports on Vernacular Education in Bengal and Behar Submitted to Government in 1835, 1836 and 1838* (1868); a more recent and more complete edition, edited by A. Basu, appeared in 1941.

[3] Sir Philip Hartog in *Some Aspects of Indian Education, Past and Present* (1939), sets out to explode the myth of 'Bengal's 100,000 schools'; attempts have been made to refute his arguments, e.g. by R. V. Parulekar in *Literacy in India in Pre-British Days* (1940).

schools in Bengal alone; he pointed out that they were terribly inefficient and that the ignorance of the people was appalling. Adam questioned the wisdom of providing, at State expense, education for the upper classes and recommended that efforts should be made to foster and improve the indigenous schools which were providing a very inadequate training for less than 7 per cent of the children of school-going age. Meantime, Mr B. H. Hodgson, the eminent Sanskrit scholar, entered the fray and in a series of letters to *The Friend of India*, over the signature of Junius,[1] he made out a very strong case for 'the pre-eminence of the vernaculars'. Neither Adam nor Hodgson saw any possibility of English ever becoming the medium of general education, and the latter argued that English would prove just as great a curse to India as Sanskrit had in the past. The Committee of Public Instruction reported that the cost of Adam's comprehensive scheme of 'national education' would be prohibitive and that his proposals were premature and impracticable. Lord Auckland eventually wrote a Minute (1839)[2] in which he sought to deal fairly with the various issues at stake. Realizing that the transfer of funds from the Oriental colleges had caused genuine hardship and alienated orthodox opinion, he decided to restore their original grants and, in place of stipends, he instituted scholarships which were to be open to competition and to be retained only on condition that satisfactory progress (as tested by annual examination) was shown. He authorized separate grants from the public treasury for the support of English education, which he considered had a very strong claim on the patronage of the Government. He appears to have been won over, by Trevelyan and others, to the view that modern knowledge would gradually 'filter' down from an educated aristocracy to the masses. He decided that there was no reason to depart from the principle of combined English and vernacular education which had been followed in Bengal since 1835, and he accepted the view of the Committee of Public Instruction, that the active encouragement of higher education in English did not imply that elementary education for the masses was 'to be necessarily rejected or- indefinitely postponed'. Although he was ready to admit that he saw no prospect of primary education 'acting

[1] Reprinted in his *Miscellaneous Essays Relating to Indian Subjects* (1880), II, pp. 255 ff.   [2] Sharp, op. cit., pp. 147 ff.

immediately and powerfully on the poor peasantry of India', he was unable to shut his eyes to the fact that vernacular education had made considerable progress in the Bombay Presidency. He concluded, therefore, that both English and vernacular education should be supported by public funds and suggested that the Government's future policy might be guided by the results of the experiments carried out in Bengal and Bombay. The Board of Directors sent out a Dispatch (1841) approving of the main principles laid down in Lord Auckland's Minute, which 'came to be regarded as an authoritative pronouncement of the educational policy of Government'[1] and which formed the basis of all subsequent reforms up to the great Dispatch of 1854.

Opinion is still divided as to the merits, even the intentions, of this famous Minute. Dr Smith's view that it is 'remarkable for its bad style and worse reasoning'[2] is obviously an exaggeration, but it may be conceded that in his efforts to reach a compromise Lord Auckland was influenced by considerations other than the mere educational needs of the country. The requirements of the public service called for a supply of young Indians with a knowledge of English and the Government, despite Adam's telling criticisms, still pinned their faith to the filtration theory. In consequence, vernacular education was quickly relegated to an insignificant place in the scheme for educational advancement. Further, the Anglicists wrongly jumped to the conclusion that the Minute indicated a reversal of the policy laid down by Lord William Bentinck, with the result that the old controversy, which had died down, was immediately revived.

When Duff returned to India (1840) he was horrified to learn that the Governor-General had been persuaded by reactionaries to sanction the expenditure of Government funds on the 're-endowment of error'; he accused him, in a series of letters which appeared in *The Christian Observer*, of vacillation and cowardice, of temporizing expediency, of anxiety to purchase peace at any price; his 'tortuous Machiavellian policy' was described as 'remarkable for its concessions and compromises, remarkable above all for its education without religion, its plans without a providence, its ethics

[1] J. A. Richey, *Selections from Educational Records*, II, (1922), p. 1; the Dispatch is given in full on pp. 3-5.
[2] Smith, op. cit., I, p. 429.

without a God'.[1] In 1852 the Bishops of Calcutta and Madras, following Duff's lead, declared that 'the Government educational system was a blot upon the honourable Company's Courts, involving the most awful guilt before Almighty God'.[2] Vernacularists, including J. C. Marshman, son of the Serampore missionary, also protested, but they were more restrained in the expression of their disapproval. The Government, however, remained unmoved by Duff's fiery outbursts, and the Afghan war soon distracted attention from domestic affairs. The Directors' Dispatch of 1841 finally brought to an end a controversy which had lasted for more than twenty-five years and in the following year the General Committee was abolished and the control of public instruction was handed over to Councils of Education in each Presidency. In Bengal the policy of establishing Zillah, or District, Schools, with junior vernacular departments attached, was continued; neither vernacular education nor Oriental learning made any noticeable progress.

Duff's second and longest period of service in India lasted ten years and is mainly notable for the steady progress which was made in the face of internal difficulties and against opposition from without. The Disruption of the Scottish Church (1843) led to a crisis in which his powers of leadership and his magnanimity were strikingly revealed. Together with the Scottish educational missionaries of Bombay and Madras he was driven to sever his connexion with the Established Church. This body, however, refused to surrender—even at a price—the property of the General Assembly's Institution and, rather than provoke a quarrel, Duff 'freely and forever' renounced his 'legal claim' to any portion of the property, although he felt (and continued to feel) that in 'moral equity' his claim was very strong.[3] In the following year, accompanied by his four missionary colleagues, entire Indian staff, and over one thousand students, he moved to a rented building. There he established a new department for the systematic training of teachers and in this important branch of educational work Duff was a pioneer. At this time there was not a single Normal School or Training College in the whole of India.[4] Duff had made

---

[1] ibid., pp. 433-4.   [2] Thomas, op. cit., p. 58.
[3] Smith, op. cit., II, p. 35.   [4] See, however, pp. 140 and 146 ff.

a special study of Pedagogy, was conversant with the works of the great educational reformers and familiar with the most recent developments in advanced countries. He used to lecture on the methods of teaching employed in Scotland, Germany and Switzerland and to expound the systems of Stow, Fellenberg and Pestalozzi —subjects of which, it is safe to say, few others in the country had even a superficial knowledge. Many of the young men whom he trained became teachers in Government or mission schools in places as widely separated as Sind and Burma. ` In 1846 the Government opened a Normal School in Calcutta, to which a model school was attached; stipends were awarded to those willing to undergo a two years' course of training, on condition that, if required to do so, they agreed to serve for at least three years in Government schools. This institution did not prove the success that was anticipated and, in efficiency, was unable to compete with the classes which had been added to the Free Church Institution; there, also, subjects such as Literature and Philosophy, Science and Mathematics were taught 'to a standard abreast of the Scottish Universities of the day'.[1] Meantime, the Established Church of Scotland appointed Dr Ogilvie as Principal of the original Institution and very soon he had some seven hundred students in attendance. This happy result of the great schism in the Presbyterian Church was more than a compensation to Duff for the loss of his fine college, for it almost doubled in the metropolis the missionary agencies at work on higher education.

During this period some notable converts were made, including Lal Behari Day, author of the well-known *Bengal Peasant Life* (1874)[2] and Professor of History and English Literature at the Hooghly College, and Dr K. M. Banerjea, who became a Fellow of the University of Calcutta and was one of the founders of the Indian National Congress. The success of Duff's proselytizing zeal inspired Debendranath Tagore, the poet's father, who had succeeded Ram Mohun Roy as leader of the Brahmo Samaj, to organize a counter-reformation against the spread of Christian propaganda, and this movement met with unexpected success. Duff, however, failed to recognize its significance and appears to

---

[1] Ogilvie, op. cit., p. 401.
[2] Also wrote *Reminiscences of Dr Duff* (1879).

have been totally unaware that a new spirit was beginning to animate Hinduism. Another section of offended Hindus resolved to open a rival college and enlisted the services of an Irish adventurer called Tuite, who was one of the few 'so-called Christians who would consent to teach English and Western science on purely secular lines'.[1]   In this way, according to Dr Smith, was established Seel's Free College, with the object of crushing Christianity and perpetuating Hinduism. Contrary to expectations, Duff welcomed the establishment of yet another secular college, and he made no secret of his conviction that the teaching of European literature and science would, sooner or later, prove fatal to Hinduism. In spite of attacks in the press and the receipt of threatening letters, his influence—and even his popularity—continued to increase and the number of his students rose to over twelve hundred, with a daily attendance of more than a thousand.

In 1844 Lord Hardinge became Governor-General and no sooner had he assumed office than he issued a Resolution[2] which gave a direct and powerful impetus to the study of English. It stated that in the selection of candidates for the public service preference would in future be given to those who had distinguished themselves in the institutions controlled, or recognized, by the Government. The Council of Education was authorized to conduct yearly examinations which were to be open to all, including students from missionary and other private colleges, and the successful candidates were to be arranged in order of merit. Indians hailed the Resolution with delight and Duff welcomed it[3] not merely as an official endorsement of the policy which he himself had persistently advocated, but as the first public recognition of missionary institutions in connexion with the service of the state. When, however, the departmental rules framed by the Council of Education were published, he protested vehemently. These, it must be frankly admitted, were not altogether in keeping either with the letter or the spirit of the Resolution. It was determined that the minimum standard of qualification for employment should be equivalent to that for gaining a Senior English Scholarship, whereas the original intention seems to have been that the annual

[1] Smith, op. cit., II, p. 60.   [2] Richey, op. cit., pp. 90-1.
[3] Smith, op. cit., II, p. 86.

returns should embrace a large number of candidates of different 'degrees of merit and capacity'. Duff's chief ground of complaint,[1] however, was that the prescribed books were chosen exclusively from the secular texts used in Government colleges and that this arbitrary limitation virtually debarred students from missionary institutions from taking the public examination. This he regarded not only as unfair to his own students, but as a slight on the work and efficiency of the missionary colleges. He also complained that the examinations had been unfairly conducted, and he even challenged the competence of the officials who had been appointed examiners. The Council defended the system of examination which had been introduced and, although 'it was carefully explained that insertion in the returns must not be regarded as a *sure pledge* of employment'[2] a place in the list came to be regarded as a substitute for a University degree. In nine years only a handful of 'certificated' students were appointed to Government posts, and these of subordinate rank; when vacancies occurred they were filled without any reference to the Council's register and Kerr states that in 1853 it had become 'a byeword that Lord Hardinge's Resolution had become a dead letter'.[3] The main effect of the proclamation was to strengthen the growing belief that English was 'the language of good appointments'; Stark points out that by attracting to Government service young men who should have become teachers of the masses it helped to undermine faith in 'the filtration theory'.[4]

The resentment of the missionaries was not unjustified, but the failure of Hardinge's scheme was only partially due to the steps taken by the authorities to put it into operation; more important were (1) the refusal of the Directors to accord their sanction to the new policy, and (2) the proposal to create a Central University, which was made by the Council of Education in the following year. The Directors, apparently forgetful of the contents of some of their earlier Dispatches dealing with higher education, pointed out that the test which had been instituted gave students in Government colleges 'a monopoly of public patronage', that

---

[1] Richey, op. cit., p. 96.   [2] ibid., p. 67.   [3] ibid., p. 68.
[4] H. A. Stark, *Vernacular Education in Bengal from 1813 to 1912* (1913), p. 65.

it was likely to discourage the general acquisition of English, and that a high degree of scholastic knowledge did not constitute an essential qualification for public service. It took them the best part of two years to arrive at these conclusions, but they were more prompt in disposing of the plan for a University. This had been drawn up, in consultation with Duff, by Dr Mouat, Secretary of the Council, and was based on the model of the University of London, which had been established a few years previously (1836). It provided for the granting of degrees in Law, Medicine and Engineering, as well as in Arts and Science, to successful candidates in affiliated colleges. The Council urged that a Central University would ensure a higher standard of advanced education, would produce a body of 'able, honourable and efficient' public servants, and bring into existence a number of well-qualified professional men. Lord Hardinge endorsed these views but, in spite of his strong support, the Directors replied very curtly 'we must decline at present to give our sanction to the proposal'.[1] This decision, which caused much disappointment among educated Indians, was unexpected, because the Board had consistently approved of the policy of promoting and improving higher English education; it may have been justified on the ground that there was no foundation of general education among the people, but it is unlikely that this was the consideration which carried most weight in Leadenhall Street.

In Calcutta the proposal continued to engage public attention and was supported by several prominent officials. Sir Frederick Halliday was of opinion that the scholarship examination to test eligibility for Government service was in itself 'the germ of a University'; while Mr C. H. Cameron, President of the Council of Education, presented an Address[2] to Parliament on the subject, and claimed that 'work like Duff's made Bengal ripe for a University'. In 1853 it was decided to replace the sectarian Hindu College by a 'Metropolitan' college, open to students of every class and creed; this proposal was sanctioned by the Directors and Lord Dalhousie, the next Governor-General, prophesied that 'the

[1] Howell, op. cit., p. 46.
[2] C. H. Cameron, *An Address to Parliament on the Duties of Great Britain to India* (1853); cf. Mahmood, op. cit., chap. xvi.

time will come when the Presidency College, having elevated itself by its reputation . . . will expand itself into something approaching the dignity and proportions of an Indian University'.[1] Duff had no misgivings on the subject and, at the very time when the question of the establishment of the Presidency College was being considered, assured Lord Stanley that the moment had come 'in Calcutta, at least, when, with comparatively little expense to Government, a University might be established, somewhat after the general model of London University'.[2] Shortly afterwards the issue was finally settled by the Dispatch of 1854, to which the Universities of Calcutta, Bombay and Madras owe their origin.

On the death of Dr Chalmers in 1847 Duff had been asked to return home and assume the leadership of the Free Church. He was reluctant to abandon, even temporarily, his work in Calcutta and, in spite of indifferent health, was with difficulty persuaded to leave India. He reached Scotland in 1850 and in the succeeding year was elected Moderator of the Free Church Assembly. Ecclesiastical duties and responsibilities occupied much of his time, but he came forward and gave very material assistance when the renewal and revision of the Company's Charter was being discussed. In 1852–3 Select Committees of Parliament examined a host of witnesses—official and non-official—and in the latter year the Charter was renewed (for the last time), not for a fixed period of years but during the pleasure of Parliament. The constitution of the Court of Directors was altered so as to give the Government a greater measure of control over Indian affairs and their patronage was withdrawn by throwing open to competition posts in the civil service.[3]

By far the most important outcome of this legislative measure was the issue of the famous Educational Dispatch of Sir Charles Wood (afterwards Lord Halifax), which even to this day is regarded as the Magna Charta of Indian education. Forty years earlier Indian administrators had been almost unanimous in holding that no attempt should be made by the State to introduce education and that interference on the part of missionaries would be dangerous.

---

[1] J. Ghosh, *Higher Education in Bengal under British Rule* (1926), p. 132.
[2] Smith, op. cit., II, p. 242.
[3] L. S. S. O'Malley, *The Indian Civil Service, 1601-1930* (1931), pp. 206 ff.

The very opposite opinions were expressed by most of the officials who now gave evidence. Instead of urging that education had no claim on public revenues, many argued that the funds so far made available for public instruction had been totally inadequate. The contributions made by missionaries to the educational and social advancement of the country were generously acknowledged, and it was declared that the success of British administration depended almost entirely on a satisfactory solution of the educational problem, because 'popular knowledge was a safer thing to deal with than popular ignorance'.[1] Many of the witnesses were able to speak from first-hand experience of these problems, and included in their number were Lord Hardinge, Sir Charles Trevelyan, Sir Edward Ryan, Dr H. H. Wilson, and Mr C. H. Cameron; missionary interests were ably represented by Mr J. C. Marshman and Dr Duff.

In cross-examination the latter had several lively passages at arms, in none of which he came off second best. He had some spirited exchanges with Lord Ellenborough who, throughout his term of office as Governor-General (1842–4), showed continued hostility to missions and was 'haunted by the fear of arousing the Hindu world by any action capable of misrepresentation as a Christian gesture'.[2] In reply to the former Governor-General's suggestion that the political ruin of the English power in India would be the inevitable consequence of the spread of Western education, Duff assured his Lordship that he had 'never ceased to declare that, if our object be, not merely for our own aggrandisement but very specially for the welfare of the natives, to retain our dominion in India, no wiser or more effective plan can be conceived than that of bestowing this higher English education in close and inseparable alliance with the illumining quickening and beautifying influence of the Christian faith'.[3] Needless to say, Ellenborough, despite Duff's obvious sincerity, was not impressed, and his 'nervous preoccupation' with what Mayhew[4] calls 'the explosive potentialities of all religions' subsequently led him to attribute the Mutiny to the misguided activities

[1] Howell, op. cit., p. 58; this view was expressed by Mr (later Sir Frederick) Halliday, First Lieut-Governor of Bengal, 1854-9.

[2] Mayhew, op. cit., p. 147.   [3] Smith, op. cit., II, p. 244.

[4] op. cit., p. 120.

of missionaries. As early as 1835 Duff had assured the General Assembly that if, in India, 'you do give the people knowledge without religion, rest assured that it is the greatest blunder, politically speaking, that was ever committed'; his subsequent experience of twenty years' missionary and educational work had confirmed him in the belief that higher Christian education was the sovereign remedy for India's moral and political advancement.

Duff's written evidence was characterized by his usual clarity and vigour, and the great Dispatch[1] not only embodies the most important of Duff's recommendations but its very language reflects his influence. It begins by stating 'that among many subjects of importance, none have a greater claim to our attention than that of education. It is one of our most sacred duties to be the means, as far as in us lies, of conferring upon the natives of India those vast moral and material benefits which flow from the general diffusion of useful knowledge'; further on it reads, 'the education which we desire to see extended in India is that which has for its object the diffusion of the arts, science, philosophy of Europe; in short, of European knowledge'. It repudiates any desire 'to substitute the English language for the vernacular dialects' or to discourage 'the traditional learning', which must always have a great antiquarian and historical importance, although 'deficient as regards all modern discovery and improvements'. It adds 'that a knowledge of English will always be essential to those who aspire to a high order of education' and declares the intention 'of extending far more widely the means of acquiring general European knowledge of a less high order, but of such a character as may be practically useful to the people of India in their different spheres of life'. Consequently, 'in any general scheme of education, the English language should be taught where there is a demand for it; but such instruction should always be combined with a careful attention to the study of the vernacular, and with such general instruction as can be conveyed through that language'.

This is a very brief summary of the general policy outlined in this memorable Dispatch and among the more specific recommendations[2] may be mentioned:

[1] Richey, op. cit., pp. 364 ff.
[2] See *Report of the Education Committee* (1883), pp. 22-3; also, Howell op. cit., p. 59.

(1) The setting up of separate provincial Departments of Public Instruction, each under a Director assisted by qualified Inspectors.

(2) The establishment of Universities at the Presidency towns, constituted on the model of London University.

(3) The maintenance of existing Government high schools and colleges and an increase in their number, where necessary.

(4) Increased attention to vernacular schools, indigenous or other, for the extension of elementary education among the masses.

(5) The establishment of institutions for the training of teachers for all kinds of schools.

(6) Increased and cordial support to female education.

(7) The introduction of a system of grants-in-aid, to all institutions imparting a sound secular education, provided they were under suitable management and subject to Government inspection, and provided, also, that fees—however small—were charged.

It is little wonder that Lord Dalhousie considered that this document 'contained a scheme far wider and more comprehensive than the Local or Supreme Government could ever have even ventured to suggest. It left nothing to be desired, if, indeed, it did not authorize and direct that more should be done than is within our present grasp'.[1]   After the Mutiny the Government of India was taken over by the Crown and in 1859 Lord Stanley issued a second important Dispatch[2] which is one of the first communications, if not the very first, addressed to the Government of India by the Secretary of State. This re-affirmed and amplified the principles and policy laid down by Sir Charles Wood. These two Dispatches 'stand out from all later documents as the fundamental codes on which Indian Education rests'.[3]

It is unnecessary to describe the steps taken by the new Department of Public Instruction to carry out a comprehensive programme of educational reform. The establishment of the Universities in the Presidency towns was responsible for a rapid

[1] Howell, op. cit., p. 59; see also Dalhousie's Minute of 1854 in Richey, op. cit., pp. 394 ff.

[2] Richey, op. cit., pp. 426-50.

[3] *Report of the Education Commission* (1883), p. 24.

expansion of English education—collegiate and secondary; the growth of elementary education, the development of girls' education and the increase in training institutions were disappointing, and in none of these directions has satisfactory progress yet been made. The most important innovation was the introduction of the system of grant-in-aid, which was copied from the English system. This 'essential feature' of the first Dispatch was warmly supported by Duff and appears to have been accepted for two main reasons: firstly, as a means of encouraging local initiative, enterprise and self-reliance, and of inducing wealthy and benevolent Indians to make liberal contributions towards the advancement of education; secondly, in the hope that, in the not distant future, many existing Government institutions, especially those for higher learning, would be closed, or transferred to the management of local bodies under the control of, or aided by, the State. Duff had argued, 'Government ought to extend its aid to all other institutions, by whomsoever originated and supported, where a sound general education is given. . . . Here at home the Government does not expend its educational resources on the maintenance of a few monopolist institutions; it strives to stimulate all parties, by offering proportional aid to those who show themselves willing to aid themselves'.[1]

The general principle was accepted, but it was decided to assign grants-in-aid irrespective of the religious teaching given in any particular institution, and this decision, in Duff's opinion, was the one serious blemish in the great charter of educational privilege. In his evidence before the Select Committee of Parliament he had said, 'I have never ceased to pronounce the system of giving high English education, without religion, a blind suicidal policy';[2] he had also given the assurance that there need be no fear of any evil political results from the extension of education, provided it is 'wisely and timeously united with the great improving, regulating, controlling and conservative power of Christianity'.[3] Had he been able to have his way the Bible would have been taught in every Government school and college and he affirmed that it was the duty of a Christian Government to give optional, if not compulsory, religious instruction in all State insti-

---

[1] Smith, op. cit., II, p. 243.   [2] ibid.   [3] ibid., p. 244.

tutions. Neither the Court of Directors nor Parliament were prepared to go to these lengths and, although Wood's Dispatch permitted the inclusion of copies of the Bible in the libraries of Government institutions, the allotment of grants-in-aid was sanctioned on the basis of 'strict religious neutrality', for all institutions managed by private bodies, whether Hindu, Mohammedan or Christian, whether indigenous or foreign. Indeed, it was expressly laid down that inspecting officers (when assessing the grant-in-aid) should take no notice whatever of the religion taught in any institution, and this injunction was repeated in the Dispatch of 1859, which emphasized that Indian educational policy had always been based on 'an abstinence from all interference with religious feelings and practices and on the exclusion of religious teaching from Government schools'.[1] Duff regarded this settlement as thoroughly unsatisfactory: at best, it was a timid compromise, at worst, an open alliance with paganism.

He was ready to admit, however, that the extension of facilities even for secular and useful education was a step in the right direction and thought that conversion to Christianity would follow in due course; this, as Trevelyan said, 'will take place at last wholesale, just as our ancestors were converted. The country will have Christian instruction infused into it in every way, by direct missionary education, and indirectly through books of various kinds, and in all conceivable ways through which knowledge is imparted. Then, at last, when society is completely saturated with Christian knowledge, and public opinion has taken a decided turn that way, they will come over by thousands'.[2] Secondly, he anticipated that the grant-in-aid system would make possible a great extension of missionary educational work, and the latter expectation was quickly realized. Although neither private bodies nor individuals showed any great alacrity to take advantage of the Government's offer of financial assistance, the missionaries were not slow to avail themselves of the help which the grant-in-aid system afforded and there was a rapid increase in the number of their educational institutions.

This expansion created fresh problems, both for the mssionaries themselves and for the Government. In the first place, the missionary schools and colleges became identified with (if not

---

[1] Richey, op. cit., p. 447.   [2] Smith, op. cit., II, pp. 244-5.

submerged in) the general educational system of the country, were forced to compete in ordinary subjects with other aided and with State institutions, and were thrown open to Government inspection as far as their secular teaching was concerned; as a result, they had to surrender a certain measure of control, to curtail the provision for religious teaching and, thus, to sacrifice something of their original and distinctive religious character. On the other hand, the rapid expansion of missionary education was viewed by the provincial Educational Departments with some concern. The institutions managed by various missionary societies were undoubtedly among the most efficient in the land, but the Government could not very well hand over State schools and colleges to bodies whose declared aim was conversion to Christianity. Consequently, in order to prevent the higher education of the country from passing, almost entirely, under missionary influence, the Government were forced to continue the maintenance of their own institutions and, even, to add to the number of State schools and colleges. Expenditure on higher education increased rather than decreased, and funds were not available for the expansion of mass education foreshadowed in Wood's Dispatch. Duff could hardly have foreseen that this would happen, nor could he have anticipated the heated controversies which were to follow.[1] He was bitterly disappointed that he had failed over the question of 'religious neutrality'; he had, however, made a spirited fight and was satisfied that no one could have done more to bring a Christian influence to bear on a Government committed to a suicidal policy. His Parliamentary work over, he visited America, where his missionary tour was in the nature of a triumphal procession. Early in 1855 he returned to Calcutta in confident expectation of that growth of missionary educational work for which recent legislation had paved the way.

The Dispatch of 1854 marks the end of an era—the age of the great educational pioneers. Thereafter, the historian is

---

[1] The Rev. J. Johnston, Secretary of the General Council on Education in India (1878), wrote several pamphlets urging the withdrawal of the Government from the field of higher education. The most important was *Our Educational Policy in India* (1879). The leader on the other side was Sir Roper Lethbridge whose *High Education in India* (1882) contains the ablest presentation of the opposite point of view.

mainly concerned with legislative measures of greater or less importance and with the working of the elaborate machinery set up by the Government to control education in its various branches. State control was inevitable and had to come sooner or later; it has achieved much that would otherwise have been impossible, but with the establishment of a system somewhat complicated and inelastic, education has become more and more stereotyped, with the result that there has not been the same scope for individual effort as there had been in the earlier part of the century. Duff's last seven years in India (1856-63) belong to the modern period, or at any rate to a period of transition, and were spent in an atmosphere very different from that in which he began his Indian career. During his extended furlough he had raised, in Britain and America, some £15,000 for a new college, which took the place of the temporary abode occupied since the Disruption and which became a worthy, but friendly, rival of the Presidency College (1854). Here Duff continued his educational and missionary work with the same zeal and energy that he had displayed as a young man, but his interests were by no means confined to the affairs of his own institution or to the welfare of his own flock.

He threw himself eagerly into a movement for the advancement of female education—a problem which had long exercised his mind. He had often dreamt of the 'halcyon period when universal theory would run parallel with universal practice'[1] in the matter of the education of Indian women. From the beginning he had claimed that his work in the Mission college 'was in reality a movement for female education also, because it would create in time an irresistible demand among men for educated wives'.[2] Until Bethune established (1849), at his own expense, a school for girls of good family, and induced Lord Dalhousie to lend his patronage and support to female education, little progress had been made. Towards the middle of the century enlightened public opinion had begun to veer round in favour of a reform, which had previously been resisted. The Dispatch of 1854 had stated that 'the importance of female education cannot be over-rated', and had authorized the Government to give it

[1] Smith, op. cit., I, p. 151.   [2] Paton, op. cit., p. 124.

'frank and cordial support' and to make girls' schools eligible for grants-in-aid. Up to this time only poor girls had been attracted to the few existing elementary schools, and the efforts made to enlist the sympathy and support of high-caste Hindus had not been very successful. As early as 1840, Dr Thomas Smith,[1] one of Duff's younger colleagues, had suggested in a magazine article that steps should be taken to give the women of India Christian instruction in the zenanas; nothing, however, was done to carry out this plan until Mrs Fordyce (the wife of a missionary) assisted by an Anglo-Indian lady, Miss Toogood, made a modest beginning in 1854. Their success prompted Duff to go a step further: he proposed that Englishwomen should be recruited in England by missionary bodies and sent out to India to popularize and extend zenana work. The proposal was strenuously opposed by the English residents of Calcutta, headed by Bishop Wilson. Duff made light of the arguments of his opponents; volunteers—most of them unmarried women—were enlisted and he was soon able to confound his critics. At first instruction was given in the families of the middle and higher classes; later, it was apparent that even Brahmans had no objection to allowing their daughters to attend missionary schools. In this way Duff was able to extend to girls the educational facilities which, a quarter of a century earlier, he had made available for boys, and in this way began zenana work, which gradually became one of the most important departments of missionary service in almost every station.

So far modern education has touched only the fringe of Indian womanhood and, judged by mere numerical standards, the results may seem disappointing. On the other hand, the policy which Duff elaborated has been more than justified, for it started a silent revolution in Indian life which still continues. If Duff was not the founder of modern women's education he was mainly instrumental in extending it to higher-class families; if he did not originate Zenana Missions he made them an instrument for carrying out one of the most important recommendations of the great Dispatch. He took no less pride in the girls' school attached to his own mission than he did in the great college which he had established for men. He played an active part in the affairs of

[1] Smith, op. cit., II, pp. 360 ff.

the Female Orphanage,[1] which developed into an efficient school and became a training-ground for women teachers. In short, not the least of his claims to grateful remembrance is the contribution he made towards the extension of education among the women of India.

His missionary work brought him into close contact with the masses, whose ignorance and poverty touched his heart. In 1858 he ventured to remind the Government of the clauses in the great Dispatch which dealt with the spread of useful and practical knowledge among those 'who were incapable of obtaining any education worthy of the name by their own unaided efforts'. He pointed out, with characteristic bluntness, that the promised 'considerable increase in expenditure' on elementary education was already overdue. He went on to say that funds could easily be made available for this purpose if, in accordance with the spirit and the letter of the Educational Dispatch, institutions for higher learning, including the Presidency College, were handed over to private management and supported by grants-in-aid. These suggestions were not acceptable to the authorities and higher education continued to enjoy a disproportionate share of Government financial support, while the Presidency College remains to this day a State institution.

It is not surprising that an educationist of Duff's eminence was appointed by the Governor-General a member of the committee which framed the constitution of the new University. Its primary aim was to test by examination the value of the education imparted by affiliated colleges; the Dispatch had made it clear that the standard required for an ordinary degree was to be 'such as to command respect without discouraging the efforts of deserving students', while in the competition for honours care was to be taken 'to maintain such a standard as will afford a guarantee of high ability and valuable attainments'; finally, the examinations for degrees were not to include any subjects connected with religious beliefs. These directions were followed by the com-

---

[1] Miss Cooke, better known as Mrs Wilson, arrived in Calcutta in 1821 and was instrumental in founding the 'Ladies Society for Native Female Education'. A Central School was built in 1824 and Lady Amherst consented to be Patroness of the Society. The Serampore trio had anticipated Mrs Wilson by starting the 'Calcutta Female Juvenile Society' in 1819.

mittee and, when the necessary legislative measures had been taken, the University was established in 1857. For six years Duff was the most influential member of the Senate and, in the words of Dr Banerjea, soon became 'the virtual governor of the University'.[1] In 1863 the Viceroy—Lord Elgin—wished to nominate Sir Charles Trevelyan as Vice-Chancellor, but Trevelyan would not accept until the honour had been offered to one whose distinguished services marked him out for this high office; he wrote[2] (March 1863):

> My dear Dr Duff,
>
> I have written to Sir R. Napier[3] requesting that he will submit to the Governor-General my strong recommendation that you should be appointed Vice-Chancellor of the University, and entirely disclaiming the honour on my part if there should have been any idea of appointing me. It is yours by right, because you have borne without rest or refreshment the burden and heat of the long day, which I hope is not yet near its close; and, what concerns us all more, if given to you it will be an unmistakable public acknowledgement of the paramount claims of national education, and will be a great encouragement to every effort that may be made for that object.
>
> Very sincerely yours,
> Ch. Trevelyan.

Unfortunately, illness prevented Duff from occupying the Vice-Chancellor's chair which was his 'by right'; his old enemy, dysentery, shattered his health, and before the end of the year he was again invalided home—this time for good.

The news of his departure prompted members of all classes and creeds, including orthodox Hindus, to do honour to the man who had occupied such a conspicuous place in the life of the capital and whose loss was a public calamity. Duff scholarships were endowed in the University, his marble bust was placed in the Great Hall of his own college, the Doveton Society and the Bethune College procured oil portraits of their great benefactor by the best painters; in addition, his Scottish merchant friends in

---

[1] Smith, op. cit., II, p. 383.   [2] ibid., p. 384.
[3] Member of the Supreme Council, 1861-5; officiated as Viceroy and Governor-General for a short period towards the end of 1863.

the East offered him £11,000 as a personal gift. He agreed to accept the interest on this sum during his lifetime, on condition that the capital was devoted, after his death, to a fund for the benefit of invalid missionaries of the Free Church. The valedictory addresses which poured in upon him would fill a volume, but only one short extract from a speech by Bishop Cotton need be quoted; 'it is quite certain that the work he did in India can never be undone, unless we, whom he has left behind, are faithless to his example'.[1] Although his health was never again robust, he lived for another fourteen years during which, in various capacities, he continued to devote his great spiritual and intellectual powers to the cause of Christian missions. He died peacefully in 1878 in his seventy-second year.

More than a century has elapsed since Duff launched his great educational experiment and it is now possible to review his policy and to criticize his methods with detachment. In attempting to do so one must always bear in mind that he was first and foremost a missionary, that with an abounding energy based on deep religious conviction he sought to make education the instrument of his supreme purpose—the salvation of souls. All his work rested on two fundamental beliefs—that the highest form of education was religious education, based on the eternal truths of the Bible, and that the end of such education was the acceptance of Him 'in Whom are hid all the treasures of knowledge and wisdom'. On theoretical grounds the validity of these assumptions might be challenged; in actual practice higher education 'saturated with Christianity' has seldom yielded results which justify the claims which have been made by its most enthusiastic supporters.

In the first place, it has led to a very small number of direct accessions to the Christian church, and among Duff's own early converts some were students from the Hindu College. One inherent weakness in his scheme was his failure to see that the mere intellectual assimilation of Biblical knowledge does not necessarily lead to a Christian way of life, much less to acceptance of Christian dogma. The great majority of Duff's students accepted with gratitude all that he had to teach them in the way of Western literature and science, but 'few were so permeated with

[1] Smith, op. cit., II, p. 395.

his spirit that they were led to assimilate his ideals'.[1]   Hundreds
of young men, attracted by the bait of free, or cheap, education,
readily submitted to daily instruction in a faith to which they were
either completely indifferent or definitely antagonistic.   It seems
fairly obvious that Christian teaching given in such an atmosphere
can never have an influence which is wholly for good.   Bishop
Whitehead[2] wisely points out that 'a lad's character is affected by
the religious truth he sincerely believes and assimilates and not
by that which he hears and rejects'.   Indeed, when the opponents
of secular education complained that the State colleges turned out
atheists, they invited the retort that the missionary colleges produced a goodly crop of hypocrites.   In so far as colleges of either
type undermined, or tended to undermine, faith in orthodox
Hinduism, the result was disbelief or scepticism.[3]   But whereas
the missionaries claimed to supply—even where conversion was
not effected—a valuable substitute for that which had been taken
away, the State colleges offered no divine sanction to replace the
old foundations of morality and religion.   Few would deny that
close contact with Christian teachers 'inspired with a deep sense
of religious vocation must count for a good deal in the education
of non-Christian students'.[4]   On the other hand, 'it is too often
assumed, as if it were an obvious truth, that the moral tone of
missionary schools and colleges must be higher than that of Government schools and colleges, simply because religious instruction is
given in the former and not in the latter.   It is certainly true
that the Government attitude of strict religious neutrality cuts
off one important instrument for the training of character . . .
but it is also true that the missionary colleges have not been able
to give their Hindu and Mahomedan students a really Christian
education.   Christian teaching is given in an atmosphere of antago-

[1] L. G. Mylne, *Missions to Hindus* (1908), p. 139.

[2] H. Whitehead, *Indian Problems in Religion, Education, Politics* (1924),
p. 184.

[3] Many Hindus who had received a modern education 'were suddenly
thrown adrift from the moorings and anchorages of old creeds and thrown
upon the wide sea of speculation and extravagance.   It was no wonder that
moral and social obligations began to share the fate of religious beliefs and
that the whole community was in alarm at the spread of the new views.'—
Howell, op. cit., p. 10.

[4] Whitehead, op. cit., p. 183.

nism or indifference which goes far to discount its moral influence'.[1] This is the verdict of one who has himself had a wide experience of missionary and educational work in India; it explains why even the great Dr Duff failed in his endeavour to give a real training in Christian life and character, and where he failed lesser men could hardly hope to succeed. The Lindsay Report (1931)[2] brings out very clearly that the creation of a truly Christian atmosphere is still a fundamental difficulty in colleges where the aims of missionary tutors do not coincide with those of the great majority of their non-Christian students.

Secondly, in his main purpose Duff undoubtedly failed—he did not 'take Brahmanism by storm', and this was what he set out to do. It is often said that he and his successors helped to bridge the gulf that had previously existed between Christianity and Hinduism and that the higher Hinduism of today owes a great deal to the spiritual movement of which Duff was one of the leaders. Farquhar, in his fascinating and authoritative work on *Modern Religious Movements in India*, dates 'the effective interpenetration of India by the West' back to 1800,[3] the year in which Carey settled in Serampore, but he regards the foundation (1828) of the Brahmo Samaj as the real beginning of the 'great awakening' which began in the early years of the last century. That modern Hinduism has been influenced by Christianity is beyond question, but the fact remains that Duff aimed at the complete overthrow of what he regarded as a false and mischievous religion; to claim that he strengthened or purified it is a criticism of his work which, even if true, is beside the mark.

Thirdly, it is permissible to argue that Duff was guilty of bringing undue religious pressure to bear on immature minds. He seems to have regarded 'the attainment of fourteen years as qualification for independent judgment, while in Bombay Wilson apparently considered sixteen a safer age'.[4] Modern missionaries would be reluctant to fix the age of discretion even at the higher of these two levels. But one might go further and make out a very damaging case against the use of any religious propaganda

---

[1] ibid.

[2] *Report of the Commission on Christian Higher Education in India* (1931); Dr A. D. Lindsay, Master of Balliol, was Chairman.

[3] Farquhar, op. cit., pp. i ff. [4] Mayhew, op. cit., p. 134.

through schools and colleges. ' "Do you think it honest to take boys and girls in their unformed years and to bring every kind of moral and spiritual pressure to bear on them while they are still immature?" When the argument is put in this form there can be only one answer.'[1] Possibly, Duff never considered the matter in this light and, even if he had, he would still have thought that he was acting in the best interests of those committed to his charge. The mere suggestion that he should withhold from the young the only wisdom worth having would have seemed outrageous to one whose conviction it was that 'the tree of knowledge without the tree of life can only tend to sin and misery'.[2]

Leaving aside these controversial issues, there can be little doubt that Duff's whole educational scheme was vitiated by one fundamental defect. He aimed at 'the supplanting of one civilization by another, the uprooting of the Indian civilization and the substitution of the English'.[3] Like many of his contemporaries, official as well as missionary, he was supremely ignorant, and arrogantly contemptuous, of Indian thought and culture. He was not, like Wilson of Bombay, an Oriental scholar and his sweeping condemnation of Hindu learning can no more be condoned than Macaulay's ill-informed condemnation of Oriental classical learning. In extenuation, it has been argued that these men saw only the worst features of popular Hinduism, with which they associated almost everything that was wicked and degrading. On the other hand, the Victorians had few misgivings about the merits of their own civilization, and in cocksureness Duff was little, if anything, behind Macaulay. It might be argued that the missionary took a sensible and statesmanlike view of the importance of the vernaculars, but this is only superficially true; although he aimed at making them the vehicles of modern knowledge and Christian teaching, his object was to hasten the advent of European civilization and, eventually, to cut India off completely from her ancient cultural heritage. Neither Duff nor

[1] Neill, op. cit., p. 117.

[2] Quoted by Ghosh, op. cit., p. 145 from a letter written by William Keane, a clergyman, to Bethune in 1850; he was asked to report on Government schools and colleges and this was the occasion of his *Present State and Results of Government Public Instruction in India* (1850).

[3] Andrews, op. cit., p. 34.

Macaulay recognized the salient fact that the real educational problem was 'one of assimilation rather than substitution', and each believed implicitly that by a process of 'filtration' India would become 'anglicized'. Each advocated, in perfectly good faith, root-and-branch methods which every modern thinker rightly condemns; each reminds one of that obstinate Caledonian whom Lamb had in mind when he said 'the twilight of dubiety never falls upon him'. These criticisms have been made not for the sake of mere fault-finding, still less with the idea of debunking an 'eminent Victorian'. When the last word has been said Duff's name stands out as the greatest in the long roll of Protestant missionaries who have laboured in the Indian mission field; amongst the makers of modern Indian education he is, beyond shadow of doubt, the most striking personality; indeed, he has left an imprint on the educational system of the country which the lapse of centuries will not efface. It is true that changing conditions have brought to light the need for certain modifications[1] in his original methods; but the system he introduced has, in its broad outlines, been followed right down to the present day. Many of his successors have rendered conspicuous services to the cause of education; none of them, however, has achieved the same success as Duff and none of them has brought such a rare combination of great gifts to bear on the work of the Educational Mission.

Many tributes have been paid to Duff's wide and varied scholarship, his eloquence and enthusiasm as a preacher, his prodigious capacity for work and his fearless courage in times of stress; the secret of his success, however, was that deep religious conviction which was the ruling passion of his life. This compelled admiration and respect, but not affection—for Duff was not a lovable man; he was austere and remote, without personal charm and completely lacking in a sense of humour.[2] He never outgrew the rugged Calvinism of his Highland home and it is significant that, next to the Bible, he owed most to Carlyle. His selfless devotion to duty cut him off from intimate contacts with his fellows and forced him to lead a life of rigorous asceticism and

[1] Lindsay Report, passim.
[2] *Memorials of Alexander Duff, D.D.*, by his son (1890), p. 10.

unnecessary self-sacrifice.[1] No hardship or deprivation was too great for one who gloried in his high calling and, though obsessed with a sense of his own weakness and unworthiness, he laboured unceasingly as a minister of the Gospel. Indians, whose religion he openly denounced, admired his spartan simplicity and saintly character, and they still hold him in the highest esteem; officials, although he condemned their misguided policy of religious neutrality, recognized his eminence as an educationist. Had he done nothing but bring his mighty influence to bear on successive Governors-General in India and on legislators in London his name would figure largely in the history of Indian education; the active part he played in the establishment of the early universities and in the introduction of the grant-in-aid system would entitle him to grateful remembrance; his efforts to extend and improve female and vernacular education were solid achievements for which, alone, a lesser man would be acclaimed an enlightened reformer. These conspicuous contributions to the development of the educational system of the country are all the more remarkable in that they were merely the work of those leisure hours in which he was free to turn aside from the evangelical labours in the performance of which he found his only joyful satisfaction. Further, his participation in public affairs was ever guided by the light of one cardinal principle—that secular education was, of itself, a poor, truncated thing, shallow, ineffective and even harmful. 'Without useful knowledge', he once said, 'a man might not live so comfortably in time; without divine knowledge, eternity must be lost.'[2] It is unflinching loyalty to a lofty ideal, rather than massive intellect or even dynamic personality, which makes Alexander Duff stand out as a grand heroic figure among the Indian educational reformers of the last century.

[1] See Paton, op. cit., pp. 218 ff.   [2] Smith, op. cit., I, p. 359.

SIR THOMAS MUNRO, 1761–1827

ADVOCATE OF EDUCATION FOR THE INFLUENTIAL CLASSES

DESPITE the widespread activities of Protestant missionaries in southern India in the eighteenth century, no steps were taken to place educational work on a systematic basis until Sir Thomas Munro became Governor of Madras in 1820. As a result of some forty years' experience—partly as a soldier, partly as a civil servant —he had gained a knowledge of Indian conditions which was unrivalled even in the days of Elphinstone and Malcolm. These three exceptional men were bound together by ties of friendship and inspired by the same lofty ideals of service to the people over whom they were called upon to rule. In some respects Munro's career was the most remarkable of the three, because he started life without the advantages of birth or wealth; also, he was a professional soldier whose fame rests not upon his military exploits, but upon his achievements as a civil administrator. If Elphinstone was a civilian who revealed many of the qualities of the born soldier, Munro was a soldier who found his true vocation in the work of civil administration.

Thomas Munro was the son of a Glasgow merchant and was born in that city in 1761. He left school at the early age of thirteen and proceeded to the local university, where he remained for three years. His academic career was not particularly distinguished, but he appears to have taken a special interest in the study of science. He was, however, an intelligent and hard-working boy and, blessed with a robust constitution, he excelled in sports and games. As a young man he cultivated a taste for reading and, although he never had any pretensions to scholarship, he remained a keen reader of miscellaneous books until his eyesight began to fail; even then he delighted in having books read to him aloud and among his favourites were the novels of Sir Walter Scott. His first ambition was to join a Highland regiment but, owing to the failure of his father's business, he had to decline the offer of a commission and to take up work in a mercantile firm. A little later he was offered, and accepted, a military cadetship in the service of the East India Company; not being

SIR THOMAS MUNRO

able to afford to pay for a passage to India he volunteered to work his way out as an ordinary seaman—an early example of his grit and determination. He landed in Madras early in 1780, a few months before his nineteenth birthday. Considering that Malcolm came to India before he was fourteen and that Elphinstone left home at fifteen, Munro started his career in the East with a decided advantage over his contemporaries in age, experience of the world and length of schooling.

His first twelve years in India were spent in military service and, although he took part in the campaigns against Haidar Ali and Tipu Sultan, were comparatively uneventful. His early letters —and he was an exceptionally good letter-writer—give many interesting details of the life of a young subaltern in India towards the close of the eighteenth century and they throw occasional sidelights on events of historical importance; they also reveal an early liking for the country in which his lot was cast and a growing sympathy with its inhabitants.

From 1792 to 1807 he was employed in civil administration as a District Officer, first at Baramahal, now part of the District of Salem, then in Kanara and, finally, in the Ceded Districts, which had been acquired by treaty with the Nizam of Hyderabad (1800). In many ways these years—excluding his short stay in Kanara—were the most pleasant and the most fruitful of his whole career. Having acquired a working knowledge of the spoken languages of the people among whom he lived (he had already attained proficiency in Persian and Hindustani), he made it a point to get into intimate touch with those with whom he had official dealings and to listen personally to the petitions and complaints of even the humblest peasant. In a country recently ravaged by war, people had many grievances and the settlement of the revenue called for the most delicate handling. Munro and his colleagues at Baramahal (where, it is claimed, his memory still lives) introduced the ryotwari system, on the lines followed later by Elphinstone in the Deccan; under this system the holding of each cultivator, who is regarded as a proprietor, is assessed annually and the revenue is paid direct to the Government. The work in which he was absorbed was interrupted by the outbreak of the third Mysore War and for a short time Munro, who had attained his captaincy, found himself on active service. After the fall of

Seringapatam and the death of Tipu, he was appointed Joint-Secretary, with Malcolm, of a Commission which was set up to arrange for the disposal of the Mysore and neighbouring territories and for the settlement of other questions arising out of the war. The short period of his secretaryship is memorable, for it led to his lasting friendship first with Malcolm and then with Wellesley.

Among the territories which were ceded by treaty to the English was the District of Kanara, on the Malabar coast, which was then inhabited by a discontented and turbulent people. Munro, now a Major, had looked forward to the resumption of his work in Baramahal, and was none too pleased to be appointed Collector of Kanara. In less than eighteen months he reduced the District to order and won the respect, even the affection of the people. He spent most of the year on tour, often without an escort, and was ever ready to grant interviews to villagers who had anything to bring to his notice. In Kanara he could not introduce the ryotwari system, because here the settlement had long been made with the zemindars and not with the cultivators direct. It was Munro's policy to interfere as little as possible with established customs and, like Elphinstone, he had little patience with what Malcolm called 'excessive innovation'.

In spite of the beauty of the scenery, Munro never grew to like Kanara, although he had the satisfaction of seeing the fruits of his extremely hard work in an enervating climate—the restoration of order and the establishment of good government. He applied for a transfer and it was with some reluctance that the authorities agreed to post him as Principal Collector of the Ceded Districts (Bellary, Anantapur, Cuddapah and Kurnool), with four Collectors to assist him. The country is almost the exact opposite of Kanara with its picturesque seacoast and great inland forests; much of it is arid, rocky and treeless, and the fertile tracts are covered with black cotton soil. It had long been the battleground of opposing armies, and when Munro arrived he found that it was studded with forts and overrun by petty chieftains (known as *polygars*), who numbered some 30,000 and lived by plunder and violence. His first concern was to bring these bandits to heel and to win the confidence of law-abiding people. This he did by moving freely about his Districts, often unarmed and sometimes unattended, and by making himself easily accessible to all. Gradually he restored order and introduced the ryotwari system, which subsequently became the principal revenue system throughout the Madras Presidency.

At this period Munro was so hard-worked that he complained he had no time for rest or relaxation. When he was asked to keep a diary and submit it periodically to the Government he caustically remarked: 'I cannot see what purpose it would answer here except to hinder me from looking after more important matters.'[1] When the Mutiny of Vellore (1806) broke out, it was attributed by many to intrigues among members of Tipu's family, who were thought to be scheming to restore Muslim rule. Munro realized from the first that the main cause of the revolt was the issue of new regulations prohibiting sepoys from wearing caste marks and prescribing changes in their uniforms and in the mode of wearing beards. He hastened to assure the Governor of Madras, Lord William Bentinck, that if these regulations were cancelled no further trouble need be feared; this actually proved to be the case, although the agitation caused by the mutiny led to Bentinck's recall.

After twenty-seven years' continuous service Munro, who had been promoted to the rank of Lieutenant-Colonel, decided that he ought to take leave, and so he resigned his appointment in 1807. He reached England early in the following year to find that his mother had died before his departure from India and that his father had grown old and infirm. He revisited the scenes of his youth, dabbled in chemistry and spent a good deal of time in London, where he mixed in society and followed with interest the political events of the day. His stay in England is memorable because, in the discussions which preceded the renewal of the Company's Charter (1813), Munro was consulted by the Court of Directors and by the Government. Before a Committee of the House of Commons he gave evidence on a variety of topics concerning the internal administration of India and he wrote a long and interesting memorandum[2] on the subject of the Company's trading privileges, which were soon to be abolished. In his evidence before the Commons he made a statement which is of

[1] J. Bradshaw, *Sir Thomas Munro* (1894), p. 119.
[2] G. R. Gleig, *Life of Sir Thomas Munro*, (abridged edition, 1849), pp. 204 ff.

interest to the educationist and one which attracted considerable notice at the time and has frequently been quoted since; 'if', he said, 'a good system of agriculture, unrivalled manufacturing skill, a capacity to produce whatever might contribute to convenience or luxury, schools established in every village, the general practice of hospitality and charity amongst each other, and, above all, a treatment of the female sex full of confidence, respect and delicacy, were among the signs which denoted a civilized people—then the Hindoos were not inferior to the natives of Europe; and if civilization were to become an article of trade between the two countries, he was convinced that England would greatly benefit from the import of cargo'. Dr Marshman, who quotes[1] this statement in full, regrets that a responsible Government official should have 'volunteered the most extravagant panegyric on the Hindoo character and institutions' and laments Munro's 'morbid admiration' for a civilization which tended to perpetuate moral and religious degradation and to impede the introduction of Christianity. More reliance may be placed on the generous verdict of one of his biographers, who writes: 'On all the matters which were brought under investigation Munro was consulted, and in most cases the information which he gave contributed to their settlement. The evidence given by him before the House of Commons, and the promptitude and clearness of his replies, produced a most favourable impression.'[2]

The Court of Directors showed their appreciation of Munro's intimate knowledge of Indian affairs by appointing him President of a Special Commission to inquire into the judicial system which had long been in operation in Bengal and Madras. After a stay of some six years at home he landed in Madras in September 1814, accompanied by his wife, having married six months earlier Miss Jane Campbell, of Ayrshire. It is hardly necessary to discuss in detail the findings of the Judicial Commission which (despite the opposition of the Governor of Madras, the Right Hon'ble Hugh Elliot, and the Members of his Council) were eventually passed into law and remain as 'a monument not only of Munro's force

[1] J. R. Marshman, *The Life and Times of Carey, Marshman and Ward* (1859), II, p. 20.

[2] A. J. Arbuthnot, *Major-General Sir Thomas Munro—A Memoir* (1889), p. 102.

of character . . . but of his high administrative ability and statesmanlike views'.[1] Suffice it to say that among the alterations made
in the Madras Code of Regulations were the transference of the
superintendence of the police and the functions of District Magistrate from the Judge to the Collector, the employment of petty
hereditary village officials and the restoration of panchayats; to the
latter Munro attached much importance because these village courts
settled disputes by mutual agreement rather than by precise judicial
procedure. He had long been of opinion that one of the worst
results of British rule had been to lower the status and to reduce
the powers of panchayats and, even though he admitted that
their decisions were sometimes corrupt and arbitrary, he maintained that they dispensed as much real justice as the law-courts
and with less delay.

The work of the Commission was completed before the lapse
of the three years for which it had been appointed and Munro
contemplated a return to army life. The outbreak of the Maratha
War (1817–18) seemed to offer a suitable opportunity for military
service and merited promotion. To his great disappointment,
however, he was appointed Commissioner of the Southern
Maratha country, ceded to the Government of Bombay by the
Treaty of Poona, and he had to proceed to Dharwar to take up
a responsible, but purely civil, appointment. He gave vent to
his annoyance in a letter to the Governor-General in which he said
that he could not but 'regret deeply to feel for the first time in
advance the army shut against him'.[2] His disappointment was
short-lived, for he was soon given command, as Brigadier, of a
division with instructions to reduce the Southern Maratha country.
Working in a military as well as a civil capacity, he set himself
to carry the war into the territories held by the enemy by expelling
the army of occupation, by reducing their strongholds and by
issuing conciliatory proclamations to the people. Fortunately, his
fame had preceded him, for the Dharwar District is bordered
on one side by Bellary and on another by Kanara and so the
cultivators had often heard of 'Thomas Munro Bahadur', whose
reputation as 'the friend of the ryot' had already been established;
they willingly assisted in the expulsion of their old masters, in

[1] Bradshaw, op. cit., p. 159.   [2] ibid., p. 162.

the defence of their own possessions and, even, in the collection of revenues for the British. Malcolm said that the success of a plan 'at once so simple and so great' could have been anticipated only by 'a mind like his',[1] while Canning said in the House of Commons that 'the population which he subjugated by arms, he managed with such address, equity, and wisdom, that he established an empire over their hearts and feelings'.[2] His combination of firmness and clemency had the approval of Elphinstone, who also took part in this campaign and, later, succeeded Munro as Commissioner of the Deccan (including the Southern Maratha country).

The battle of Sholapur brought hostilities to an end and Munro, whose health was now seriously impaired, decided to submit his resignation and to return to England. On his arrival in London he was received with the greatest cordiality in social and political circles, and honours were showered upon him. Before his departure from India he had been gazetted Companion of the Bath and promotion to the rank of Major-General soon followed; he was one of those suggested by Canning for the governorship of Bombay—the others being Elphinstone, who was selected in 1819, and Malcolm, who succeeded Elphinstone in 1827. Munro, however, had not long to wait for a tangible recognition of his services, and within a few months he was elevated to the governorship of Madras in succession to the Right Hon'ble Hugh Elliot with whom his relations, as President of the Judicial Commission, had been somewhat strained. Prior to his departure for India, he was created K.C.B. and given an official banquet, at which his old friend the Duke of Wellington was present to applaud Canning's eulogistic references to the Governor-designate. Munro, ever a modest and unassuming man, was rather over-whelmed by these proceedings, but a day or two before he sailed for Madras he confessed, in a letter to a friend, 'it is worth while to be a Governor to be spoken of in such a manner by such a man'.[3]

In May 1820 Sir Thomas and Lady Munro landed in Bombay, where they spent two weeks as the welcome guests of the Hon'ble Mountstuart Elphinstone. Munro then proceeded to Madras to

---

[1] ibid., p. 166.   [2] Gleig, op. cit., p. 260.   [3] Bradshaw, op. cit., p. 178.

assume his high office and, as events turned out, the period of his governorship proved quiet and uneventful. Throughout he acted on his own maxim that 'the superintending influence of a Governor should be felt in every corner of his province'. It is not surprising, therefore, that he made extensive and prolonged tours through the Presidency, so that he could come into personal contact with the people and local officials. He took particular delight in revisiting the places in which he had served his apprenticeship as an administrator, and it was on a tour in the Ceded Districts that he died in harness. In 1826 he had submitted his resignation; this was accepted and Lady Munro returned to England. Owing to unforeseen circumstances, his successor, the Hon'ble Stephen Lushington, was unable to come to India to relieve him before the break of the monsoon in 1827 and so Munro, in spite of the hot weather and the prevalence of cholera, decided to pay a farewell visit to the Ceded Districts. Although he appeared to be cheerful and in good health, he soon fell a victim to the epidemic and after a short illness passed quietly away. He was buried in Gooty, but a few years later his remains were removed to St Mary's Church, Madras. His loss was mourned by all classes and creeds, for he had already earned the appellation of 'father of the people'. In a special Government notification it was stated that 'his sound and vigorous understanding, his transcendent talents, his indefatigable application, his varied store of knowledge, his attainments as an Oriental scholar,[1] his intimate acquaintance with the habits and feelings of the native soldiers and the inhabitants generally, his patience, temper, facility of access and kindness of manner, would have insured him distinction in any line of employment'.[2] Many tributes to his worth as a soldier, as an administrator and as a man have been paid by eminent persons and that by Elphinstone (in a letter to his friend Strachey, written as early as 1821) deserves quotation: 'You greatly undervalue Munro, who has more marks of genius than most men I have seen, a clear sagacious head in peace and war, original and correct views on all subjects, a real love of the natives and of mankind, without cant or sentiment, firmness approaching to inflexibility, great

[1] This is a tribute to Munro's colloquial knowledge of several Indian languages; he was not a scholar in the strict sense of the term.
[2] Bradshaw, op. cit., p. 211.

indulgence for others, good taste, candour, frankness and simplicity that make one at home with him in a minute.'[1] His equestrian statue by Chantrey was erected in Madras in 1839, but this is not such a fitting memorial as the esteem with which the name of this great and kindly man is still remembered.

This brief sketch of Munro's life merely draws attention to some of the more important events in his varied career, but it does not bring out with any fulness those traits of character, that largeness of sympathy and that breadth of vision which characterized all his dealings. It certainly would not lead one to suppose that Munro held advanced views on the subject of education, which he regarded as a matter of first-rate importance for the administrator and the social reformer. Fortunately, his minutes and official papers have been admirably edited by Sir Alexander Arbuthnot[2] and many quotations from them (as well as from the letters reprinted in Gleig's *Life*) have found their way into modern books on Indian history. For the educationist, three of these documents have a special significance for, taken together, they give a true picture of the ideals which lay behind Munro's desire to improve and expand education in southern India and of the efforts which he made to translate those ideals into practice.

The first, addressed to the Board of Revenue and dated 2 July 1822, is of historical importance because it marks the first attempt to carry out in India a reliable educational survey. It begins: 'Much has been written, both in England and in this country, about the ignorance of the people of India and the means of disseminating knowledge among them. But the opinions on this subject are the mere conjectures of individuals unsupported by any authentic documents, and differing so widely from each other, as to be entitled to very little attention. . . . We have made geographical and agricultural surveys of our provinces. We have investigated their resources and endeavoured to ascertain their population; but little or nothing has been done to learn the state of education.'[3] Munro had made up his mind that it was desirable

[1] T. E. Colebrooke, *Life of the Honourable Mountstuart Elphinstone* (1884), II, p. 125.

[2] *Major-General Sir Thomas Munro—Selections from his Minutes and other Official Writings*, 2 vols. (1881).

[3] Arbuthnot, *Selections*, op. cit., II, p. 328.

that the Government should have trustworthy information about educational activities throughout the province, and a circular order was issued to Collectors directing them to supply details regarding the number of schools in their respective Districts, the number of pupils in attendance, the quality and methods of instruction, and the like. He warned them, however, to observe the principle of non-interference: 'It is not my intention', he concluded, 'to recommend any interference whatever in the native schools. Everything of this kind should be carefully avoided, and the people should be left to manage their own schools in their own way. All that we ought to do is to facilitate the operations of these schools by restoring any funds that may have been diverted from them, and perhaps granting additional ones where it may appear advisable.'[1] The Court of Directors warmly approved of the inquiry into the state of indigenous schools, also of the warning 'against exerting any fear in the people that their freedom of choice in matters of education should be interfered with'; they added, somewhat pompously, that 'it would be equally wrong to fortify them in the absurd opinion that their own-made institutions of education were so perfect as not to admit of improvement'.[2]

It took more than two years to collect and collate the reports of the Collectors, which formed the basis of Munro's great educational Minute[3] of 10 March 1826. They showed that there were 12,498 schools for a population of 12,850,941 persons or, roughly, one school with an average attendance of 15 pupils for every 1,000 people; but, 'as only very few females were taught in schools, we may reckon one school to every 500 of the population'. Taking into consideration the fact that many children were receiving private tuition at home, the total number of children of school-going age was estimated at nearer one-third than one-fourth of the whole It must be admitted that too much reliance cannot be placed on the accuracy of these figures, because the unsettled conditions of the country and the lack of adequate machinery for the collection of statistics hardly permitted of exact estimates of population, schools or pupils. Speaking of children

[1] ibid., p. 330.
[2] S. Satthianadhan, *History of Education in the Madras Presidency* (1894), p. 2.
[3] H. Sharp, *Selections from Educational Records*, I (1920), pp. 73-6.

who were educated privately, Munro himself says that, for Madras city, 'the number taught at home is 26,903, or above five times greater than that taught in schools'; he adds that 'there is probably some error in this number' and that 'the number privately taught in the provinces does certainly not approach this rate', though it is 'considerable'. Again, the report of Mr A. D. Campbell,[1] Collector of Bellary, shows that for a population of 927,857 there were only 553 schools with 6,641 pupils; on the basis of Munro's calculations there should have been about 927 with over 13,000 pupils. The results of the survey carried out by Elphinstone in Bombay (1824) would also appear to strengthen the inference that Munro overestimated the number of schools and of pupils under instruction, though he discovered that the number of indigenous schools in the south was far greater than was commonly supposed. The conclusions of Sir Philip Hartog[2] on this controversial issue seem convincing, despite the efforts which have been made to rebut them.

Among other interesting facts[3] which the reports of District Officers brought to light were:

(a) that of the total number of pupils attending existing schools only about 13,500 were Muslims and only some 4,500 were girls; of the Hindu pupils under instruction 1 in every 4 was a Brahman;

(b) that few schools had been endowed by the public, the majority being supported by parents or by grants from ancient rulers or zemindars;

(c) that fees varied from 1 anna to 4 rupees a month, the average being about 4 annas;

(d) that teachers did not earn more than Rs. 6 to Rs. 7 per mensem.

As regards content and methods of instruction, valuable details were supplied by the Collector of Bellary (Mr Campbell), who reported that teachers were inefficient, that discipline was harsh, and that learning was restricted to mere memorization—in a high-flown language which differed considerably from the 'dialects of business' and was, therefore, unintelligible to children.

---

[1] Sharp, op. cit., pp. 65-8.

[2] P. J. Hartog, *Some Aspects of Indian Education, Past and Present* (1939), pp. 72-4.

[3] J. M. Sen, *History of Elementary Education in India* (1933), pp. 92 ff.

In the light of the information before him Munro was forced to the conclusion that 'the state of education was low compared with that of our own country'; he was not, however, unduly pessimistic for he went on to say that 'it was higher than in most European countries at no very distant date'.[1]

In the second part of his educational minute the Governor made concrete proposals for the expansion and improvement of education throughout the province. Before turning to these proposals, attention may be drawn to the second of the three documents to which reference has been made—the Minute of 31 December 1824 on Internal Administration.[2] This was written after some four years' experience of the duties and responsibilities of the Governor of a large province and it states, clearly and frankly, the liberal principles which guided all Munro's administrative work. Having disposed of some of 'the well-intended but visionary plans' which had been suggested for 'the improvement of India', he proceeded to lay particular emphasis on what he had come to regard as the chief means of uplifting a people who had earned his sympathy and respect. He advocated, with great sincerity, the employment of Indians in the administration of the country; indeed, his conviction that it was the duty of the Government, even in its own interests, to train Indians for high office, lies at the back of all his schemes for educational reform. A few quotations will reveal the firmness and liberality of his views on this subject—views which he shared with Elphinstone and Malcolm:

(a) 'How can we expect that the Hindoos will be eager in the pursuit of science, unless they have the same inducements as in other countries? If superior acquirements do not open the road to distinction, it is idle to suppose that the Hindoo would lose his time in seeking them; and even if he did so, his proficiency, under the doctrine of exclusion from office, would serve no other purpose than to show him more clearly the fallen state of himself and his countrymen.'[3]

---

[1] Sharp, op. cit., p. 73.

[2] Arbuthnot, *Selections*, I, pp. 237 ff. The Minute is quoted in full under the heading, 'On the State of the Country and the Condition of the People'. Copious extracts will be found in Gleig, op. cit., pp. 299 ff.

[3] Gleig, op. cit., p. 308.

(b) 'The great number of offices in which the natives are employed, is one of the strongest causes of their attachment to our Government. In proportion as we exclude them from these, we lose our hold upon them; and were the exclusion entire we should have their hatred in place of their attachment.'[1]

(c) 'We should look upon India not as a temporary possession, but as one which is to be maintained permanently, until the natives shall in some future age have abandoned most of their superstitions and prejudices, and become sufficiently enlightened to frame a regular government for themselves, and to conduct and preserve it. Whenever such a time shall arrive, it will probably be best for both countries that the British control over India shall be gradually withdrawn.'[2]

No further extracts are needed to show that Munro was sincere in his conviction that it was morally, as well as politically, necessary for the Government to take immediate steps to educate the people. He openly confessed that he was 'impressed with favourable sentiments' towards Indians and had nothing but contempt for those who spoke of them 'as men utterly unworthy of trust'; but 'if', he wrote, 'we are sincere in our wishes to protect and render them justice, we ought to believe that they deserve it. We cannot easily bring ourselves to take much interest in what we despise and regard as unworthy'.[3]

It is important, however, to remember that, in expressing these sentiments, Munro had chiefly in mind the upper classes, whose support and co-operation he was anxious to win; 'One of the great disadvantages of our government in India', he wrote, 'is its tendency to lower or destroy the higher ranks of society, to bring them all too much to one level, and, by depriving them of their former weight and influence, to render them less useful instruments in the internal administration of the country'.[4] He was wise enough to recognize that class, no less than caste, distinctions had existed in India from time immemorial and had the sanction of traditional usage; hence, in all his proposals for the administrative and educational advancement of the country, he had mainly in view the upper and middle classes, whose privileged posi-

---

[1] ibid., p. 309.   [2] ibid., p. 316.   [3] ibid., p. 316.   [4] ibid., p. 314.

tion made them the acknowledged leaders of the masses. This is the true explanation of what he called the 'doctrine of exclusion from office' and failure to appreciate this fundamental fact renders it impossible to assess at their proper value the proposals for educational reform which are embodied in his Minute of 1826.

Addressing the Court of Directors, he recommended the establishment at each District headquarters of a higher Hindu and a higher Mohammedan school and, as there were twenty Collectorates in the province, this meant 40 *superior*, or *principal*, schools; he also proposed the setting up of 15 *inferior* (*elementary*) schools, one in each *tahsil* (sub-division) of every Collectorate— making a total of 300. He estimated that these 340 schools would provide for the education of about 7,400 boys, at a cost to the Government of Rs. 4,000 a month; this figure included (*a*) salaries of 40 teachers (at Rs. 15 p.m.) in Collectorate schools —Rs. 600; (*b*) salaries of 300 teachers (at Rs. 9 p.m.) in *tahsildari* schools—Rs. 2,700; (*c*) a monthly grant of Rs. 700 to the Madras School Book Society, which had been founded (1823) on the model of the sister institution in Calcutta. Munro anticipated that the teachers in *tahsildari* schools would each receive at least another Rs. 9 p.m. from pupils and would, therefore, be as well off 'as a parish school master in Scotland'. Presumably, he expected that the official salaries of teachers in Collectorate schools would be supplemented in the same way and in the same proportion—otherwise teachers in elementary schools would have been at a decided financial advantage.

The Governor explained that, in his opinion, the decline in education had been due partly to poverty caused by the unsettled conditions resulting from war and partly by the lack of official encouragement. He pointed out that without Government endowment of schools little could be done to further the spread of education and he argued that the trifling expenditure required to put matters right would be 'amply repaid by the improvement of the country: for the general diffusion of knowledge is inseparably followed by more orderly habits, by increasing industry, by a taste for the comforts of life and by the growing prosperity of the country'.[1] The Directors were impressed by the cogency of his arguments (and by the cheapness of his scheme) and they authoriz-

[1] Sharp, op. cit., p. 75.

ed, in their Dispatch of 1828, the appropriation of half a lakh
of rupees and the appointment of a Committee of Public Instruction, which was to superintend and direct educational activities
throughout the province. They also approved courses of studies
for the Collectorate schools, and these included English, Tamil
and Telugu, with Grammar, Arithmetic and Geography, and,
perhaps, Sanskrit and Arabic. It may be explained that the *higher*
schools were roughly equivalent to what are now called *middle*
schools, and that their aim was to impart, through the languages
of the people, a sound elementary education, including a working
knowledge of simple English.

Without waiting for the sanction of the Directors the local
Government approved the appointment of a Committee of Public
Instruction (1826) and operations were started on a small scale.
The School Board had already recommended the establishment
of a 'school for educating teachers' and the new Committee began
by organizing in Madras a Normal School for the training of 40
teachers—two for each of the proposed Collectorate schools. (This
institution developed into the Madras High School and, subsequently, into the Presidency College.) The selection of teachers,
to be deputed for training on a monthly stipend of Rs. 15, was
left to the more important inhabitants of the principal towns
in each District, and the few schools which were eventually
established were placed under Indian management, though
Collectors were given (on the recommendation of the Directors)
powers of general supervision.[1]

The eagerness of the Committee to set to work, and their
insistence on the importance of having qualified teachers, would
seem to indicate that a promising start had been made. Within
a few years, however, it became quite obvious that both central
and *tahsildari* schools had proved a failure. The commonly
accepted explanation is that these schools 'died out for want of
pupils'[2] and 'lack of efficient supervision',[3] but that is not the
whole story. In 1827, the year of Munro's death, the normal
class numbered only 10, and only 8 schools had been established
—all of them in the neighbourhood of the city of Madras. It is

---

[1] Satthianadhan, op. cit., p. 9.

[2] A. J. Richey, *Selections from Educational Records*, II (1922), p. 432.

[3] Satthianadhan, op. cit., p. 9.

true that, eventually, some 60 *tahsildari* schools were started in the Districts and that the Normal School attracted a considerable number of would-be teachers for the Collectorate schools. The majority of these, however, underwent the prescribed course of training not because they wished to become teachers, but because they welcomed the opportunity of acquiring, as stipendiaries, a knowledge of English, which had come to be regarded as indispensable for a successful career in many walks of life. Little or nothing seems to have been done to provide trained teachers for *tahsildari* schools and, outside Madras itself (where they were subject to inspection), they were a signal failure. The Committee, with the best of intentions, had decided that these schools should be open to 'Brahmins and Sudras alike', and this decision can hardly have been acceptable to the leading citizens of up-country towns—and it was on their sympathy and co-operation that the success of Munro's scheme ultimately depended. It was to the principal inhabitants of each town that the selection of candidates for deputation to the Normal School in Madras was entrusted, and this method of securing suitable teachers, though laudable in theory, resulted in the selection of many unqualified and unenthusiastic young men; most of them were Brahmans and they owed their appointment to the fact that they were able to bring influence to bear on the appointing authorities. It is true that in the selection of Hindu candidates for deputation to Madras it was the policy of the Committee to give preference to Brahmans. As regards the recommendation that low-caste Hindus should be admitted to *tahsildari* schools, the Government appear to have felt some uneasiness; it was feared that, if the lower classes were encouraged to attend these schools, the upper classes would show resentment and withdraw their support.

Meantime, in their Dispatch of 1828, the Directors had approved Munro's scheme; a few years previously (1825) they had informed the Governor-General that plans to provide schools with efficient teachers were 'worthy of great encouragement, since it is upon the character of the indigenous schools that the education of the great mass of the population must ultimately depend'.[1] In a subsequent Dispatch, however, written in 1830, they com-

---

[1] Sharp, op. cit., p. 50.

plained that the Madras scheme had failed to provide higher education for the upper classes; 'by raising the standard of education among these classes', they wrote, 'you would eventually produce a much greater and more beneficial change in the ideas and feelings of the community, than you can hope to produce by acting directly on the more numerous class'.[1] It is little wonder that, deprived of Munro's leadership, the Committee of Public Instruction were at a loss to know what policy they should adopt. Their perplexity was ended by the receipt of Lord William Bentinck's Resolution of 1835; this was interpreted as a prohibition against the use of the vernaculars as media of instruction in State institutions and, accordingly, aid was withdrawn from the few remaining 'superior' and 'inferior' schools.

Munro had hoped that Government patronage of education would find favour among the more influential classes, who would welcome the starting of new and efficient schools for the education of their sons; he had also hoped that the establishment of State institutions, which would serve as models for indigenous schools, would improve standards of teaching throughout the province. Unfortunately, his scheme to set up a network of good schools did not materialize and its failure was due to many contributory causes. It is true that the author's untimely death, just when his energetic leadership was most needed, was a severe blow to the advancement of education in southern India; other factors were the inconsistency of the Directors, the hesitancy of the Committee, the apathy of officials and the indifference of the people —most of whom were too ignorant to appreciate the benefits which would accrue from the education of their children. It may even be said that Munro's plan, admirable though it was in general conception, contained within itself the seeds of its own dissolution. In the first place, he failed to realize the magnitude of the task of setting up an organized system of public instruction, with the result that the financial provision which he proposed for the payment of teachers, expert supervision and the printing of textbooks was totally inadequate; secondly, the emphasis, rather over-emphasis, which he laid on the principle of 'non-interference' served to deter officials from taking those active measures which

---

[1] ibid., p. 51.

were necessary to ensure success, and, also, allowed too much scope to private persons to exert their influence in places where educated public opinion was almost non-existent. There is certainly much truth in Sir Alexander Arbuthnot's verdict that 'the measure was essentially faulty in its design and its failure was inevitable'.[1] On the other hand, it must be admitted that, despite inherent defects, Munro's scheme embodied educational views far in advance of those commonly held in his day and that, if he failed, he failed splendidly.

It might be argued that, even if the Governor's plans for the establishment of elementary and middle schools (staffed by efficient teachers) came to nothing, yet the Court of Directors and the Central Government soon came round to his way of thinking as regards the higher education of the upper and middle classes with a view to their employment in Government service. No one had advocated with more sincerity than Munro the acceptance of this policy, which is stressed in his comprehensive Minute of 1824; it is significant that this was penned at a time when his mind was much occupied with thoughts of educational reform and it contains the most explicit statement of his deep-rooted conviction that 'improved education and higher employment should go together'.[2] Indeed, this was the main ground on which he based his argument that the British Government in India must recognize its obligation to educate the people under its rule. Elphinstone and Malcolm shared this enlightened view and the influence which these liberal administrators exerted on the Directors was effectual. In Dispatches sent out to India there began to appear frequent references to the importance of 'useful knowledge', by which was meant knowledge that would fit members of the upper classes to hold responsible posts under the Government. For instance, in their Dispatch of 1830, the Directors reminded the Government of Madras of 'their anxious desire' to have at their disposal a number of Indians 'qualified by their habits and acquirements to take a larger share and occupy higher situations in the civil administration of their country than has hitherto been the practice'.[3] They urged the local Government to concentrate upon the encouragement of English education, by adopting measures similar to those which

---

[1] Arbuthnot, *Memoir*, op. cit., p. 154.   [2] ibid.
[3] Sharp, op. cit., p. 51.

had proved so successful in Bengal. At first sight, this would appear to be an adequate answer to the question which Munro had raised a few years previously: 'With what grace', he had asked, 'can we talk of paternal government, if we exclude the natives from every important office?'[1]   On closer examination, the policy which eventually found favour marks a departure from that advocated by Munro, and the over-insistence which came to be placed on the importance of higher English education for the privileged few soon led to the utter neglect of vernacular education, which was of basic importance in Munro's educational scheme. Several references have been made to his desire to uphold the established institutions of the people, to promote education through their own languages and to respect their sentiments and feelings. He had no objection to the study of English or to the spread of Western knowledge, but he realized, as clearly as Elphinstone, that the foundations of the educational edifice must be well and truly laid in a manner intelligible and acceptable to the people, whose traditions and usages it would be folly to ignore.

As years went on the wisdom of Munro's recommendations was forgotten, his schools dwindled to nothing, and the principles advocated by the Anglicists prevailed, in Madras as elsewhere. No one could have had less sympathy than Munro with the plans of his successors to concentrate on the spread of higher English to the exclusion of elementary education, which had the first claim on the Government's patronage, for it was best calculated to improve the character of the people and to raise the standard of social life throughout the community.   It must never be forgotten that Munro's scheme for primary and middle schools was designed— in the first instance, at any rate—for the benefit of sons of the upper and middle classes rather than for the children of the poor or the lower orders.   He never contemplated 'mass education', in the sense in which that term is interpreted today; for instance, in his Minute of 1826 he wrote: 'We ought to extend to Mahomedan the same advantages of education as to our Hindoo subjects, and perhaps even to a greater degree, because a greater proportion of them belong to the middle and higher classes.'[2] His first object was to conciliate the acknowledged leaders of the

---

[1] Gleig, op. cit., p. 307.   [2] Sharp, op. cit., p. 74.

people, those whom the masses had for centuries regarded as their superiors. It is true that he foresaw that education would eventually be extended 'by means of an increased demand for it, and this must arise chiefly from its being found to facilitate the acquisition of wealth or rank, and from the improvement in the condition of the people rendering a larger portion of them able to pay for it';[1] he had the good sense to realize that it was impossible to 'educate those who do not seek, or cannot pay for education'[2] and, therefore, his first appeal was made to the upper classes. By slow degrees, however, he anticipated that a taste for knowledge would spread and that education would extend even to remote villages, though progress 'must of necessity be slow'.

The Anglicists also set themselves to conciliate the higher classes, but whereas they pinned their faith to filtration, in the belief that 'the light must first touch the mountain tops before it can pierce the levels and depths',[3] Munro realized that a national system of education must have its basis in efficient schools—for without good schools at the bottom, higher education, whether Oriental or Western, would be little more than moonshine. True it is that, after Munro's death, the English schools which sprang up in profusion aimed at providing educated candidates for Government service; but even this gain (he would have argued) was won at the sacrifice of something more valuable—the welfare and progress of the nation's schools; these had the first call on the patronage of the Government because they had the first call on the esteem of the people, who for generations had cherished and supported them and regarded them as institutions which belonged to themselves and as instruments of their own welfare and advancement.

Bentinck's Resolution of 1835 dealt a final blow to the progress of Munro's schools, but (strangely enough) it did not spur the Madras Government to take energetic steps to pursue the policy of anglicization which had been forced upon them. Indeed, the history of education in southern India for the next

[1] ibid., p. 76.   [2] ibid.

[3] This picturesque enunciation of the filtration theory was made by Mr Norton, Advocate-General and President of the University Board; *vide* Satthianadhan, op. cit., p. 25.

twenty years is a sorry tale of hesitancy and indecision on the part
of the local Government. As Richey[1] points out it consists
'chiefly of Minutes by successive Governors, Lord Elphinstone,
Lord Tweeddale and Sir Henry Pottinger, outlining policies which
were never fully adopted, of reports from the educational board
submitting schemes which were never brought into effect, of
orders of the local Government constituting new educational
authorities, each of which was short lived, together with despatches
from the Court of Directors criticizing the policies framed by
the Governors, rejecting the schemes submitted by the educational
board and dissolving the new educational authorities constituted
by the local Government'.

It seems desirable to amplify this verdict, not with a view to
showing the futility of official attempts to advance education but
with a view to showing that official lukewarmness, coupled with
the energetic efforts of missionaries, served to bring about a gradual
recognition of the soundness of Munro's original scheme.   In
1836 the Committee of Public Instruction was replaced by a
Committee of Native Education, consisting of a Member of Council
(President), a Presbyterian Presidency Chaplain, the Maratha
Translator to Government, the Hon'ble Company's Astronomer
and the Hon'ble Company's Solicitor.[2] In the instructions given
to this strangely constituted body, no mention was made of the
'English College' which had been proposed by the Supreme
Government nor of the necessity of providing facilities for higher
education; the Committee was merely asked to submit proposals
for the establishment of a Normal School at the Presidency for
the training of teachers for English schools to be set up in different
parts of the province. In reply, the Committee submitted a much
more elaborate scheme, including the establishment of four English
schools in Madras (and its suburbs) and the establishment of a
college as well as of a Normal School. They proposed that a
beginning should be made with the schools and said that the
establishment of a college, or even of a Normal School, might
well be postponed because 'there were probably not a dozen natives
who were capable of profiting by a college education'.[3] The
Government took no notice of these proposals and educational

---

[1] op. cit., p. 177.   [2] ibid., p. 178.
[3] Satthianadhan, op. cit., p. 18.

activity remained at a standstill until Lord Elphinstone issued his Minute of 1839.

The new Governor brushed aside the recommendations of the Committee, which were clearly at variance with the suggestions of the Supreme Government, and elaborated a scheme of his own. He was a keen advocate of higher education on Western lines and, although he did not oppose the promotion of vernacular education, he had come to the conclusion that the time had come to discontinue 'the system of frittering away the sums allowed for educational purposes on mere elementary schools and upon eleemosynary scholars'.[1] (Incidentally, he was the nephew of Mountstuart Elphinstone and was Governor of Madras from 1837–42 and of Bombay from 1853–60. He was the first Chancellor of the University of Bombay (1857) and he lies buried in the same country churchyard as his more illustrious uncle.) The main feature of his plan was the establishment in Madras of a collegiate institution, or University (as it came to be called) with two departments—a college giving instruction in the higher branches of learning and a high school teaching English, the vernacular languages and elementary science. This institution, although nominally open to 'members of all creeds and sects' was intended for the children of upper-class and well-to-do parents. It was based on the model of the Scottish universities and the Governor quoted with approval the considered judgement of Dr John Wilson, of Bombay, who had said 'the connexion between the school and college divisions of our institution is most intimate, for they are both taught under the same roof and are placed under the same superintendence. This connexion I shall ever seek to maintain. . . . I would earnestly recommend [these arrangements] to the conductors of all educational institutions in India, and to the Government itself'.[2] For the promotion of education outside the capital Lord Elphinstone proposed the establishment of four superior schools, as feeders to the University, in which English was to be the medium of instruction; they were to be located at Trichinopoly, Masulipatam, Bellary and Calicut for the benefit of the Tamil, Telugu, Kanarese and Malayalam peoples, respectively. The Directors sanctioned these proposals in 1842, whereupon rules of management were drawn up and local committees formed; these

[1] Richey, op. cit., p. 185.   [2] ibid., pp. 187-8.

local authorities were empowered to charge fees and were informed that 'the projected schools should not be thrown open to all classes, as it was the principle of the Court of Directors that the education of the higher classes should be first considered'.[1]   Unfortunately, the schools were not opened, as competent headmasters could not be secured on salaries of Rs. 100 p.m. (which had been sanctioned) and, once again, matters were allowed to drift.

In 1841 the Committee of Native Education was replaced by a University Board, with the Advocate-General, Mr Norton, as President and fourteen Members or Governors, of whom seven were Indians representing the most influential and respected members of the community.   In the same year the institution commonly known as the Madras University was formally opened as a high school, with Mr E. B. Powell, a Cambridge mathematician, as its first Principal.   It is worth noting that, at the opening ceremony, the President of the Board said that although the institution 'excludes no class or quality of the people, yet it obviously concerns most that order of the public who have the means and leisure to profit by such [higher] education'.[2]   In his reply the Governor said that if the people of the country remained 'unconvinced of the importance of education in the true sense of the word, not merely elementary instruction, but that mental training and culture which leads to higher attainments, it is idle to declare their political equality—worse than idle to advocate their participation in political power'.[3]   This policy had the approval of the Directors who wrote, in their Dispatch of 1842, 'we entirely agree in the view taken by the President that the object of the Government should be elevation of the standard of education and the instruction of those classes which can spare time sufficient to acquire more than a mere rudimental learning, rather than the multiplication of mere elementary schools'.[4]

Within a couple of years the University Board reported to the Government that the progress of the new institution had been disappointing and they attributed the paucity of scholars in the higher classes to (a) the frequency with which boys discontinued their studies as soon as they had acquired the small amount of learning which led to profitable employment, and (b) the heavy

---

[1] Satthianadhan, op. cit., p. 22.   [2] ibid., p. 24.   [3] ibid.
[4] Richey, op. cit., p. 193.

rate of fees (Rs. 4 p.m.) which had been sanctioned. They urged the opening of classes in Medicine and Engineering with a view to extending the scope of the University and in the hope of attracting more students, especially to the collegiate classes. As regards the provincial schools, the Board recommended the appointment of headmasters, preferably from England, on Rs. 250 p.m., and, also, a substantial reduction in the rate of fees. Although Lord Elphinstone himself was inclined to favour all reasonable proposals for the advancement of education, his Government entered into a protracted correspondence with the Board on matters of principle and, even, of detail. In 1843, the Marquis of Tweeddale, Elphinstone's successor, reviewed the whole position: and, as the Board's proposals involved considerable expenditure, he decided to refer them to the Court of Directors. They summarily rejected (1845) the scheme for establishing provincial schools and pointed out that the proposals for the establishment of Medical and Engineering Colleges (or Departments) were premature and unwarranted; they added, 'the further development of the branch of the University now established should be the exclusive object of attention'.[1]

This decision came as a shock to the members of the Board, who, to do them justice, had taken their responsibilities seriously. They had more than once complained that the unsatisfactory state of affairs in the University was largely due to the lukewarm attitude taken by the Government towards this institution and to their reluctance to sanction progressive measures of reform. The Members of the Governor's Council refused to accept this explanation and Lord Tweeddale himself came to the conclusion that the failure of the University had been due to the indifference of the public and to the existence of other and cheaper schools— presumably missionary. He argued that the University had been founded in the expectation of popular support, an expectation which was based on the fact that Lord Elphinstone's scheme had been prepared after the receipt of a petition signed by 60,000 Indians promising pecuniary help. He pointed out that the Government had been disappointed in their anticipation that the public would support the University, by sending their sons to it in large numbers, and that leading citizens would contribute handsomely to its funds. It is hardly surprising that the Court of Directors con-

[1] ibid., p. 180.

curred with the Governor's views and, rather than accept heavy financial commitments, rejected the Board's proposals for expansion.

Nothing daunted, the Board decided to continue the struggle with the Government. With more earnestness than tact they urged that the failure of the University had been mainly due to official apathy and they pointed out that their own activities had, from the beginning, met with governmental disfavour amounting to active opposition. Members of the Government resented this plain speaking and took exception to the wording of certain passages in the Board's Annual Reports. Matters came to a head when, on the promulgation of Lord Hardinge's Resolution of 1844, the Board were asked to submit proposals regarding the examination and selection of candidates for the public services. These did not accord with the views of the Government, and so the latter appointed a new educational authority called the Council of Education (1845) and transferred to it some of the functions of the University Board. The primary object of the new Council was to organize and superintend examinations for entrance to Government service and, in order to afford facilities to candidates from the mofussil, they proposed the establishment of nine provincial schools, to be placed under local committees. They suggested that the syllabus should be restricted to English, one vernacular, Arithmetic, History and Geography. There were differences of opinion regarding the inclusion of Bible teaching in the English course, and so the establishment of the provincial schools was postponed, pending the decision of the Directors on this issue. The Marquis of Tweeddale, who himself supported the proposal, received a sharp rebuke from the Court of Directors: 'we cannot', they said, 'consider it either prudent or expedient to introduce any branch of study which can in any way interfere with the religious feelings and opinions of the people. All such tendency has been carefully avoided at both the other Presidencies. . . . We direct you, therefore, to refrain from any departure from the practice hitherto pursued' (1846).[1] The scheme drawn up by the Council had to be abandoned, because the Directors not only refused their sanction but even recommended the dissolution of

[1] ibid., p. 201.

the Council itself. This body had enjoyed a short life of only two years (1845-7) and during that time its half-hearted efforts had achieved nothing of any practical value.

On the abolition of the Council its duties were again entrusted, perhaps reluctantly, to the University Board. This body was now (1848) much reduced in number and had for five years been involved in frequent controversies with the Government 'to whose proceedings and want of support it ascribed the ill-success of the only institution under its charge'.[1] In this year Sir Henry Pottinger succeeded to the governorship and, acting on the suggestion of the Directors, he decided to appoint a new Council of Education of some twenty members, with a member of the Governor's Council as President. At this time there was considerable difference of opinion between the Governor's Council and the Board (and even between the Members of Council themselves) regarding the policy of providing higher education for the few, rather than elementary education for the many. In 1851 Sir Henry Pottinger wrote a long Minute in which he recorded his views on the topics under discussion and reviewed the state of education throughout the province. He proposed the establishment of a Normal School to be attached to the University, the establishment of eight provincial schools (with a somewhat lower standard of instruction than that given at the so-called University) and the adoption of a system of grant-in-aid; he also recommended the postponement of the opening of the collegiate department of the University until 'the advancement of the scholars might be considered to justify it'.[2] One of the Members of Council, Mr Thomas, emphasized, in an able Minute, the importance of vernacular education and the futility of aiming at the higher education of the few through the medium of English. 'It appears to me', he wrote, 'to reverse the natural order of things, and that the attempt to educate and enlighten a nation through a foreign language is one opposed to the experience of all time and countries. English must ever be, in this land, to the mass, an unknown tongue.'[3] His colleague, Mr Eliott,[4] agreed that elementary education was a responsibility of the Government, but concurred with Sir Henry Pottinger that the original plans for the development of the University should

---

[1] ibid., p. 181.   [2] ibid.   [3] ibid., p. 206.   [4] ibid., pp. 209 ff.

be followed up so that 'in fitting time' a collegiate department might be established, with provision for the teaching of Medicine, Engineering, and the like. Differences of opinion on these and other topics (including Bible teaching in State institutions) gave rise to much noting and discussion and, eventually, the Governor abandoned his plan for setting up a Council of Education and contented himself with reorganizing the University Board (now reduced to four members) by the addition of thirteen new members (1852).

Inside a few months the newly constituted Board submitted to the Government comprehensive proposals for the extension of education; these included the establishment of high schools and primary schools in the Districts and of Normal Classes (English and Vernacular) at the Presidency, and the appointment of paid examiners for public examinations and of one or more inspectors of schools. The total cost of the scheme was estimated at Rs. 1 ½ lakhs. After the usual lengthy discussions with the Government, who considered the proposed expenditure excessive, it was eventually decided to attach a primary school, as well as a collegiate department, to the 'University High School', to form Normal Classes, English and Vernacular, to appoint paid examiners to conduct governmental examinations and to introduce a limited system of grant-in-aid. The total cost of the revised scheme was estimated at one lakh of rupees a year, of which the University was to get Rs. 50,000, while Rs. 30,000 was allotted to the establishment of five provincial schools and Rs. 20,000 was set aside for the award of grants-in-aid to existing schools. In 1853 the Governor sanctioned the opening of the collegiate department, with a Professor of English and a Professor of Political Economy and Philosophy.

Within the next couple of years three other provincial schools were started and two primary schools, both at Cuddalore. These schools, together with 'the collegiate institution under the designation of an university at Madras', represented the sum total of the Government's achievements over a period of some twenty-five years. They duly came under the control of the first Director of Public Instruction, Mr (later Sir) Alexander Arbuthnot, Munro's biographer, who subsequently became Governor of Madras. Apart from the significance which had always been attached by the

authorities in the South to the training of teachers, the only
redeeming feature in this dismal record of ineptitude is the fact
that, towards the end of the period under review, Sir Henry
Pottinger began to revert to Munro's views regarding the importance of vernacular education and to question the wisdom of the
anglicizing policy which had been imported from Bengal. The
Governor's colleague, Mr Thomas, also recognized the importance
of a thorough education of the people in the vernacular tongues
and said that 'the course now pursued, and advocated by some, seems
to me to ensure a waste of time and of funds' because higher
English education for the few 'must fail to produce any good or
general effect on the national mind'.[1]   Although Wood's Dispatch
(1854) directed attention to the educational needs of the masses,
the question of furthering the spread of elementary education was
shelved until the early seventies, and then it was decided to build
on the foundations which Munro had laid nearly half a century
earlier.

Several reasons have been advanced to explain the reluctance
of the Government to take energetic measures to promote education
in southern India; it would seem that their hesitancy and indecision
were in no small measure due to the vigorous educational activities
of missionary bodies, who had established many good schools—
elementary and secondary—in various parts of the province.
These institutions were run with a view to making converts and,
even if Biblical teaching was compulsory, this apparent disadvantage
was offset by the readiness of missionaries to admit pupils without
payment of fees. It may well have been that the Government,
remembering Munro's principle of non-interference, were uneasy
at the thought of establishing schools of more or less the same type
as those conducted by missionary effort. Officials, doubtless,
feared that, had they followed the lead of the missionaries, they
might be suspected of aiming at conversion; they certainly realized
that, even if this fear proved to be groundless, they could not run
schools without incurring a heavy financial burden. They probably
argued that as long as missionary effort provided a reasonable
number of efficient schools (which supplied the Government with
recruits for subordinate posts) it was safer for the State to hold

[1] ibid., p. 206.

itself aloof and to avoid the expense which a bold and energetic educational policy would necessarily involve. Another point, which did not escape the notice of the Government, was that missionary schools admitted pupils of even the lowest castes, whereas the official policy was to cater primarily for the requirements of the upper and middle classes. It was felt that, if educational institutions were established under State control, it would be difficult to refuse admission to children belonging to any class or creed; if, however, low-caste boys were admitted it was feared that high-caste parents would refuse to send their sons to State schools, and so the efforts of the Government to conciliate the higher and 'middling' classes would be frustrated. These apprehensions were never explicitly stated, but casual references in official documents (including some of those written by Munro himself) seem to justify the inference that missionary educational activity in the south served to check, rather than to spur, the Madras Government in their attempts to formulate and to carry out a comprehensive scheme of education for the whole province.

It may be well to quote a few figures to indicate the extent of missionary activity in the days when, in the words of Lord Elphinstone, the educational backwardness of the province was 'a matter of regret, and of reproach to Madras'.[1] Satthianadhan states that in 1852 'the total number of mission schools in this Presidency amounted to 1,185 with 38,005 pupils; while in other Presidencies, where the Government schools were more numerous than here and more had been done in the higher branches of education, the aggregate number of mission schools was only 472 with 26,791 children in attendance'.[2] These figures approximate fairly closely to those given (p. 11) in the Hunter Commission's Report (1882), which indicate that in 1854 about 30,000 children were being educated in mission schools in Madras, of whom about 3,000 were receiving secondary education in English. Either group of figures shows pretty conclusively that the missionaries were up and doing, while the Government, to put it euphemistically, were 'busy biding their time'. It is only fair to add, however, that Government officials appreciated the services rendered by missionary bodies to the cause of education and did not hesitate to make generous references to the good work they had

[1] ibid., p. 184.   [2] Satthianadhan, op. cit., p. 39.

done throughout the province. In 1839 Lord Auckland could truthfully say that 'the Madras Presidency is remarkable in India as being that in which the knowledge of the mere English language is most diffused among all who are attached in public or private capacities to European officers'.[1] By this time Munro's schools had disappeared and the local Government, despite the recommendations of the Directors and of the Supreme Government, had not made any progress with their plans to provide English education for the upper classes. The fact is that school education, primary and secondary, was almost the monopoly of missionaries, who continued to carry on in the first half of the nineteenth century the work which had been begun by Schwartz and other well-known pioneers of missionary effort.

It is true that, for obvious reasons, missionaries attached the greatest importance to elementary education through the mother-tongue, but it has already been pointed out that, in the middle of the century, about one-tenth of the pupils in mission schools were receiving the elements of a liberal education in English. Indeed, even before Lord Elphinstone established the Madras University, the Rev. John Anderson had founded (1837) the Free Church Mission Institute. Like Duff in Calcutta and Wilson in Bombay, he decided to make a frontal attack on Hinduism, and in the original prospectus he stated that the object of his institution 'is simply to convey through the channel of a good education as great an amount of truth as is possible to the native mind, especially Bible truth. Every branch of knowledge communicated is to be made subservient to this desirable end'.[2] His school proved a great success and, despite the importance attached to Bible teaching, was popular from the beginning. It had, as the years went on, to pass through critical times, but, eventually, as the Madras Christian College under the inspiring leadership of Dr Miller, whose services to this great college extended over almost half a century (1862–1909), it attained an eminence second to none among the great collegiate institutions of India. As the so-called University was not established until 1841, Anderson may fairly be regarded as the founder of higher English education in Madras.

The success of the missionaries is all the more remarkable because they did not, and could not hope to, receive any official

---

[1] Sharp, op. cit., p. 170.   [2] Satthianadhan, op. cit., p. 39.

backing. The local Government, however, could not remain blind to the public services which they continued to render and their activities were duly brought to the notice of the Court of Directors. Recognition of their selfless work is recorded in the Dispatch of 1854[1] which states that 'in Madras, where little has yet been done by Government to promote the education of the mass of the people, we can only remark with satisfaction that the educational activities of Christian missionaries have been more successful . . . than in any other part of India'. The Dispatch notes 'with equal satisfaction' that 'Thomason's plan' for the encouragement of indigenous schools has a fair prospect of success in Madras, 'where the *ryotwari* settlement offers a similar practical inducement to the people for the acquisition of elementary knowledge'. This plan, despite important modifications, does not differ greatly in certain essentials from the scheme drawn up by Munro in 1826, and, it will be remembered, the Directors had approved his original proposals for the encouragement of elementary schools; they said at the time, 'it is upon the character of indigenous schools that the education of the great mass of the people must ultimately depend' and that, therefore, such schools were 'worthy of great encouragement' (p. 141 *ante*). As time passed, however the subject of elementary education was allowed to fade into the background and the attention of the Honourable Court was diverted to the expansion of higher English education. It is fitting that Wood's Dispatch should contain convincing evidence that the Directors had finally realized that the time had come for a change of educational policy and that it should conclude with a further tribute, belated and implicit though it was, to the wisdom and foresight of a Governor who had given Madras a lead which his successors had hesitated to follow.

[1] Richey, op. cit., p. 392.

MOUNTSTUART ELPHINSTONE

MOUNTSTUART ELPHINSTONE
1779-1859

SUPPORTER OF INDIGENOUS LEARNING

As in Bengal, so in other parts of India, the beginnings of education under the East India Company's rule were isolated and spasmodic. Although the Governor-General at Fort William was vested in 1774 with a certain measure of control over the Governments of Madras and Bombay, the educational policy which was followed in Calcutta during the early years of the nineteenth century had little or no direct influence outside Bengal and the other Presidencies were, for a time, allowed to work out their own educational salvation without any interference from the distant capital. Gradually, however, the policy of anglicization was forced upon provinces, which had already made considerable progress along altogether different lines and, with the approval of the Court of Directors, was finally accepted by other provincial Governments.

Turning to Bombay, it is usual to trace back the beginnings of English education to the old Charity School, which was founded in 1718 by the Rev. Richard Cobbe, Chaplain of St Thomas's Church, for 'the education of poor European children in the Christian religion'. This institution was supported by voluntary subscription until 1807, when the Company assumed direct control and sanctioned an annual grant of Rs. 3,600 for its maintenance. In 1815, however, members of the Church of England founded the 'Society for Promoting the Education of the Poor within the Government of Bombay' (afterwards called the Bombay Education Society); the Company handed over the management of the Charity School to this private organization and undertook not only to continue but to increase their financial support.

Within a few years the members of the Education Society, prompted by missionary and humanitarian zeal, decided to extend their educational activities and to open schools for Indian children. With this end in view a special sub-committee was appointed (1820) which drew up elaborate schemes for the improvement and expansion of elementary schools for Indian children and, also, proposed the establishment of a Central English School for Indian boys. The expenditure foreshadowed in the sub-committee's report caused the members of the Education Society considerable uneasiness and they decided (1822) to approach the Government for more liberal financial assistance. Only a few years previously (1819) the Hon'ble Mountstuart Elphinstone had been appointed Governor and his keen interest in educational problems was a guarantee that the Society's appeal would receive very careful and sympathetic consideration. Indeed, it is to this remarkable man that Bombay owes the original organization of its educational, as well as of its administrative, system.

On the whole, Elphinstone has been lucky in his biographers and the main incidents in his distinguished career are so well known that only a passing reference to them is needed here. He was the fourth son of General Lord Elphinstone, Governor of Edinburgh Castle, and was born in 1779. He was educated first at Edinburgh High School and then sent to a fashionable private school in Kensington, where he spent two years prior to his departure for India, while still under 16 years of age. Considering his subsequent eminence as a scholar and as an administrator, it is interesting to note that his career at school was undistinguished. At most he carried away with him a love of books, which remained his chief recreation during his active life in India and during the many years of his retirement in England. On arrival at Calcutta in 1796, he was posted to Benares as assistant to Samuel Davis, an experienced civil servant and a Sanskrit scholar of repute. Here he began his devotion to reading, which developed into a passion and covered fields unexplored by such an omnivorous reader as Macaulay; his acquaintance with Greek and Latin literature was matched by his appreciation of English, Italian and Spanish writers; added to this, he acquired an intimate knowledge of Persian, Hindustani and Marathi. In later years he used to travel with two camel-loads of books, so arranged that he could quickly lay his hand on any volume he happened to want. Many entries in his diary are quoted in Colebrooke's *Life* which reveal a width of knowledge, a critical appreciation, and a universality of interest which are remarkable in one who commenced his career with such a slender educational equipment.

After four years of routine work at Benares, where he began the study of Persian and Hindustani and made strenuous but

pleasurable efforts to repair the deficiencies of his early education,
he was posted to Poona as the Assistant to the Resident at the
Court of Baji Rao, and thus began his association with the province
of which he subsequently became such a distinguished Governor.
He soon acquired a good working knowledge of Marathi and
during the Second Maratha War he was attached to Wellesley's
staff as Political Officer (in the place of Malcolm, who had
suddenly fallen ill) and he displayed such bravery at the battle
of Assaye (1803) that his commanding officer remarked that he
had mistaken his calling and ought to have been a soldier.   At
the end of the campaign Sir Arthur Wellesley brought to the
notice of his brother, the Governor-General, the satisfactory manner
in which Elphinstone had conducted negotiations with Maratha
statesmen and, as a reward for his services, he was appointed
Resident at Nagpur.   Here he spent some four years (1804–8)
devoted, for the most part, to sports such as hunting, coursing
and tiger-shooting and to quiet but extensive reading.   He was
next sent on a mission to Kabul to conclude a treaty with the Amir
of Afghanistan; to his great disappointment he got no further
than Peshawar and there negotiations broke down.   Although his
mission proved fruitless from a diplomatic point of view, it enabled
him to collect material for his history of Afghanistan,[1] which was
published in 1815 and laid the foundations of his fame as a
scholar and a man of letters.   In 1811 he returned to Poona as
Resident and there he spent four uneventful years quietly watching
the intrigues which were going on at the Courts of the Peshwa
and other Maratha princes; during this period he gave himself
up to study, particularly to the study of the history of ancient
India.   It is unnecessary to relate the events that led up to the
Third Maratha War, which culminated in the battle of Kirkee
(1817) at which Elphinstone again displayed the courage and
calmness of a veteran soldier.   On the conclusion of hostilities
the Peshwa's territories were annexed and Elphinstone was the
obvious choice for appointment as Commissioner of the Deccan.
He proved himself to be not only an exceptionally able but an
unusually sympathetic administrator of the newly acquired territories and his promotion to the Governorship of Bombay (1819)

[1] The full title is *An Account of the Kingdom of Caubul and its Dependencies in Persia, Tartary and India.*

was as deserved as it was popular. Historians and biographers have paid ample tribute to his work as Governor, which lasted exactly eight years; it was marked by skillful administration, based on an intimate acquaintance with the language and history, the customs and traditions of the people, which was unique even in those days.

For several years he had given much thought to educational problems and had corresponded on the subject with his cousin John Adam (who set up the first Committee of Public Instruction in 1823, during the brief period in which he officiated as Governor-General) and with Sir Thomas Munro, whose views were almost identical with his own; on one point, indeed, they were in complete agreement—that the ultimate aim of education was to fit Indians to take a large and responsible share in the administration of their own country. It is not surprising, therefore, that as soon as Elphinstone became Governor he set on foot a scheme for the training of Civil Servants. He proposed that a college should be established in Bombay on the model of the college at Fort William, but with this important difference—that provision should be made for the training of young Indians who were considered suitable for employment in the higher ranks of Government service and not solely for the training of junior Civil Servants from England. The members of his Council opposed the scheme, partly on account of the estimated expenditure and partly on the score of the unsuitability of the climate. The matter was referred to the Directors, who, much to Elphinstone's disappointment, refused to sanction his scheme (1821).

In the following year the sub-committee of the Bombay Education Society applied to the Government for financial assistance which would enable them to proceed with their plans for the expansion of primary education for Indian children. The application was referred to the Governor himself and he decided to take immediate action. In the first place, he advised the sub-committee to break away entirely from the parent body and to form itself into a separate association, which was originally called the 'Bombay Native and School Book Society', but afterwards (1827) the 'Bombay Native Education Society'.[1] This step was welcomed

---

[1] The change of title would seem to indicate a determination to concentrate on elementary vernacular education; this policy, if not inspired by Elphinstone himself, certainly had his approval.

by members of the parent body, not only because they realized that they could not possibly meet the expenditure which the recommendations of their own sub-committee involved, but because these proposals were clearly at variance with their original aims —the education of European and Anglo-Indian children. The change was also welcomed by the Government because the new society was a purely secular organization and the fact that it had separated from a body pledged to further Christian education would, Elphinstone hoped, render its aims 'particularly agreeable' to the public. He, therefore, consented to be the first President (1822) of a body primarily concerned with the spread and improvement of elementary secular education. Further, he came to the conclusion that, before embarking on ambitious schemes, it was essential to find out as accurately as possible what was the present state of primary education throughout the province. Accordingly, he issued instructions that Collectors were to make a survey of indigenous schools in the various Districts. Too much reliance cannot be placed on the figures which were submitted; it was estimated that for a population of (roughly) $4\frac{2}{3}$ millions, there were 1,700 schools with rather more than 35,000 pupils, or, approximately, one school for every 2,750 inhabitants. These figures strengthened Elphinstone in his opinion that education was 'in a very low state throughout the country' and this view was confirmed by a report of the Native Education Society that the main defects were paucity of suitable books, inefficient teachers and lack of funds.

. The survey which was carried out was an important, and unforeseen, consequence of the representations made by the sub-committee, but a still more important consequence was the Governor's famous Minute of 1824. Elphinstone had already written several minutes on this subject, and many of them may still be consulted in the Bombay Secretariat, but he seized the opportunity which the Society's representation offered of reconsidering his views and of drawing up a more comprehensive and statesmanlike scheme of public instruction than had previously been formulated under British rule. It is surprising that this most important document is not, save for a few brief extracts, represented in the admirable volume of *Selections from Educational Records, 1781–1839*, edited by Sir Henry Sharp. Not a few competent authorities would regard

11

this Minute as the most important document on Indian education in the British period to have been written prior to the issue of Wood's Dispatch.   The rough draft was circulated among Elphinstone's colleagues, who protested against the expenditure which the acceptance of such a far-reaching scheme would involve. Warden felt compelled to outline a scheme of his own which limited the Government's responsibility to higher English education, advocated non-interference with indigenous schools and suggested the desirability of cautious and indirect support to missionary endeavour.   This scheme did not appeal to Elphinstone, who wrote, 'the great defect, it appears to me, of Mr Warden's plan, is, that every improvement among all classes of the Natives is to be postponed until they shall have acquired English'.[1]   Much 'noting' over the various important points at issue followed and in March 1824 Elphinstone decided to submit his Minute[2] (modified, perhaps, in the light of the discussions which had taken place) to the Court of Directors.   This contains the clearest and most exhaustive statement of Elphinstone's educational policy and, as it formed the basis of operations in Bombay for some thirty years, it is deserving of careful examination.

In the first place, it is well to remember that Elphinstone made no secret of the fact that he considered education the most important of all the problems which confronted the English in India and he even went so far as to impress upon the Directors that 'it is difficult to imagine an undertaking in which our duty, our interest and our honour are more immediately concerned'.[3] The welfare of the people was his chief concern and education was the only remedy he could see for the improvement of their material conditions, for the eradication of superstitious beliefs and for the abolition of cruel practices.   But, unlike many who had neither his vision nor his sympathy, he was wise enough to realize what is a commonplace of modern thought, that education must be brought into the closest possible touch with the general life of the community.   'It would surely', he said, 'be a preposterous way

---

[1] J. A. Richey, *Selections from Educational Records*, II (1922), p. 26.

[2] G. W. Forrest, *Selections from the Minutes and other Official Writings of the Honourable Mountstuart Elphinstone* (1884), pp. 77-116.   Forrest regards this Minute as 'a model of what a state paper ought to be'. (p. 66.)

[3] Forrest, op. cit., p. 101.

of adding to the intellectual treasures of a nation to begin by the destruction of its indigenous literature,' and he went on to argue that the future attainments of Indians must be 'grafted on their own previous knowledge and imbued with their own original and peculiar character'.[1] At a time when this obvious truth was not clearly realized and when it was the custom to disparage the vernaculars, Elphinstone had the good sense and the courage to stand by his conviction that education could make no headway unless it were imparted through the living languages of the people. He himself had a command of Marathi and Hindustani and, although he was well aware that these languages could be improved and refined, he never even suggested that they were unsuitable as media of instruction. On the other hand, one of his proposals for the enlightenment of the country was the translation into the languages of the people of Sanskrit tales and fables (calculated to improve morals) as well as of English books suitable for use in schools. It is significant that the controversy between the Anglicists and Orientalists, which caused such a stir in Bengal, never arose in Bombay; indeed, had the policy laid down by Elphinstone been followed by his successors, the later conflict between Anglicists and Vernacularists, which came to a head about 1848, would never have arisen in western India. He, at any rate, would have disagreed with Macaulay's pontifical verdict that the 'spoken dialects' were 'so poor and rude' that it would be difficult to translate into them any valuable work. In fact, when Macaulay was still an undergraduate he had, as the result of his experience in the Deccan, come to the very opposite conclusion, and one from which he never wavered.

Although he himself was an accomplished Persian scholar, he had no knowledge of Sanskrit. Yet he realized the importance of encouraging the classical literature of the Hindus and warmly supported the establishment of a Sanskrit College at Poona. This had been proposed by Mr Chaplin, his successor as Commissioner in the Deccan, as a modification of Elphinstone's original plan to found Oriental Colleges at Nasik and Wai, and the opening of the college was sanctioned by the Government of Bombay in 1821. In this institution Elphinstone defended the maintenance

---

[1] Forrest, op. cit., pp. 110-11.

of a professorship of Sanskrit poetry in a noble plea, which Cotton[1] rightly believes was inspired by his own enthusiasm for the Greek and Latin classics: 'Even without the example and enthusiasm of a more civilized nation, the science possessed by every people is gradually superseded by their own discoveries as they advance in knowledge, and their early works fall into disuse and into oblivion. But it is otherwise with their poetry; the standard works maintain their reputation undiminished in every age, they form the models of composition and the fountains of classical language; and the writers of the rudest ages are those who contribute most to the delight and refinement of the most improved of their posterity'.[2] It is not a little surprising that the Court of Directors were persuaded, however reluctantly, to accept this part of Elphinstone's educational scheme, because in their Dispatch of 1824, addressed to Bengal, not to Bombay, they had said 'it has never been thought necessary to establish colleges for the cultivation of poetry'.[3] Elphinstone's championship of Sanskrit, however, was not based entirely, or even mainly, on the poetic or literary beauties of a language with which he himself was unfamiliar. He realized as clearly as the most ardent Orientalist that in this ancient tongue were preserved the traditional learning and the religious beliefs of the Hindus. He pointed out that under British rule encouragement to the advancement of knowledge had been withdrawn, so much so that 'the actual learning of the nation is likely to be lost and the productions of former genius to be forgotten' and, he added, 'something should surely be done to remove this reproach'.[4] It had long been the custom in India for rulers and princes to patronize higher learning and Elphinstone very wisely determined to continue an admirable practice, which the Peshwas had supported with lavish generosity. They had set aside a sum of five lakhs of rupees to be distributed primarily among learned Brahmans, but as 'every claimant, however ignorant' was awarded a handsome sum, the practice was discontinued by the British. This saving of 'an enormous waste' proved very unpopular and Elphinstone

[1] J. S. Cotton, *Mountstuart Elphinstone* (1896), p. 193.

[2] Forrest, op. cit., p. 111.

[3] H. Sharp, *Selections from Educational Records*, I (1920), p. 92; the Dispatch of 18 Feb. 1824 is believed to have been drafted by James Mill.

[4] Forrest, op. cit., p. 102.

persuaded the Supreme Government to sanction an annual expenditure not exceeding two lakhs of rupees for the promotion of Brahmanic learning and this was awarded by the Commissioner of the Deccan to deserving students of the Poona Sanskrit College (1821). In support of his recommendation to re-establish the original *dakshina*, Elphinstone argued: 'As it is the object of our enemies to inculcate the opinion that we wish to change the original manners and customs of the Hindus, it seems equally popular and reasonable to apply part of that sum to the encouragement of their learning.'[1] It is evident that the preservation of India's ancient lore was not the only motive that prompted him to take this course; he candidly admitted that he was anxious to conciliate the people, and particularly the higher classes, who, by reason of the recent change in Government had lost property, power and prestige. He felt confident that the patronage of Sanskrit learning would allay any uneasy feeling that his Government were scheming to interfere with age-long religious beliefs, least of all that there was the remotest intention of trying to make converts. On this point Elphinstone was emphatic: 'To the mixture of religion, even in the slightest degree, with our plans for education I must strongly object.'[2]

It has been held that Elphinstone's hostility to missionary enterprise was largely due to his own unorthodox religious beliefs. There is little doubt that he himself was utterly devoid of those ardent religious feelings which inspired so many of his great contemporaries;[3] his friend and biographer admits that as a young man, he was an avowed sceptic and that to the end, 'he exhibited in his life the better side of the Stoic's character'.[4] Yet, it would be rash to conclude that his own religious, or anti-religious, views

---

[1] ibid., p. 107.   [2] ibid., p. 105.

[3] *Vide Dictionary of National Biography;* cf. E. L. Woodward, *The Age of Reform, 1815-1870* (1938), p. 390.

[4] Sir T. E. Colebrooke, *Life of the Honourable Mountstuart Elphinstone,* II (1884), p. 173. Bishop Heber in *Narrative of a Journey through the Upper Provinces of India* (1838), attempted to defend Elphinstone from the charge of being 'devoid of religion and blinded to all spiritual truth' (III, p. 134) and ascribed to him, 'greater orthodoxy than he ever professed'; see Cotton, op. cit., p. 216. James Douglas says that 'if Elphinstone had lived in the Middle Ages' he would have been 'burned for heresy or witchcraft'—*Bombay and Western India,* II (1893), p. 49.

were entirely responsible for his educational policy. A careful study of his great Minute shows that anxiety to preserve and encourage the indigenous culture of the people was a far more important factor than mere personal belief, or unbelief; there is no ambiguity in such statements as 'it was desirable for its own sake to encourage the learning of the people'[1] and 'at no time could I wish that the purely Hindu part of the course should be entirely abandoned'.[2] Indeed, his attitude towards Hindu learning was merely one example of his general attitude towards the whole problem of Indian administration; this was based on the deep-rooted conviction that due respect must always be shown to social and political usages which had stood the test of time and were part and parcel of the heritage of the people. Perhaps the best-known example of his desire to establish a 'system of government in all things, as much as possible, in conformity with the genius of the people'[3] was his determination to base revenues and judicial procedure on systems which had long been in use and to which the people had grown accustomed. He argued that institutions which had lasted for centuries (e.g., *panchayats*) could not be altogether devoid of merit and that just government would not prove a blessing unless it were adjusted to the habits and character of the governed. 'It is not enough', he said, 'to give good laws, or even good courts; you must take the people along with you and give them a share in your feelings, which can only be done by sharing theirs'.[4] Far from regarding the overthrow of the Maratha power as an unmixed blessing he 'knew that foreign domination must ever be a hardship, and that the most that conquerors can do is to take care that the yoke presses as lightly as possible, and galls at the fewest points'.[5] In order to gain the confidence of those who were prone to resent even beneficial innovations, he resolved to interfere as little as possible with established practices and to trust to time for the introduction of reforms 'which should appear to develop themselves naturally from within, rather than ingraft themselves on the system by the force of external dictation'.[6] Soon after he became Governor, he appointed a committee for the codification

---

[1] Forrest, op. cit., p. 109.   [2] ibid., p. 111.
[3] J. W. Kaye, *Lives of Indian Officers*, I (1873), p. 402.
[4] Cotton, op. cit., p. 191.   [5] Forrest, op. cit., p. 57.
[6] Kaye, op. cit., p. 405.

of the law and he issued instructions that in this work one guiding principle should be adherence to the legal, traditional as well as written, customs of the people. With Malcolm and Munro he shared that 'policy of sympathy' which led him, as early as 1823, to substitute the vernaculars for Persian as the language of the Courts and to insist that the evidence of witnesses should be taken in their own mother-tongue. This progressive measure anticipated by some fourteen years the decision of the Government of India to abolish throughout British India the use of Persian as the language of the law courts.

Another, and perhaps a more striking, instance of Elphinstone's desire to 'make no innovations' may be seen in his liberal treatment of the hereditary nobles and landlords of the Deccan. Not only were they given assurances that their possessions, rank and dignity would be respected, but they were exempted from the processes of the Civil Courts and, in criminal cases, could be proceeded against only with the consent of the Collector, acting in his capacity as Political Agent, and the approval of the Commissioner. Judged by modern standards, the grant of such privileges seems arbitrary and unjustifiable, but it was extremely popular at the time, for the lower classes regarded it as a concession to those whom they had long regarded as their superiors and as a boon to the whole community. No less an authority than Sir John Malcolm[1] went so far as to say that in his long administrative experience he had known of no institution so prized by those who enjoyed its benefits or more gratifying to the people as a whole. This was Elphinstone's solution of the problem of how to preserve a contented upper class, intermediate between the ryots and the officials, by calling to his aid accepted usage and ingrained sentiment. There is much truth in the verdict of Kaye that 'to the very end of his life he protested against rash innovations and experiments, by precipitating which a new race of statesmen, bent upon anglicising everything, in season and out of season, were piling up for themselves and their country, a mountain of future difficulty and disaster'.[2]

On the other hand, he was not opposed to provision for English education, least of all in places where there was a genuine demand for it. 'If English', he said (1823), 'could be at all diffused

[1] Cotton, op. cit., p. 133.   [2] Kaye, op. cit., p. 427.

among the persons who have the least time for reflection, the progress of knowledge, by means of it, would be accelerated in a ten-fold ratio.'[1] He realized as clearly as Warden that the spread of English would bring inestimable benefits to India and he even looked forward to the foundation, in the distant future, of colleges for the promotion of a knowledge of Western science. Where he differed from so many of his contemporaries was in the view that English education must always be subordinate to a well-planned system of primary education and, also, to adequate provision for higher Oriental learning. He readily admitted that in Bombay itself, and perhaps in a few other centres, there was a growing demand for a knowledge of English, but he thought it was limited to a small number of people who hoped that it would help them in their business pursuits or qualify them for service under the Government. He realized that there was much force in Warden's contention that many Indians belonging to the higher classes 'were anxious that their children should be thoroughly grounded in the English language'[2] and he had no hesitation in approving the establishment (1824) of an 'English School at the Presidency where English may be taught classically'.[3] In short, English education was merely an appendix, though an important one, to his wider plan, which was based on the fundamental conviction that education in India must be based on India's 'original and peculiar character'. Even if it be argued that he had in view an ultimate synthesis of Eastern and Western learning, it still remains true that he believed, and rightly believed, that the foundations must be laid on Indian thought and culture and not on knowledge, however valuable in itself, imported from abroad.

There can be no reasonable doubt, however, that the chief reason why Elphinstone found a place for English in his general scheme of education was his desire to man the public services with highly educated recruits. As Commissioner in the Deccan, as Governor of Bombay and as a scholarly recluse living in retirement, he never ceased to emphasize the importance of throwing

---

[1] Sharp, op. cit., p. 176.

[2] Syed Mahmood, *A History of English Education in India, 1781-1893* (1895), p. 41.

[3] R. B. Bhagwat, *A Short History of the Elphinstone High School, 1824-1924* (1925), p. 3.

open official careers to educated Indians. It was not with the utilitarian object of cheapening the cost of administration that he urged this very desirable reform though, it must be admitted. financial considerations induced others to lend him their support. Elphinstone's statesmanlike views went far beyond those petty economies which seem to have carried so much weight with the Court of Directors. Like his great contemporary, Sir Thomas Munro, he believed that the main object of British rule in India was to prepare the country for self-government and that, for the accomplishment of this end, education was the most important instrument. In 1819, while still in the Deccan, he wrote to Malcolm: 'I see nothing to threaten the safety of our empire [in India] until the natives become enlightened under our tuition. and a separation becomes desirable to both parties.'[1]   A month or two later he said, in a letter to Mackintosh: 'A time of separation must come; and it is in our interest to have an early separation from a civilized people, rather than a violent rupture with a barbarous nation.'[2]   In his *Report on the Deccan* he advocated the appointment of Indians to posts carrying £1,200 a year and urged that 'economy, no less than policy, requires liberal pay when there is considerable trust'.[3]   Writing to Munro in 1822, he went even further and said, 'the system of government and education which we have already established must, some time or other, work such a change on the people of this country that it will be impossible to confine them to subordinate employments'.[4]   In his great Minute on Education he emphasized that care should be taken to train Indians for the highest official posts and he made light of the objection that, if they were admitted to a share in the government of their own country, they would never rest until they had made good their claim to the whole.   Other quotations in a similar strain might be made, but it is only necessary to add that, as late as 1850, he wrote: 'I conceive that the administration of all the departments of a great country by a small number of foreign visitors, in a state of isolation produced by a difference in religion, ideas and manners, which cuts them off from all intimate communion with the people, can never be contemplated as a permanent state of things'; and he concluded that the progress of

[1] Cotton, op. cit., p. 185.   [2] ibid., p. 186.
[3] Forrest, op. cit., p. 320.   [4] Cotton, op. cit., p. 187.

education rendered such a scheme impracticable, even if it were otherwise free from objection. The letter from which this extract is taken is, very appropriately, included in Cameron's well-known *Address to Parliament on the Duties of Great Britain to India*[1] (1853) which makes out a strong case for the employment of Indians, even in the covenanted services, and for the establishment in India of modern universities. It is significant that Elphinstone retained, even in his old age, those liberal educational and political beliefs which had inspired his work as an active administrator, anxious to promote, as best he could, the interests of the Indian people.

Holding views such as have been described, it is in no way surprising that he attached the greatest importance to the part which the Government must play in the establishment of a sound system of elementary schools. At a time when few people, even in Europe, were willing to countenance any interference by the State in educational matters, Elphinstone reminded the Court of Directors that Adam Smith had recognized 'the instruction of the poor to be among the necessary expenses of the sovereign' and had expressed the opinion that elementary education 'must in all stages of society be in a good measure the charge of the Government'.[2] He realized, however, that to rest his case on the general principles of political theory would be merely academic and he was careful to bring to the notice of the Court that there were very special practical reasons why, in Bombay, the Government should assume responsibility for the spread of education. He pointed out that in territories recently devastated by war education had inevitably declined and that there were few private persons qualified, or willing, to devote themselves to the work of reconstruction; also, the number of Europeans was much smaller than in Bengal and it was undesirable to have resort to the help of missionaries. For practical as well as for theoretical reasons, therefore, he was 'perfectly convinced that, without great assistance from Government, no progress can be made in that important undertaking'[3]—the advancement of education. Although Elphinstone regarded the responsibility of the State for education as almost self-evident, he hesitated to suggest anything in the nature of

---

[1] p. 173.   [2] Sharp, op. cit., p. 48.   [3] Forrest, op. cit., p. 79.

complete Government control. A desire to please the people, by aiding them in the support, or revival, of ancient institutions, led him to the conclusion that a combination of official and private effort was likely to yield fruitful results. He knew that the inhabitants of the larger villages had a sense of pride in the ownership of their schools, many of which were partly supported out of village funds, and he realized that such people would resent the handing over of these schools to official control. He wisely decided to build on foundations which were already there and to restrict to a minimum direct interference by the Government. The problem, as he saw it, was how to provide State assistance without offending the susceptibilities of the people, and the solution he arrived at was to work through the agency of existing bodies, such as the Bombay Native Education Society. He, therefore, proposed[1] that the Government should assume responsibility for the improvement of existing schools and for the opening of new ones, should guarantee the salaries of teachers by setting apart for this purpose sums out of village or other local funds, and should bear the cost of printing textbooks and of awarding prizes for proficiency. On the other hand, the actual preparation of suitable textbooks was to be entrusted to the Native Education Society, who were also to undertake the training of teachers and the appointment of qualified superintendents (inspectors), to work under the supervision of District Officers.   In this way the Government were to be made responsible for the provision, maintenance and control of schools and, at the same time, able to secure the cooperation of private agencies, such as the Education Society, which were to be liberally subsidized.

The policy which underlies the comprehensive scheme of education which Elphinstone embodied in his great Minute may be briefly summarized under three heads:

(1) To diffuse knowledge among the people, mainly through the improvement of existing schools and by the starting of new ones in towns and villages.

(2) To provide for the training of recruits for Government service, by combining a knowledge of English with a knowledge of India and its people.

[1] J. M. Sen, *History of Elementary Education in India* (1933), p. 109.

(3) To expand education by a combination of direct Government management, with aid to voluntary (excluding missionary) organizations.

In view of subsequent developments, not to mention the turn which events had already taken in Bengal, it is significant that Elphinstone's comprehensive programme is based on the conception of a sound system of elementary education for the diffusion of knowledge through the spoken languages of the people. He was by no means oblivious of the necessity of encouraging both higher Oriental learning and a knowledge of Western literary and scientific thought, but he rightly believed that first things should come first. Finally, he realized the contribution which the State must make to advancement of higher as well as of primary education and his principle of 'partial support' contains the germs of the grant-in-aid system, which was introduced at a later date.

Perhaps the greatest defect in Elphinstone's elaborate scheme was his limited conception of the scope of primary education. Meston tells us that while he 'was keenly interested in higher education, his thought constantly turned to the education of the great masses of the people'.[1] Statements such as these must be accepted with caution, because Elphinstone did not think in terms of universal, or mass, education in the sense in which they are understood today. Indeed, he made it quite plain that he intended to provide elementary education principally for the sons of the better classes and that 'a mixture of ranks' would prevent high-caste Hindus from sending their children to school. Again, one of his objections to utilizing the help of missionaries was that they found the lowest castes their best pupils and he feared that, if the Government were to encourage men 'of that description', schools would be boycotted by the upper and middle classes, whom he wished to conciliate. Whatever ultimate end Elphinstone may have had in view, there is no doubt that his immediate object was to provide facilities for the education of their children to parents of wealth and position, to those who were the acknowledged leaders of public opinion and to those who might reasonably be expected to provide recruits to fill positions of trust under the Government.

[1] W. Meston, *Indian Educational Policy, Its Principles and Problems* (1936), p. 17.

If Elphinstone was an idealist he was also essentially practical, and it is hardly fair to blame him because he was unable to escape the influence of the age in which he lived and to regard popular education, including the education of girls, in the light of subsequent thought. Only the sentimentalist will agree with Thomas when he says, 'to us it cannot but seem a hard saying that those who had been from time immemorial condemned from birth by religion and by circumstances to a life of ignorance and oppression should be shut out from their only chance of improving their condition'.[1] Few statesmen have been more solicitous than Elphinstone for the welfare of the masses of the people of India, but he was firmly convinced that, if education were to be made an instrument of social uplift, it was desirable to begin by making it attractive to those who claimed the respect and esteem of the populace. It may be argued that Elphinstone, no less than his colleague Warden, was wedded to the 'filtration' theory, and extracts from his writings might be quoted to substantiate the charge. But when all is said on either side, the conclusion is irresistible that he appreciated more fully than any of his predecessors, or contemporaries, what were the real problems which confronted the educationist in India and the solutions he proposed (whatever their defects) were far ahead of anything which had been previously suggested; indeed, for many years, perhaps for more than half a century, no carefully thought-out scheme for the reorganization of Indian education showed any marked deviation from the statesmanlike views which are associated with the name of Mountstuart Elphinstone.

One of the original recommendations of the sub-committee of the Bombay Education Society had been the establishment, at the Presidency, of an 'English School where English may be taught classically'. This proposal was warmly supported by Warden, who had consistently 'urged the policy of directing our chief effort to one object, to a diffusion of a knowledge of the English language, as best calculated to facilitate the intellectual and moral improvement of India'.[2] Elphinstone realized the force of this argument and he also felt that the establishment of an institution

[1] F. W. Thomas, *The History and Prospects of British Education in India* (1891), p. 50.

[2] Syed Mahmood, op. cit., p. 42.

to meet the demand for English would not only tend to conciliate advanced public opinion but would also meet his own wish to provide the services with highly educated recruits. Without waiting for the approval of the Honourable Court, he sanctioned on his own responsibility (1824) the opening of the Society's Central English School, which was subsequently called after him and of which the Elphinstone College is an offshoot. In the following year the Society secured a suitable plot of ground and erected a spacious building for the accommodation of its English and Central Vernacular Schools. No part of Elphinstone's comprehensive scheme for educational advancement was more warmly applauded by the Directors, who stated (1826) that they 'were disposed to attach considerable importance to the establishment of an English School at the Presidency';[1] they had been greatly impressed by the phenomenal success of the Vidyalaya in Calcutta, which they considered 'in the highest degree satisfactory'.

Their expectations were more than fulfilled because, owing to the enthusiasm of the Governor himself and to the energy of Capt. Jervis (Secretary of the Society), the English School made a very promising start. To begin with no fees were charged and, in order to attract pupils, prizes and medals were awarded on the results of annual examinations. It is interesting to note that soon after the arrival of Dr Wilson (1832) there was a considerable increase in the number of applications for enrolment, because many parents, from religious scruples and fear of attempts at conversion, withdrew their boys from mission schools. It was not until 1840 that tuition fees were levied, but even this distasteful innovation failed to reduce the number of applications for admission. Although the school was, nominally, open to members of all communities, it was attended almost exclusively by the sons of rich and better-class Hindu and Parsi parents; in Bombay, as elsewhere, the 'new' education did not find much favour among Muslims, who looked with suspicion on the secular instruction which was patronized by an alien Government. At first recourse was had to the Bell, or monitorial, system, but in the early thirties qualified Indian assistants were appointed to the staff and efforts were made to improve the standard and scope of the teaching. From these modest beginnings has sprung the oldest English school in western

[1] ibid., p. 44.

India, which has sent forth a continuous stream of learned scholars, wise legislators and captains of commerce and industry, who have held an honoured place in the history of modern India.[1]

The retirement of Elphinstone in 1827 deprived the Society of its chief support. To commemorate his services to the Presidency, citizens of every class and creed subscribed over two lakhs of rupees for the endowment of Elphinstone Professorships, intended primarily for the encouragement of Western literature and science. Out of sympathy with the views of the departing Governor it was decided that these appointments were 'to be held first by learned men invited from Great Britain and to continue so to be held until the happy period arrive when natives of this country shall be found perfectly competent to undertake the office'.[2] At the suggestion of Sir John Malcolm, Elphinstone's successor and a keen supporter of his educational policy, his predecessor's illustrious name was definitely associated with the Society's English School, and it was he who first proposed that the Elphinstone Professorships should form the nucleus of a higher, or collegiate, department of the Central School. This proposal did not meet with the approval of the Court of Directors, who recommended the foundation of a new institution modelled on the Anglo-Indian College, Calcutta. A final settlement was not reached until 1834 when the Government sanctioned the foundation of the Elphinstone College and very fittingly expressed the hope that it would raise up 'a class of people qualified by their intelligence and morality for high employment in the civil administration of India'. A council of management, representative of the Government and the Society, was appointed, and in the following year Professors Harkness and Orlebar (whose selection in England had been approved by Elphinstone himself) arrived and delivered their first lectures in the Town Hall. For the next few years there was very considerable friction between the college, working under its own council, and the school, still under the management of the Society. Petty jealousies and domestic squabbles tended to keep the two institutions apart and in 1838 it looked as if the college were bound to prove a complete failure, for only three students were attending professorial lectures. After much anxious

[1] Bhagwat, op. cit., p. 2.   [2] ibid., p. 9.

consultation a union was effected, and in 1840 Malcolm's original proposal was accepted and the professorships were attached to the Elphinstone High School, which was renamed the Elphinstone College School and later the Elphinstone Institution (1845).

At the same time a very radical change was made in the whole educational machinery of the province. As the college had ceased to be a separate institution the Council was dissolved; on the other hand, the Native Education Society was not only too large to form a suitable board of management, but it was felt that increasing preoccupation with higher education had diverted its attention from its first responsibility—the spread of primary education. Further, the expenditure of public funds on education now very greatly exceeded the voluntary contributions paid through the Society, and so the Government considered it imperative to exercise direct financial supervision and control. Accordingly, a Board of Education was created consisting of a President, Secretary and six members—three nominated by the Government and three elected annually by the Society. To this body were entrusted the funds of the Elphinstone Professorships and of the Native Education Society and control over all public institutions, English and vernacular, throughout the Presidency. The Society, however, continued to exist as a purely voluntary and private association, and its main function appears to have been to stimulate interest in education and to keep the Government in touch with popular opinion regarding educational matters generally. As a consequence of these changes the Society's school became a purely Government institution and the internal management was entrusted to a sub-committee, containing members of the college staff and representatives of the Board of Education. These arrangements, with slight modifications, lasted until a Department of Public Instruction was set up (1855). By this time the increasing demand for English education had made the numbers on the roll of the Elphinstone Institution so unwieldy that it was decided to separate the college from the school, and to house the former in a rented building at Byculla (1856). In the following year the University of Bombay was incorporated and this gave a still further impetus to higher English education, which continued to receive generous financial support from the Government.

There can be no doubt that the popularity of English education increased far more rapidly than Elphinstone, or even Warden, had ever anticipated, and the result was a rather lop-sided development of the policy laid down in 1824. Even the Sanskrit College at Poona gradually succumbed to the process of 'anglicization'; as early as 1825 it had been induced to accept, at the suggestion of Warden, the gift of a valuable library of English books in all branches of literature, and some twenty years later the English department had grown so strong that it overshadowed the Oriental side and the institution developed into the famous Deccan College. It is true that Elphinstone had from the first provided for the development of English education, because he regarded the diffusion of modern knowledge as essential for the progress of the country at large and, secondly, because he was anxious to enlist in the service of the State those who combined a knowledge of Indian life and culture with a knowledge of what was best in Western thought. After his retirement (1832) he defended the growth of English education on the grounds that it contributed to general improvement and that it appealed to the better classes by uniting their interests with those of the Government. It might be argued that Elphinstone had been won over to the Anglicist camp, for these views do not seem altogether consistent with those expressed in his famous Minute. At most, however, they merely indicate a change of emphasis, for Elphinstone never intended that English education should develop to such an extent that its growth would retard the growth of elementary schools. As early as 1824 he had expressed the cautious opinion 'that English will ever be so generally known as to be the instrument of diffusing knowledge through all ranks, may be wished, but certainly should never be calculated on'.[1] Indeed, he never expected that English would ever be 'more than a learned language, or at best a language spoken among people of education, as Persian is now in some parts of India'.[2] His anxiety to enlist in the public services the most highly qualified Indians available is the real explanation of any change of front (if such there was) on the part of Elphinstone, and by the public services he did not mean only the revenue and judicial departments of the Government.

[1] Richey, op. cit., p. 26.
[2] Appendix to the *Report from Select Committee of Affairs of E. I. Company* (1832), p. 203.

His early plan to establish a Civil Service College in Bombay came to nothing and a subsequent scheme, fostered by Capt. Sutherland, to found a somewhat similar institution in Poona (1825) was supported by Elphinstone, but does not seem to have made much headway. It was mainly due to the Governor's enthusiasm that an Engineering Institution was founded (1824) in Bombay and maintained at Government expense. In 1826 the Directors complained that this had been opened without their express authority, but as it was reported that the institution had given 'high satisfaction' to the Government and as it had been able to supply the Company with a large number of trained subordinates, the Court did not press their objections.[1] In 1825 a Medical School was founded (on the model of that in Calcutta) and munshis were engaged to translate into Gujarati and Marathi modern scientific treatises. This institution had to satisfy the needs of the public until the foundation of the Grant Medical College (1845), called after Sir Robert Grant, the late Governor and second son of the elder Charles Grant. The beginnings of professional education were made by Elphinstone and, prior to the establishment of the University, public-spirited and philanthropic citizens, notably Sir Jamsetjee Jeejeebhoy (1783-1859), had come forward to further the good work which he had begun. In the meantime the great institution connected with his name continued to be the centre of almost every new educational development in Bombay. In 1845 a Normal class for the training of primary teachers was added and, in 1855, a Law class was opened. Perhaps this year is more memorable in the annals of the Elphinstone College because of the fact that in it the first Indian, the late Sir Dadabhai Naoroji, was appointed to a Professorship (of Mathematics). Up to the time of the foundation of the University the Elphinstone Institution (school and college combined) dwarfed all the other educational institutions in Bombay and continued to keep green the memory of a Governor who had, since his retirement, gained a considerable reputation as a man of letters and a historian. For many years the pre-eminence of this famous college was unchallenged and this was, in no small measure, due to a succession of distinguished Principals. Of these mention may be made of Sir Alexander Grant (1862-5), whose fame mainly rests on his well

[1] Richey, op. cit., p. 197.

known *Ethics of Aristotle* (1857), which ran through several editions; he became Director of Public Instruction and Vice-Chancellor of the University of Bombay, but, shortly afterwards, left India on his appointment as Principal of Edinburgh University (1868). His most famous successor was Dr William Wordsworth, grandson of the poet, who was Principal from 1874 to 1890. He was twice Vice-Chancellor of the University of Bombay and took a keen interest in all questions pertaining to social and political reform. In the eighties, his lively contributions to the press created a stir in Bombay and caused no little embarrassment to the local Government. After his retirement to Italy, he published a slender volume entitled *Gleanings from Verse* (1899).

In view of later developments, it is interesting to recall the warm approval given by the Board of Directors to the proposals embodied in Elphinstone's original Minute. The most remarkable passage in their Dispatch of 1825 states that 'the grand attention of Government should be in the first instance devoted to affording means to their subjects to acquire simply the elementary parts of literature, reading, writing and arithmetic,'[1] and this was obviously a tribute to Elphinstone's wisdom in insisting upon the importance of furthering primary education. It is curious, however, that just about the same time the Directors informed the Government of Bengal, in no uncertain terms, that they regarded elementary education as of 'subordinate importance' and a little later (1830) the Government of Madras were told that their chief aim should be the spread of a knowledge of European literature and science, conveyed through the medium of English, among the higher classes of society. It is little wonder that Thomas writes, 'it is characteristic of letters written to the different Governors by the Directors that, while taken separately models of wisdom, they are not always consistent with each other. . . . An enemy might have suspected them of holding no fixed principle on the question'.[2] Most students of the period would agree that the Court of Directors had never any clearly defined educational policy, but no satisfactory explanation of their inconsistencies has been advanced. It is true that, in spite of a sprinkling of former Indian officials, the Board was mainly composed of men who regarded the Company as

---

[1] Thomas, op. cit., p. 47.   [2] ibid.

essentially a business concern, and it is also true that they had no experts on their staff to whom they could refer the educational proposals which were sent to them from India from time to time. They appear to have been duly impressed by the arguments, logical or persuasive, of different Governors-General or Provincial Governors and to have found it easier to accord their sanction to conflicting proposals for educational reform than to draw up a consistent scheme for the guidance of officials in India. Indeed, one is sometimes tempted to conjecture that, prior to 1830, correspondence with the Governor-General and with different local Governors was dealt with by different departments at Leadenhall Street and that each worked independently of the others. There is certainly no record of any central educational authority and it is extremely unlikely that the Directors, as a body, gave much thought to education, beyond regarding it as a financial burden. However this may be, Elphinstone, despite the opposition of his own Council and the indifference of the Court, had the satisfaction of carrying through a scheme which remained the basis of educational activity in Bombay until the issue of Wood's Dispatch, and even later. With the co-operation of the Society, the Government were able to achieve better results than the optimistic Elphinstone had anticipated. Indigenous schools which had fallen into decay were revived and in less than twenty years over 100 new schools were established, teachers were trained, textbooks prepared, schools inspected, prizes and certificates awarded, with the result that the judicious combination of official and private effort led to a considerable diffusion of knowledge and an increasing appreciation of the value of education. Indeed, it was the success of the 'Bombay experiment' which was largely responsible for inducing Lord Auckland to modify (1839) his predecessor's policy and to restore Government grants to elementary schools, as well as to institutions for higher Oriental learning. In 1842 there were 120 Government primary schools with 7,750 pupils, as against 4 secondary schools (outside Bombay City) with about 175 pupils.

Unfortunately, as years passed, the rate of progress slowed down and by degrees Bombay was forced to follow the example of Madras and to pursue the policy which had long prevailed in Bengal. In 1840 the Board of Education superseded the Native Education Society, which had done such admirable pioneer work in the field of elementary education. In 1844 Lord Hardinge issued his well-known Resolution, which virtually made a knowledge of English essential for employment in the higher ranks of the public service, and this gave a fillip to the growing popularity of English education in western India, as in Bengal. By this time Elphinstone and Malcolm had gone and the educational destinies of Bombay were being controlled by Sir Erskine Perry, Chief Justice, who was President of the Board of Education from 1843 to 1852 and a stout champion of English education and the filtration theory.

It was during this period that the controversy between the Anglicists and Vernacularists became acute. The leader of the former party was Sir Erskine Perry himself, who advanced the old hackneyed arguments in favour of higher English education and who claimed, with considerable justification, that 'the prospects of education were never so flourishing at this Presidency as they are now, under the present system and at the present moment' (1847).[1] His chief opponents were Col. Jervis, formerly Secretary of the Council and now a member of the Board, and Juggonath Sunkersett, also a member of the Board and one of the most highly educated Hindus of his day. The former's criticism of the view that instruction should be conveyed exclusively in English was, briefly, that it 'must at once be felt by every reasonable mind as chimerical and ridiculous'[2]—a piece of plain speaking which caused the President no little annoyance. His Indian colleague was more tactful; he argued[3] that Elphinstone's plan had aimed at the fostering of the vernacular languages and the promotion of vernacular schools and that knowledge could not be diffused save through the medium of the mother-tongue. He did not wish to discourage English, which was acquired by a small minority in the expectation of public employment and for the sake of facility of intercourse with Europeans, but he held it to be beyond the reach of the masses and incapable of extending the benefits of education to Indian women. This animated controversy, which almost led to the resignation of Sir Erskine Perry, was settled by a letter from the local Government (1848), addressed to the Board of Education, authorizing the use of both English and the vernaculars as media of instruction. The letter was so

[1] Richey, op. cit., p. 16.   [2] ibid., p. 13.   [3] ibid., pp. 16-17.

indecisive that Perry claimed that it settled nothing and that members of each party 'will refer to this Government letter as an authority for their favourite views'.[1]

Up to 1844 the Board had gone on steadily increasing the number of elementary schools and in that year they proposed (1) the creation of three Divisions—in Gujarat, the Deccan and the Southern Maratha country—each under the control of an Inspector, (2) the levy of a fee of 1 anna per mensem in Government elementary schools. The latter measure was only very partially responsible for the gradual decline of these schools. The main reason was the change that had come over Government policy, which was influenced by the increasing clamour for more and better English education and by constant pressure on the part of the Supreme Government. During the nine years of Perry's presidentship only 43 new vernacular schools were started but, despite this slackening of effort, there were in 1852 (apart from missionary and private institutions) 235 vernacular schools with 11,629 pupils, as against 10 English schools with just over 200 scholars.[2] Judged by modern standards, the figures may seem to be of trifling magnitude, but they may well be regarded as 'very creditable to the Presidency of Bombay'[3] where the foundations of a State system of elementary education had been laid according to the plans prepared by Elphinstone. It is true that his successors, perhaps through no fault of their own, had failed to develop the system on the lines which had been marked out in 1824 and that zeal for the promotion of English education blinded them to truths which are obvious today. They forgot that although Elphinstone himself had openly acknowledged that the impact of Western thought and culture would lead to momentous changes in the educational, no less than in the political, development of India, he had never ceased to adhere to the conviction that the promotion of higher education must always be strictly subordinate to the wider policy of spreading elementary education in the spoken languages of the people.

[1] ibid., p. 22.

[2] The figures quoted in Wood's Dispatch (§ 94)—216 schools and over 12,000 pupils—show a slight decline in the number of schools, which is counterbalanced by a slight increase in the number of pupils.

[3] Richey, op. cit., p. 291 (§ 94 of Wood's Dispatch).

All things considered, the progress of education in Bombay during the thirty years between 1824 and 1854 compared very favourably with developments in other parts of India. The foundations of a system of State education had been laid by Elphinstone and the policy which he had advocated in his great Minute had, with the passage of time, gained a considerable measure of approval, both inside and outside the western Presidency; indeed, Wood's Dispatch was in the nature of a reminder to the Bombay Government that they should revert to a policy which, even if it needed modifications, was essentially sound. Unfortunately, this reminder did not lead to any marked improvement as far as tangible recognition of the importance of elementary education was concerned, and such progress as was made was largely due to the efforts of private individuals and societies, including missionary bodies. Although the latter could hope for no direct financial support and no direct encouragement (excepting an occasional free grant of land for building purposes) from the Government, they had been very active ever since the American Marathi Mission commenced operations in Bombay in 1813. Two years later this body opened their first primary school for boys and, more important still, their first girls' school in 1824. The Church Missionary Society's first boys' school was established in 1822 and, six years later, its first girls' school. In 1837 this Society opened an Anglo-Vernacular School, which was called after Robert Money, an officer of the East India Company who was prompted by evangelical zeal to resign his official position and to devote his life to missionary work. More important still, in 1832 the Rev. J. Wilson, the greatest of all the Protestant missionaries whose names are associated with educational work in western India, founded, on behalf of the Scottish Missionary Society, a school which developed into the Wilson High School and the Wilson College.

With the exception of his great contemporary Duff, there is no more outstanding figure in the annals of missionary education in India in the last century. Each pursued exactly the same methods and worked for the attainment of exactly the same end. It is true that in Bombay Wilson had to face less hostility to his evangelical work than Duff had to encounter in Calcutta; on the other hand, we do read of parents whose religious scruples compelled them to withdraw their children from Wilson's school and of riots in the late thirties, which followed the conversion of a few Parsi lads. Wilson, however, even if he lacked Duff's vigour, had a kindly and tactful nature and he won the respect of members belonging to all classes of society; also, he had more sympathy than Duff with Indian thought and feeling. He was himself an Oriental scholar and among his achievements may be mentioned his classic work, the first of its kind in English, on the Parsi religion (1843) and his authoritative *History of the Suppression of Infanticide in Western India* (1855). He was elected a member of the Royal Society in 1845 and Vice-Chancellor of the University of Bombay in 1868. But, first and foremost, Wilson was a missionary and, at a time when the claims of primary schools were being ignored, he stood forth as the champion of the education of the people through the media of their own languages. He may not have had Duff's magnetic personality and he may not have captured the popular imagination to the same degree as his impetuous fellow-countryman, but in his own quiet and thorough way the results which he achieved were hardly less remarkable. Few missionary educational institutions in India hold a more honoured place in public esteem than the college which commemorates the name of the scholarly and pious Dr Wilson.[1]

In spite of the efforts of missionary bodies and of the Native Education Society, the progress of primary education was painfully slow. Outside the large towns people were inclined to look with suspicion on missionary effort and in the outlying stations officials, according to the Hunter Report, 'regarded the schools as of trivial importance'[2] and took no pains to remove the indifference of the people towards the education of their children. Further, as Elphinstone had foreseen, there were few individuals on whose 'spontaneous zeal' the Government could rely to stimulate an appreciation of the benefits of schooling. But, as in Bengal, the most important factor which militated against progress was the growing demand for a knowledge of English, which was encouraged, first by Warden and later by Perry, to such an extent that adequate funds were not available for the advancement of primary education on a large scale. Private persons were not slow to read the signs of the times, and in the year 1849 as many as nine private English schools were opened in the city of Bombay. It

[1] The standard *Life* (1878) is by Dr G. Smith, Duff's biographer.
[2] Sen, op. cit., p. 111.

is true that in 1853 the Board undertook to open a primary school
in any village in the Presidency, provided the people agreed to
meet half the pay of the teacher and to provide a schoolroom and
textbooks. In the following year a Department of Public Instruction
was set up and Mr C. Erskine, the first Director, proposed to
organize a system of elementary and English education comprising
three types of primary schools: (1) indigenous schools, which were
to be offered grants to encourage them to accept departmental
control; (2) village schools, to be established and maintained by
the Government; (3) town schools (departmental) in which pupils
were to have the option of learning English in the highest class.
His health broke down in 1856 and he was succeeded by Mr
E. I. Howard, who made energetic efforts to carry these proposals
into effect. In 1858 the Central Government ruled that Wood's
Dispatch empowered the local Government to allot grants only to
indigenous schools and not to subsidize the establishment of new
village or town schools on a partially self-supporting basis, and
they directed that no such schools should be opened without their
sanction. As a result of this bombshell the extension of primary
education came to a standstill and the good work initiated by
Erskine, who was building on the foundations laid by Elphinstone
(supported by the authority of Wood's Dispatch), came to little or
nothing. The interpretation put by the Government of India on
the Dispatch of 1854 is open to' question, but it is hardly unfair
to say that their real intention was to divert more money towards
the promotion of higher English education. Whatever the truth
may be, a second attempt (Elphinstone's being the first) to spread
a network of primary schools throughout the Presidency proved
a failure and the Government gradually drew further and further
away from the policy which had been laid down more than thirty
years previously by a Governor whose vision and enthusiasm were
still an inspiration to all who were interested in education.

By this time Elphinstone had become an old man; nearly
thirty years had elapsed since he laid down the reins of office and
for long he had been living in a quiet country seat and devoting
himself, despite failing eyesight, to his favourite literary pursuits.
As early as 1841 he had published his *History of India—Hindu
and Mahometan Periods* and so brought to fulfilment a design
he had vaguely conceived, twenty-five years earlier, when he was

Resident in Poona. This is the book on which his reputation as
a scholar mainly rests and it is doubtful whether he himself would
have consented to the publication of *The Rise of the British Power
in the East* which Colebrooke brought out in 1887. It is based on
papers which Elphinstone left behind, but it is a tedious, and
even inaccurate, book which has failed to win the appreciation
of historians. Apart from his literary pursuits, he continued to
take a lively interest in Indian affairs and was always glad to see
visitors with whom he could discuss Indian problems. He had
twice refused the offer of the Governor-Generalship, for reasons
which have never been satisfactorily explained, nor would he consent to serve on the Board of Control or to enter Parliament. He
steadfastly declined even 'to take part in those semi-public duties
which are expected from a country gentleman' and 'gradually
retired more and more into the seclusion of his own library'.[1]
As time went on his health grew worse and he suffered from failing eyesight and deafness, but to the end his intellectual faculties
remained unimpaired. He lived to see the issue of Wood's
Dispatch, the transfer of the Government of India to the Crown,
and the foundation of the University of Bombay (Warden's final
triumph, which he can hardly have grudged him). He died in
1859—the year in which Stanley's Dispatch was issued and that
in which the Bombay University (with Lord John Elphinstone
as Chancellor) held its first Matriculation examination.

It has been thought strange that Elphinstone, whose pre-eminence as an administrator and a scholar was universally acknowledged, should have received no marks of titular distinction.
Honours were showered on Malcolm, Metcalfe and Munro
and on others whose careers were far less distinguished, but
Elphinstone was not elevated to the peerage, nor made a Commander of the Bath, nor admitted to the Privy Council. Oxford,
it is true, conferred upon him the honorary degree of D.C.L., but
the most fitting honour he received was the association of his
name with the great educational institutions in Bombay which
will long perpetuate the memory of a Governor whose insight into
the educational problems of his day, whose sympathy with the
people whom he governed and whose vision of the coming destiny
of India entitle him to grateful remembrance.

[1] Cotton, op. cit., pp. 208-9.

JAMES THOMASON

JAMES THOMASON, 1804–53

CHAMPION OF ELEMENTARY EDUCATION

In the history of the Church of England few men have exercised such a great influence on the religious life of their time as the scholarly and devout Charles Simeon, Fellow of King's College and Vicar of Holy Trinity Church, Cambridge. He was the most outstanding clerical figure of the Evangelical Movement and he fired with missionary zeal many pious young men of great intellectual attainments—persons of 'godliness and good learning'. Among them were the Evangelical Chaplains[1] who came to India, as servants of the Company, between the years 1787 and 1815, to minister to the religious needs of their fellow countrymen. At that time the Directors were most reluctant to allow missionary activities within the territories under the Company's jurisdiction and officials were exceedingly apprehensive of the effects of preaching Christianity either to Hindus or Mohammedans. These Chaplains, therefore, were not permitted to take any direct part in efforts to proselytize, but they were able to advance the cause of missions by arousing enthusiasm for missionary work among Europeans, by preaching to Indian congregations and, above all, by aiding in the translation of the Bible into various Eastern languages. The most notable of this group of distinguished men were Claudius Buchanan, the first to suggest the desirability of an Ecclesiastical Establishment for India, Henry Martyn, the most remarkable of them all and translator of the Bible into Urdu, and Thomas Thomason, Simeon's closest friend and most devoted disciple. The last named, who had been Fellow and Tutor of Queens' College, Cambridge, and had worked for twelve years as Simeon's curate, came to India in 1804 accompanied by his wife and young son—James, aged four—who was destined to become Lieutenant-Governor of the North-Western Provinces.

[1] A good account of these chaplains is given in Eyre Chatterton's *History of the Church of England in India* (1924); it is strange, however, that the learned Bishop should state (p. 120) that no biography of the Rev. T. T. Thomason was ever written.

As Chaplain of the Old[1] Church, Calcutta, the Rev. Thomas Thomason soon established a reputation for his piety and learning. He devoted himself to the study of Arabic, Persian and Urdu and utilized his mastery of these languages in making translations of the Scriptures. He took an active part in various movements for the welfare of Indians and even went to the length of drawing up a scheme of general education, higher and lower, for the whole country. The Governor-General, Lord Moira, was so impressed with the Chaplain's proposals that he invited Thomason to accompany him on one of his extended tours in Northern India, so that he could discuss the details and practicability of a plan for national education. According to his biographer, the Rev. J. Sargent, the outline of Thomason's scheme was 'that schools should be established in every part of India; one English one in every district for the natives in the English language and science; under the school, and subordinate to the master, village schools, where the children should be instructed to read and write in their own language. The books to be selections from the moral and sacred writings of Christians, Mahometans, and Hindus. To supply the district schools, that there should be a school for schoolmasters in Calcutta, under the direction of a ·man of science and literature, the whole to be under a head, called Agent, for the superintendence of schools throughout India'.[2] Sir Richard Temple's summary has a rather more modern ring, though it omits one or two important particulars mentioned by Sargent; he says that Thomason proposed that some system of national instruction 'was to be imparted in the several vernaculars of the country and was to have its literary foundation in the learned languages of the East. But it was to embrace Western knowledge also, and the ideas of European civilization. The superior portions of it were to extend to instruction in English. It was to include higher institutions, central and urban schools, and village schools. It was to utilize all existing and indigenous resources of an elementary character, and to engraft on them such organization as European experience might suggest'.[3]   There

[1] Kiernander's Church was so called to distinguish it from the Church of St John, the New Church, which was built towards the end of the eighteenth century.

[2] J. Sargent, *Life of the Rev T. T. Thomason* (second edition, 1834) pp. 224-5.

[3] Sir Richard Temple, *James Thomason* (1893), p. 29.

can be little doubt that, in framing the scheme, Thomason was actuated by the belief that sound secular education would pave the way for religious teaching and the acceptance of Christianity; there can be little doubt, also, that the Governor-General's enthusiasm began to wane as soon as he realized that the Chaplain's ulterior aim was conversion. Thomason had not been long on tour with Lord Moira 'before he perceived with no little regret, that, instead of being more earnest respecting education as he beheld the accumulated proofs of its necessity, he became, *in appearance*, less alive to it as a matter of excellent policy and imperious obligation'.[1] On his return to Calcutta, highly placed officials impressed upon Lord Moira the dangers of a plan which had at first seemed so harmless, and Thomason vainly tried 'to rouse the governor to a sense of the importance of the crisis, and of the high duties to which he was called'.[2]

In the end, nothing came of the plan and the tour is remembered chiefly on account of the rebuke which Thomason, a strong Sabbatarian, administered to the Governor-General for moving his camp on the Lord's Day. Oswell, however, considers that although 'his suggestions were not carried into effect at the time, they eventually bore fruit . . . he had been the pioneer in the field of elementary education, and his son James was destined to carry on his work to fruition'.[3] It is not outside the bounds of probability that the influence of the elder Thomason may be traced in Lord Moira's Minute of 1815, which ends with the memorable words: 'To be the source of blessings to the immense population of India is an ambition worthy of our country. In proportion as we have found intellect neglected and sterile here, the obligation is the stronger on us to cultivate it. The field is noble: may we till it worthily!'[4] However this may be, Thomason, in spite of disappointment at the failure of his plans, did not allow his interest in educational reform to flag: he was one of those who actively encouraged the foundation of the Hindu College and of the School Book Society. Even if the contribution which this sincere and kindly man made to the cause of Indian

[1] Sargent, op. cit., p. 224.   [2] ibid., p. 225.

[3] G. D. Oswell, *Sketches of the Rulers of India*, II (1908), p. 175.

[4] H. Sharp, *Selections from Educational Records*, I (1920), p. 29. This minute is said to have been largely the work of H. T. Colebrooke, a noted Sanskrit scholar and President of the Asiatic Society of Bengal.

education proved ineffectual, it is none the less deserving of record. The fame of the father has been eclipsed by that of his more illustrious son, but few would dissent from the verdict of Sir Richard Temple that, 'take him all in all', Thomas Thomason 'was a person for good in the land where he pitched his tent, and a beacon for his generation in India'.[1]

At the age of ten young James was sent to England and placed in charge of his godfather, Charles Simeon, whose 'sense of the awful importance of earnest and sincere religion' made a lasting impression on Thomason's mind. He was first sent to school at Aspeden, in Hertfordshire, where he had as schoolfellows Macaulay and William Wilberforce. Four years later, he was sent to Stansted Hall, in Sussex, where Samuel Wilberforce, the future Bishop, was a pupil. Having obtained an appointment as writer in the East India Company, he proceeded to Haileybury in 1820 and there he distinguished himself in various branches of study. He returned to Calcutta in 1822, soon after his eighteenth birthday. In the following year, having completed the prescribed course in the College of Fort William and acquired a good knowledge of Oriental languages, he was appointed Assistant Registrar of the Sadr Adalat or Supreme Court. He devoted himself to the study of Mohammedan law and his proficiency in this subject, coupled with his mastery of Persian and Arabic, earned the encomium of his examiners. He also became interested in Hindu law and acquired a tolerable knowledge of Sanskrit, so that his acquaintance with Eastern classical languages was exceptional. Even if Thomason is not remembered as a scholar, or as a linguist, there is little doubt that his early acquaintance with Oriental classical lore gave him an insight into the thoughts and feelings of the people, and a sympathy with their outlook and ways of life, which stood him in good stead throughout his career. In 1826 he was appointed Judge of the Jungle Mahals and there the bad climate brought about a serious breakdown in health, and he was forced to go home to England on leave.

On his return to Calcutta, in 1828, he was posted to the Secretariat and in the following year he married Miss Maynard Eliza Grant, who was related to Charles Grant, the pioneer of English education in India. In 1832 he came to a decision in

[1] Temple, op. cit., p. 33.

every way honourable to himself, for he asked to be transferred to the executive branch of the administration, so that he might have opportunities, as a District Officer, of coming into closer touch with the people. His work in the Secretariat had been so highly appreciated that it earned the approbation and thanks of the Government, which were communicated to him by Sir Charles Metcalfe, Vice-President of the Supreme Council. It is worth noting that for a short time, after his return from leave, he was a Member of the Committee of Public Instruction, which had been set up by John Adam, Elphinstone's cousin, in 1823.

Thomason's first post as an executive officer was that of Collector and Magistrate of Azamgarh, an agricultural District some eighty miles from Benares. He threw himself with energy into the work of Revenue and Settlement Officer and took particular care to see that the proprietary rights of the cultivators were respected and safeguarded. He toured his District from end to end, acquired a thorough knowledge of village life and learned a great deal about various families, including some which belonged to primitive tribes. He always retained the happiest recollections of his pleasant life and congenial work at Azamgarh, which ended in 1837. In the previous year Sir Charles Metcalfe had been appointed first Lt-Governor of the newly created North-Western Provinces, with Agra as capital, and he selected Thomason to act as Secretary in the Judicial and Revenue Departments. Two years later his wife fell seriously ill and he decided to send her to England. He went with her to Calcutta with the intention of seeing her safely on board, but her health had become so precarious that he obtained permission to sail with her as far as the Cape of Good Hope, which was then the limit of the Company's authority regarding the sanction of leave to covenanted officers. On arrival there his wife's health gave rise to much anxiety and Thomason, at the risk of dismissal, decided to accompany her to England. On reaching home he entrusted her to the care of one of her sisters and then threw himself on the clemency of the Court of Directors; they pardoned his technical breach of discipline and ordered him back to India.

He returned by the overland route and landed in Bombay early in 1840, only to learn that his wife had died the previous November. He proceeded to Agra, where he was made permanent in the post of Secretary to Government which he had previously held.   Within the next few years he gained rapid promotion, becoming Member of the Board of Revenue and, later, Foreign Secretary to the Government of India (then regarded as the 'blue ribbon of the Indian Service'[1]).   In 1843, at the early age of thirty-nine, he was made Lt-Governor of the North-Western Provinces and he held this office until his death in 1853. These Provinces still formed part of the Bengal Presidency and included portions of what are now known as the United Provinces, the Central Provinces and the Punjab (including Delhi); as recon-stituted in 1858 they became the United Provinces of Agra and Oudh, with Allahabad as capital.[2]

The years of Thomason's Governorship were quiet and peaceful and no one was more fitted than he to guide the destinies of a province in ordinary times.   From the beginning he set himself to the accomplishment of two important ends—to make the administration thoroughly efficient and to forward every measure calculated to increase the welfare and happiness of the people.   He took a particular interest in the training of his Indian subordinate officers and 'effected many improvements in their status, emoluments and promotion'.[3]   He also paid much attention to the training of European officers and prepared 'mostly with his own hand' two manuals—one entitled *Directions to Collectors*, which dealt with the collection of land revenue, and the other called *Directions to Settlement Officers*, relating to the assessment of the land tax and the registration of tenures.   These manuals, which were used for many years throughout India, set forth the duties of District officers 'on the broadest principles and in the minutest details'.[4]   In spite of their somewhat forbidding titles, they were intended for guidance rather than as orders which were to be blindly followed; as Thomason himself put it, 'I like better to address myself to the reason of my fellow servants, than simply to their sense of obedience'.[5]   There is no better testimony to the success of Thomason's 'training school of the North-Western Provinces' than the success of many great administrators who served their apprenticeship under him; they included John Lawrence

[1] Oswell, op. cit., p. 179.

[2] For many years afterwards they were commonly called the N.W.P.

[3] Oswell, op. cit., p. 181.   [4] ibid.   [5] ibid.

and Robert Montgomery, William Muir and John Strachey, and
several others who caught Thomason's inspiration and, by virtue of
character and capacity, rose to positions of great honour and
responsibility.   When the Punjab was made a separate province
(1849), Lord Dalhousie insisted that the organization of the new
administration should be entrusted to some of the best men who
had been trained under Thomason's supervision.   The Lt-Governor,
despite this unsolicited tribute to his thoroughness and efficiency,
complained of the drain made on his own province—'It has been
a heavy tax, nineteen men of the best blood!   I feel very weak after
so much depletion'.[1]   Yet in 1853, the year of Thomason's
death, Kaye was able to claim 'there is a freshness, a vigor, a
healthy robust youth, as it were, apparent everywhere in the
administration of these provinces . . . what Thomason and his
associates have done for Upper India can only be fairly appreciated
by those who know what was the state of the Ceded and Conquered Provinces of India fifty, or even twenty, years ago'.[2]

Of no less importance, and more characteristic of Thomason
the man, was his fixed determination to show consideration and
kindliness to the people, by safeguarding their interests, by vindicat-
ing their rights and upholding their ancient institutions.   His
policy may be summarized in his own maxim, 'Support old
institutions and do not distract the people by attempting a new
one'.[3]   It should not be inferred that he was the enemy of progressive measures, or that he opposed reforms.   Far from it, for
it was his constant aim to introduce, 'cautiously and gradually,
beneficial measures, though he was careful not to offend Indian
susceptibilities by rash and hasty innovations.   As he himself said
of the civil administration of which he was the head, 'we
examined the existing systems and retained whatever of them
were found to be right and just, and then engrafted on this
basis new maxims derived from our own institutions'.[4]   Of the
reforms which are associated with his name, some were originated
by others and some were initiated by himself.   On assuming
office, he found that completion of the settlement operations

[1] Temple, op. cit., p. 102.
[2] J. W. Kaye, *The Administration of the East India Company* (1853),
pp. 267-8.
[3] Temple, op. cit., p. 161.   [4] ibid., p. 184.

demanded his attention. These had been commenced in 1833 by Robert Merttins Bird, a former Member of the Board of Revenue, who had undertaken the gigantic task of fixing the settlement for the Upper Provinces. On the eve of his retirement, Bird said that his only desire was that the good which had been effected would be maintained; fortunately, his work was carried to a successful issue by Thomason, whose reputation as an administrator of land revenue is second only to Bird's. 'Whoever', he said, 'may be the proprietor of land in India, the absence of all actual restriction in the supreme power in the amount of its demand left all property in land virtually dependent on its will. . . . But when the Government limits its demand to a reasonable amount, and fixes that amount for a term of years, a marketable property is thereby created, and it becomes of much importance that the person be named in whose favour this property is recognised or created.'[1] The intention of making any change in the disposition of property was disclaimed by the Government, but in many cases private proprietary rights did not exist, or were so vague as to be useless. Designing persons had often usurped property that did not belong to them, and subordinate officials, inefficient if not corrupt, had failed to protect the rights of the weaker parties. The consequence was that Settlement Officers had not only to establish rights, but also to create rights which did not exist before. It is significant that these officers were instructed to base their decisions, as far as possible, on the 'voice of the people'—on general public recognition of those who claimed to be proprietors; only in cases where no claims could be found to exist, or to have been exercised at any time, was the final decision to rest with the Government.

Thomason's determination to do justice to peasant proprietors, particularly those who had been illegally deprived of their rights, did not cause him to neglect the landed gentry, whose value, as an instrument of social stability and progress, he fully realized. One of the most delicate problems which he had to tackle, and one which aroused considerable controversy at the time, was in connexion with the large landowners, or taluqdars. The decision which he came to was 'that existing facts should be recognized where the taluqdars had securely established themselves as land-

[1] Oswell, op. cit., p. 184.

lords; but, where doubt existed, the original proprietors were to be supported and in such a case the settlement was to be made with them; the original proprietors were to pay the land tax direct to Government, while the taluqdars concerned were to be allowed a certain percentage of the land tenure in lieu of the profits they formerly got from the assignments of the revenue after the defrayal of all their charges'.[1] This decision was equitable for, even if certain taluqdars felt that their social status had been lowered, they could not complain that their financial interests had been seriously affected. Thomason has been severely criticized because he came to the conclusion that, in dubious cases, the benefit of the doubt should be given to peasant proprietors rather than to taluqdars, but his proposals were, with slight modifications, eventually sanctioned by the Court of Directors. Originally, taluqdars had been merely contractors for the collection of land revenue, but many of them had abused their power and their privileges and elbowed small owners out of their proprietary rights; they had thus become superior landowners and had come to regard the land tax which they collected as rent due to themselves and, having met the Government's demands, they retained the balance in their own hands. There can be little doubt that Thomason succeeded in mitigating definite hardships which afflicted small owners and he did so without weakening, to any appreciable extent, the position and prestige of the territorial aristocracy. In his own day many critics, including experienced officials, considered that he was partial to the lower and middle classes when their interests clashed with those of the upper classes, and they felt that this policy was fraught with danger to the Government.

It was only natural that, in a province containing some 40,000 villages, Thomason should pay close attention to village communities which, in the words of his predecessor, Sir Charles Metcalfe, had 'contributed more than any other cause to the preservation of the people of India through all the revolutions and changes which they have suffered'.[2] He did much to preserve and foster these ancient communities and he held them to be bodies of proprietors holding their estates in partnership and jointly responsible to the Government for the payment of revenue.

[1] ibid., p. 186.   [2] ibid., p. 185.

The acceptance of this policy proved a great boon, for each individual villager became a corporate peasant proprietor, responsible for his share of a lump-sum payment to the Government; as a result, disputes between members of the same community were reduced to a minimum, the sale of land in default of payment of revenue was prevented, and needless litigation was stopped. Such differences as arose were usually amicably settled by the villagers themselves, or settled in an equitable but informal manner by executive officers in the course of their periodical tours of inspection.

Only a passing reference need be made to the steps which Thomason took to combat outbreaks of small-pox and plague and the interest which he evinced in irrigation and communications, particularly the Ganges Canal and the Grand Trunk Road. The foundation of the Engineering College, Roorkee (1847), was a product of irrigation and other schemes initiated by the Lt-Governor himself. Although the primary aim of this institution was to provide officers, Indian and European, for the Irrigation Department, it was part of Thomason's original plan that the new college 'should work in connection with village schools, aiding and stimulating their work and preparing boys for ultimate admission within its own walls'.[1] He, therefore, proposed 'the improvement of village schools in a circle of 40 or 50 miles round Roorkee in order to provide pupils for the 3rd or lowest Department of the College',[2] which consisted of a vernacular class for Indian boys who might look forward to employment in the subordinate ranks of the Public Works Department. The establishment of the college was duly sanctioned and, in the year following its founder's death, his name was permanently associated with the institution which was officially designated (1854) the 'Thomason College of Civil Engineering at Roorkee'.

Of even greater importance was Thomason's carefully planned system of education, which was his greatest contribution to the progress of a backward province and that on which his fame principally rests. Although the North-Western Provinces were made a separate administrative unit in 1836, the control of its educational institutions was not transferred to the local Government

---

[1] ibid., p. 188.
[2] J. A. Richey, *Selections from Educational Records*, II (1922), p. 361.

until 1843. In this year there were in the new province three colleges — at Agra, Delhi and Benares — and nine Anglo-Vernacular schools maintained by the Government. From the very beginning, it was decided to adopt a policy radically different from that which had been followed in Bengal, and the reasons for this departure from the practice which had been followed in the Lower Provinces are clearly stated in the first report on the progress of education: 'In estimating the progress which has been made in the Educational Department in these Provinces, as well as in framing schemes for its future management, it must never be forgotten how much less encouragement there exists here for the study of English than in the case of the Lower Provinces and in the Presidencies of Madras and Bombay. There are here very few European Residents, except the functionaries of Government. There is no wealthy body of English merchants, transacting their business through the English language and according to the English method. There is no Supreme Court where justice is administered in English, no English Bar or Attorneys, no European sea-borne commerce, with its shipping and English sailors, and constant influx of foreign articles and commodities; even in the Public Service, the posts are very few in which a knowledge of the English language is necessary for a discharge of their functions.'[1] In view of local conditions the Government very wisely decided to introduce and foster education 'through the medium of the vernacular and not through any foreign tongue', because it was felt that in no other way would it be possible 'to produce any perceptible impression on the general mind of the people of this part of the country'.[2] Only a few months before Thomason assumed office his immediate predecessor, Sir George Russell Clerk, had asked the Supreme Government to sanction the new policy and had proposed that a beginning should be made by attempting to improve the indigenous schools in and around Agra. This letter is interesting mainly because it lays special emphasis on the fact that, in the Upper Provinces, the higher classes did not patronize institutions for higher English education, nor 'take the slightest interest in their existence'; the result was that Government colleges and schools were 'filled or supplied . . . from a lower rank and from the hangers-on of

[1] ibid., p. 228.   [2] ibid., p. 229.

public offices, the inferior shop-keepers, the children of our *burkandaz* and with individuals with whom the respectable classes would not desire their children to associate'.[1]

As early as 1844 Thomason appointed a Curator of School Books and instructed him to make a catalogue of all books used in the province (in English, Hindi and Urdu, as well as in the classical languages) and to submit to the Government from time to time proposals for the printing of new, or the reprinting of standard, books. In the following year he issued a circular calling on District Officers to submit details of the actual state of education throughout the province; he pointed out that it was important for their own protection that all who had any interest in land should be able to read the settlement papers, so as to satisfy themselves that the entries concerning their holdings were correct. 'There is, thus,' the circular runs, 'a direct and powerful inducement to the mind of almost every individual to acquire so much of Reading, Writing, Arithmetic and Mensuration, as may suffice for the protection of his rights . . . when the mind of the whole people has thus been raised to a sense of the importance of knowledge, it is natural to suppose that many from the masses will advance further and cultivate literature for the higher rewards it offers, or even for the pleasure which its acquisition occasions'.[2] It is noteworthy that Thomason, who had had firsthand experience of the official attitude towards education which prevailed in Calcutta and had served as a member of the Committee of Public Instruction, had the wisdom to realize that an educational edifice must be built from below upwards, not from the roof to the foundations. Whether he was influenced by the scheme which his father had drawn up many years before, it would be hazardous (in the absence of reliable evidence) to express any opinion; there is no doubt, however, that he was greatly impressed by Adam's Reports (1835-8), for he openly acknowledged his indebtedness to this sturdy champion of vernacular education.

The reports submitted by District Officers showed that 'less than five per cent of the youths who are of an age to attend school obtain any instruction, and the instruction, which they do receive is of a very imperfect kind'.[3] Thomason, therefore, set to work to frame (1846) a comprehensive scheme of vernacular education

---

[1] ibid., pp. 233 ff.   [2] ibid., p. 237.   [3] Temple, op. cit., p. 173.

which he submitted to the Central Government; they, in turn, forwarded it to the Court of Directors. He proposed the endowment of a school in every village containing not less than 200 houses, 'the Government giving up its revenue from the land, which constitutes its endowment, on assurance that the zemindars have appropriated the land for the purpose of maintaining a school-master'.[1] 'It is a standing reproach', wrote Thomason, 'of the British Government that, whilst it continually resumes the endowments of former sovereigns, it abstains from making any, even for those purposes which it considers most laudable. The present measure will in some degree remove this reproach and that in a manner acceptable to the people at large.' The Directors were duly impressed but, although they admitted 'the necessity for giving some powerful impulse to elementary education', they rejected the proposal that teachers should be remunerated by grants of land (*jaghirs*) and they asked the Lt-Governor to prepare a revised scheme. This was drawn up[2] and submitted to the Directors in 1848.

The most important feature of the new scheme was the establishment, at each of the sub-divisional headquarters of eight Districts (out of a total of 31), of a *tahsildari*, or middle, school, which was to serve as a model for neighbouring indigenous schools and was to be conducted by a headmaster on Rs. 10 to 20 p.m., in addition to the usual fees paid by pupils. For each District there was to be a Zillah Visitor (Inspector) on Rs. 100 to 200, and for every two subdivisions (*tahsils*) there was to be an Assistant, or Parganah, Visitor (Deputy Inspector) on Rs. 30 to 40. It was proposed that these inspecting officers should be instructed not to confine their attention to the model schools maintained by the Government; they were also to be required to inspect indigenous schools and to report on the methods of instruction and the progress of pupils and to encourage deserving headmasters by monetary rewards; finally, and not least important, they were to be encouraged to induce people to start schools of their own, or to revive old ones. Thomason also suggested the appointment of a Visitor-General, preferably a member of the Civil Service, on a salary of Rs. 1,000 a month to supervise and co-ordinate the educational activities of the Government in the eight selected

[1] Richey, op. cit., p. 241.   [2] ibid., pp. 24␣

Districts, and, eventually, in the whole province. To these proposals the Directors gave their assent and they sanctioned, in their Dispatch of 3 October 1849, an annual educational expenditure of half a lakh of rupees. In 1850 the local Government resolved to put the scheme into operation and sanctioned the appointment of a Visitor-General.[1] They also approved a fairly comprehensive syllabus, higher than that followed in indigenous schools and comprising, in addition to the three R's, History, Geography, Geometry, Accounts and Mensuration, which were to be taught through the media of the chief languages of the province (Hindi and Urdu). Assistant Visitors were asked to inspect existing schools—provided, always, that no village teacher was to be compelled to submit to Government inspection—and to submit reports on their efficiency; finally, in places where there were no schools, they were instructed to 'explain to the people the advantages that would result from the institution of a school'[2] and to offer help in finding qualified teachers and in providing suitable books.

Thomason's plan has been highly praised, particularly in recent years, as being liberal, far-reaching and economical. Whatever its merits, it was not original, for it is confessedly an attempt to apply, with modifications, to the Upper Provinces the recommendations which had been made by Adam for the encouragement of indigenous education in Bengal and Bihar and which had been summarily rejected as impracticable. The success of the plan ultimately depended on the co-operation of the people themselves; as Thomason said, 'The scheme contemplates the drawing forth of the energies of the people for their own improvement, rather than actually supplying to them the means of instruction at the cost of Government: persuasion, assistance and encouragement are the means to be principally supplied'.[3] Again, in a letter to a friend, he wrote, 'I want to do something consonant with native institutions and ideas, and also to induce its people to work with me, and exert themselves in the cause'.[4] His own earnestness and enthusiasm triumphed, for he had to overcome opposition— even from his friends and colleagues. Some feared that the people would resent even the slightest interference with indigenous schools,

---

[1] ibid., pp. 249 ff.   [2] ibid., p. 250.
[3] Temple, op. cit., p. 173.   [4] Temple, op. cit., p. 174.

while others urged that, without Christian teaching, his scheme would be a waste of energy and money. The former critics had to be content with the Lt-Governor's assurance that he himself had a more intimate knowledge than anyone else in the province of the outlook and feelings of the people; to the latter he replied that, sincere believer though he was, he was precluded by his official position from teaching Christianity: 'My business as Governor', he said on one occasion, 'is to enlighten people, not to teach religion.'[1]

As things turned out, his optimism was scarcely justified, for the people showed little inclination to co-operate and progress was anything but rapid. In 1851 the Visitor-General (Mr H. S. Reid, who became Director of Public Instruction in 1855) reported that at every step he had had to encounter blind distrust and suspicion; 'his survey, which covered eight districts with 50 towns and 14,572 villages, showed 3,127 schools of all sorts and 27,853 scholars. Twenty of the schools included English in their courses. Vernacular schools numbered less than half the total, being outnumbered by Persian. . . . The highest type of school was the Arabic *madrasa*, in which students might linger till well advanced in manhood'.[2] In his second report Mr Reid made the first reference to the system of *halkabandi* (or circle) schools—'a school in every cluster of villages in that village which enjoys the most central position'.[3] The following account of these schools is given in the Report of the Hunter Commission (1883) and is quoted by Richey: 'The *halkabandi* or primary vernacular schools which now throng the North-Western Provinces in thousands originated[4] about 1857 in an experiment made by Mr Alexander, Collector of Muttra. The plan was this. A *parganah* being chosen, it was ascertained how many children of a school-going age it numbered, what revenue it paid, and what expense it could therefore bear. A cluster of villages, some four or five, was then marked out and the most central of the villages was fixed upon as the site of the school. The rate in aid originally varied a good deal in different districts, but ultimately the

---

[1] Oswell, op. cit., p. 191.

[2] O'Malley, op. cit., p. 152.   [3] Richey, op. cit., p. 231.

[4] Stark says that 'the circle system' was started by Protestant missionaries in Bengal as early as 1822; *Vernacular Education in Bengal* (1916), p. 14.

Zamindars agreed to contribute towards education at the rate of one per cent on their land revenue.'[1] It appears that 'Mr Alexander's idea was quickly caught up by other Collectors' and that in 1854 there were about 760 of these *halkabandi* schools, with some 17,000 pupils.

In the preceding year Dr F. J. Mouat, Secretary of the Council of Education, Calcutta, was asked to inspect the various educational institutions in the Upper Provinces and he submitted a valuable report in which he praised the energetic steps which the local Government had taken to accomplish an up-hill task. 'The prejudices which had to be overcome, the difficulties which encumbered the path of a more systematic order of general instruction among a singularly suspicious, benighted and bigoted population, rendered it absolutely necessary to construct the novel scheme upon the pre-existing base so as to work with materials already familiar to the people, and thus startle them as little as possible with strange innovations.'[2] He went on to speak highly of the efficiency of the *tahsildari* schools (which were far superior to the indigenous schools) and of the enthusiasm of the teachers and the attainments of the pupils. Having paid a tribute to the 'energy, zeal, ability, and rare tact and discretion' of Mr Reid, he concluded, 'I am convinced that the scheme, above referred to, is not only the best adapted to leaven the ignorance of the agricultural population of the North-Western Provinces, but is also the plan best suited for the vernacular education of the mass of the people of Bengal and Behar. It can be efficiently worked out at a smaller cost than any other scheme, it contains nothing to shock the prejudices or rouse the passions of an ignorant people; it includes in its practical introduction an admirable system of check and supervision, and its whole organization is so simple and complete, as in my humble estimation to merit extension in the North-Western Provinces and gradual introduction into Bengal and Behar'.[3] The generous tribute paid to the energy and enthusiasm of the Visitor-General was well deserved, but there is abundant evidence to show that he derived his inspiration from the Lt-Governor himself. Also, it is noteworthy that Dr Mouat, an experienced educationist and a keen advocate of the establishment of universities in India,

---

[1] Richey, op. cit., p. 231.   [2] ibid., p. 259.   [3] ibid., p. 262-3.

was convinced that, despite the rejection of Adam's proposals regarding vernacular education and the failure of Lord Hardinge's *halkabandi* schools in Bengal, the education of the masses was a responsibility which the Government could no longer afford to evade. It is sometimes forgotten that Lord Hardinge's famous Resolution of 1844, which was issued within three months of his accession to the Governor-Generalship, aimed at throwing open to qualified young men appointments in the subordinate, as well as in the higher, ranks of Government service. It stated that in the selection of persons to fill even the lowest offices under Government 'a man who can read and write be preferred to one who cannot'.[1] This sudden change in official policy, which does not appear to have met with the approval of the Council of Education, forced the authorities to turn their attention to elementary, including indigenous, schools and to the diffusion of education in rural areas. The Bengal Government, therefore, decided to establish independently of the Council 101 'Circle Schools', which came to be called the 'Hardinge Schools'.[2] They were placed under the control of the Board of Revenue and located in places where the inhabitants were willing to provide suitable buildings and to pay the modest tuition fee of one anna a month for each pupil. In the beginning the scheme aroused a measure of popular support, but it soon proved to be a complete failure. The Board of Revenue was not a suitable, still less an enthusiastic, controlling agency and it was not prepared with books, teachers or inspectors; again, some schools were set up in places where facilities for obtaining elementary education had already been provided by indigenous schools, while others were established in villages in which the people showed no interest in the education of their children; finally, the demand for English had gathered strength and was already spreading from the towns to the larger villages. It is hardly surprising, therefore, that at the end of ten years only twenty-six of the original schools survived—and even they were in anything but a flourishing condition. Fortunately, about this time Henry Woodrow decided to follow Thomason's example and 'to make the greatest possible use of existing schools

[1] ibid., p. 91.
[2] A. Howell, *Education in British India prior to 1854* (1872), pp. 44-53; H. A. Stark, *Vernacular Education in Bengal from 1813 to 1912* (1916), pp. 66-70.

and of the masters to whom, however inefficient as teachers, the people have been accustomed to look up to with respect'.[1] He introduced the 'circle' system into Bengal in 1856 and encouraged the establishment of new, and the revival of old, indigenous schools, with the result that the number of vernacular schools in the province rose to nearly 1,000 in 1863[2] (an increase of 2,000 per cent) and to more than 5,000 in 1876.[3]

Woodrow's sudden death in the latter year deprived Bengal of one of the most distinguished and versatile educationists who have ever given their services to that province. Born in 1823, he was educated at Rugby, where he was one of the six boys who had supper with Dr Arnold on the evening before his death,[4] and at Cambridge, where he had a brilliant mathematical career and was elected Fellow of Caius College. In 1848 he accepted the post of Principal of the Martinière College, Calcutta, and six years later he was appointed Secretary of the Council of Education. Subsequently, he became Inspector of Schools in Eastern Bengal and in 1855 he introduced his system of 'circle' schools. His plan differed considerably from Thomason's, under which a central school was established for a group of villages within a radius of two miles; under Woodrow's scheme 'a superior teacher visited, in turn, for one or two days' teaching, each among a cluster of village schools'.[5] In the *Report of the Indian Education Commission* (1883) it is said that 'improvement was aimed at by employing certain State pandits, each of whom was attached to a circle of three or four village schools under their own gurus or masters' (p. 96). It soon became apparent that elementary education was making slow progress and in 1862 the 'circle' plan was abandoned in favour of a scheme for the training, as stipendiaries, of teachers for village schools. Woodrow, however, had some success in raising the standard of teaching in these humble schools, which he made more attractive by adding practical subjects, such as surveying and drawing, to the syllabus. In his efforts to

---

[1] Educational Dispatch (1859), § 48.

[2] Stark, op. cit., p. 88.   [3] Richey, op. cit., p. 481.

[4] Many of the incidents of Woodrow's school life are recounted in *Tom Brown's Schooldays*, though Judge Hughes has divided them among different characters (Richey, op. cit., p. 480).

[5] W. F. B. Laurie, *Sketches of Some Distinguished Anglo-Indians*, second series (1888), p. 144.

popularize education he used to impress upon the people that elementary education tended to give a boy a good start in life, and villagers appreciated the advice of the kindly man who erected for their benefit sun-dials in many remote hamlets.   It is said that even Collectors caught his enthusiasm and began to take more active measures to foster village schools in their several Districts.[1]

Woodrow's educational work was not confined to elementary schools. Before becoming Director of Public Instruction (1876) he acted for a short time as Principal of the Presidency College and, as a Member of the Syndicate, he took an active part in the affairs of the University of Calcutta.   He had already earned a reputation as a popular lecturer on scientific subjects and he was one of the first to realize that one of the greatest defects of higher education was the disproportionate attention devoted to literary studies, to the neglect of the sciences.   Indeed, he endeavoured (without success, as far as can be seen) to induce the University 'to extend its courses in Physical Science by curtailing its studies in Metaphysics'.[2]   He is now chiefly remembered as editor of *Macaulay's Minutes on Education in India*, which he extricated from a mass of old records in the Department of Public Instruction.   These were published privately (1862),[3] in an edition limited to fifty copies, and for this work he was warmly thanked by the Governor-General, Lord Canning.   Clearly, Woodrow was a man of boundless energy, and his sympathy with the people of India made him extremely popular.   On his death his admirers collected funds to found a scholarship in Calcutta

[1] It appears that many Collectors 'held the opinion that the introduction of education would give the people ideas beyond the sphere in which they would have to earn their bread, would make them dissatisfied, and render them more troublesome to manage' (Laurie, op. cit., p. 142).

[2] ibid., p. 142.

[3] Shortly afterwards the public edition followed; it included, besides the historic Minute of 1835, Macaulay's Minutes on Indian education written in 1836 and 1837.   The great Minute was first published in full, with 'the authority of the distinguished author' (p. 64) in C. H. Cameron's *Address to Parliament on the Duties of Great Britain to India* (London, 1853).   Two years later it appeared·in India in A. J. Arbuthnot's *Selections from the Records of the Madras Government*, though extracts had been published as early as 1838 in C. E. Trevelyan's *The Education of India* (in which Macaulay's name is not mentioned).

University to perpetuate his name and for the erection of a marble bust.[1] Perhaps the most notable memorial to the 'Nestor of Education in Bengal' are the appreciative references to his public services which are to be found in the Dispatch of the first Secretary of State for India, Lord Stanley, who had been his schoolfellow at Rugby.

Bengal was not the only, nor even the first, province in which attempts were made to carry into effect a modified form of Thomason's plans for the improvement and expansion of primary education. In the first Administration Report (1849–50) of the Punjab it was stated that the Government placed 'much reliance on the new system of settlement, as an engine for good and a medium for the diffusion of knowledge'[2] and a little later a recommendation was received from the Supreme Government that the local Government 'should consider whether the system of vernacular education in the North-Western Provinces might not beneficially be introduced into the Punjab'.[3] In 1854 a complete scheme, including the establishment of four Normal Schools and fifty *tahsildari* schools, and the appointment of a Visitor-General and assistants, was prepared; this was based mainly on the plan which Thomason had worked out for the neighbouring province and was sanctioned by the Government of India. Before the new system could be carried into effect Wood's Dispatch arrived; thereupon, a Department of Public Instruction was set up and William Delafield Arnold (son of the great Dr Arnold and brother of Matthew Arnold) was appointed Director (1856). His first report (for 1856–7)[4] of which extracts are reprinted in *Selections from Educational Records, Part II*, contains an interesting account of popular education in the newly created province. Details are given of indigenous schools—Hindu, Sikh and Mohammedan. It appears that the latter were of two kinds— *Koran* which were 'educationally worthless', and *Persian* which were 'the most genuine educational institutions in the country', and were largely attended by Hindu pupils. The explanation

---

[1] There is another bust in the library of Caius College and a mural tablet in the chapel of Rugby School.

[2] Richey, op. cit., p. 280.   [3] ibid., p. 281.

[4] This was not published until 1917 when J. C. Godley, D.P.I., Punjab, brought out an edition with a short prefatory note; this is now out of print.

is that Persian was still the official language of the recently
annexed territories and, consequently, some acquaintance with
this language was the hall-mark of an educated person and the
prerequisite of a successful career. (As English became more
prevalent, many of these Persian schools were gradually transformed
into Anglo-Vernacular schools.) It is also reported that, in the
first year of its existence, the Educational Department had started
17 girls' schools and that, of the 306 girls attending them, no
less than 296 were Mohammedans—the other 10 being Hindus.
Hopes were held out that the establishment of *Zillah* schools would
raise the general standard of education in the province and that
they would provide English education 'as an accomplishment
for those who are willing to pay for it'. Here, however, it is
more important to record that the scheme which Arnold drew
up for the Punjab 'was in its main features the same as that
which had been introduced in the North-Western Provinces a few
years before. The existing indigenous schools were to be
improved, the cost being met out of the one per cent cess on
land revenue which was being levied at the time from most of
the districts. The Halkabandi system of the North-Western
Provinces was also adopted, a school being established in the
centre of each group of six villages'.[1] Mr R. N. Cust who,
prior to his transfer to the Punjab, was one of Thomason's own
officers, says 'the conception of utilizing indigenous teachers and
training them was a master-stroke. In Lower Bengal the Government, with a flourish, started some hundred brand new schools.
Thomason improved and rendered effective several hundred old
ones. Of course, we took the system with us to the Punjab and
had it from the beginning; but Thomason was its founder'.[2]

On Arnold had fallen the heavy work of organizing the
Educational Department in the Punjab and of planning for the
future. No sooner had a beginning been made than the Mutiny
broke out and, after a period of disorder and confusion, a fresh
start had to be made. The severe strain, increased by sorrow at
the death of his wife, caused a breakdown in health and Arnold

[1] Richey, op. cit., p. 283.
[2] Quoted by H. Morris, *Heroes of Our Indian Empire*, I (1908), p. 122.
Cust was afterwards Hon. Secretary of the Royal Asiatic Society and author
of *Life Memoir* (1899).

had to take sick leave. He died at Gibraltar on his way home and his memory is preserved in his more famous brother's *A Southern Night* and *Stanzas from Carnac*.[1] Meantime, attempts to make effectual the Punjab Government's adaptation of the Thomason plan, like the efforts to work the original in the Upper Provinces, proved a failure. This was partly due to the inadequacy of the income derived from the one per cent cess and partly due to the lack of local support in many places. From the beginning Arnold had realized that 'the number who are eager for education is very small', and it soon became apparent that the fanatical views of teachers belonging to the different communities, and appointed mainly for their priestly qualifications, rendered steady progress impossible. Further, the growing demand for a knowledge of English, especially in large cities such as Lahore and Amritsar, caused a setback to the spread of vernacular education, which, in the troublous days of the Mutiny, had come almost to a standstill. But, in spite of the failure of the early attempts to make the Thomason plan operative in his own province, in the Punjab and in Bengal, the verdict of history must be that Thomason's encouragement of vernacular education—for simple cultivators, petty shopkeepers and even humbler folks— entitles him to be regarded as the father of elementary education in India. This claim has been made on behalf of others, but not with anything like the same justification.

James Thomason's solicitude for the poorer and more unfortunate members of society, and his determination to advance their moral and material well-being, did not lead him to underestimate the value and importance of higher, even English, learning. He was firmly convinced, however, that the provision of primary education for the masses was a direct responsibility of the Government, whereas higher education was largely a matter for private enterprise in which Government assistance should, for the most part, be restricted to financial support by way of grants-in-aid. He also held that higher education, of whatever kind, must always be based on Indian culture and he strongly disapproved of the policy of sweeping innovation, which aimed at the wholesale

---

[1] W. D. Arnold was the author of a somewhat tedious novel of Anglo-Indian life, *Oakfield or Fellowship in the East* (1853), which enjoyed considerable popularity in its day.

substitution of English for Indian learning; by all means, he argued, let India have the benefit of Western knowledge, but in such a way that new light will be thrown on the Indian traditional outlook upon man and his place in the universe. As early as 1841, before his accession to the Governorship, he had recommended the amalgamation, under the same Principal, of the Oriental and English Departments of the Delhi College on the ground that 'great facilities will thus be afforded for the simultaneous acquisition of Oriental and European learning, which may be expected to exercise a salutary influence on the former'.[1] A similar amalgamation was sanctioned for Benares and Mr J. Muir was appointed (1844) first Principal of the reconstituted college. He was succeeded (1846) by Dr J. R. Ballantyne who wrote some interesting reports on Sanskrit studies in Benares, but is remembered (if at all) for his 'conviction that European knowledge could be conveyed to the vernaculars only through Sanskrit'.[2] He strongly deprecated the borrowing of English words to express ideas for which there were no vernacular terms, and made an attempt (which did not prove successful in practice) to provide a scientific terminology based on Sanskrit words and their derivatives. By a strange coincidence, Dr K. M. Banerjea, who was working just about the same time on his *Encyclopaedia Bengalensis*, took exactly the opposite view and freely borrowed English scientific terms 'when the Sanskrit fails to produce any either readymade or capable of being easily invented'.[3] It is hardly necessary to enter into a discussion of the merits of these rival schools of thought, but it is interesting to notice, in passing, that an Indian scholar in Calcutta—the stronghold of the Anglicists—advocated the wholesale adoption of English scientific terms, while English officials in the Upper Provinces were eager to produce, with the aid of Sanskrit, a modern vernacular literature suitable for the communication of scientific knowledge to the people of the country. Indeed, this was the original aim of the Government colleges in Agra, Delhi and Benares, and throughout his Governorship Thomason took a lively interest in these colleges, as well as in

[1] Richey, op. cit., p. 253.
[2] F. W. Thomas, *The History and Prospects of British Education in India* (1891), p. 42.
[3] ibid.

14

the educational institutions conducted by missionary bodies throughout the province.

One of the last public functions which Thomason attended was the opening (1853) of the new buildings of Queen's College, Benares, which was housed in one of the most beautiful public edifices in Upper India. In a notable speech he spoke of 'the natural effect upon the mind of architectural beauty', of the opportunity which the new college would afford of supplementing Hindu learning by the infusion of Western thought, and of the need for religious toleration, or, in the words of Lord Morley, 'reverence for all the possibilities of truth'. In an eloquent peroration he said, 'unhappily, human opinions on the subject of religion, are so irreconcilable that we cannot concur in any one act of worship. The more necessary it is, then, that each man in his own breast, should offer up his prayer to the God whom he worships, that here morality may be rightly taught, and that here truth, in all its majesty, should prevail'.[1] The Lt-Governor was known to be a devout and orthodox Christian, and so his liberal advocacy of religious tolerance caused a mild sensation. Objection was taken by narrow-minded (but, possibly, well-meaning) persons to words which acknowledged the existence of Gods other than 'the one and only true God'; his critics had failed to distinguish between statements which Thomason made in his official capacity and those which were expressions of his personal beliefs. It was well known that the Lt-Governor was a regular churchgoer and a strict observer of the sabbath; occasionally he attended vernacular services in missionary churches and he even translated some of the Psalms into 'elegant Hindustani'. Again, as a private individual, he did not hesitate to lend liberal support to missionary work, particularly that of the Church Missionary Society with which he had hereditary associations and which had important stations at Agra and Benares. Sir Richard Temple states that 'his munificence embraced churches, colleges, schools, medical dispensaries, orphanages, and the like. He set aside a tithe of his large official income for good works, but this limit was often exceeded'.[2] A man of rare piety and sincere religious convictions, he was always careful to observe, in his

[1] Temple, op. cit., pp. 184-5.   [2] ibid., p. 132.

official dealings, the policy of strict religious neutrality which had been adopted by the Supreme Government and which, from the political point of view, had his warmest approval.

Thomason's fame as an able and sympathetic administrator spread far afield and his services, as was only natural, attracted the appreciative notice of the Governor-General and of the Court of Directors. In 1853 he was nominated to the governorship of Madras, 'but on the very day on which the Queen signed the paper giving her sanction to his appointment, September 27th 1853, he passed peacefully away, dying at the post of duty'.[1] Many tributes were paid to his conspicuous ability, his devotion to duty and his high moral character. That of Sir William Muir, who had been formerly one of his officers and subsequently became Lt-Governor of the North-Western Provinces, deserves quotation. 'It may well be inquired what secret charm it was, which lent to every department of his administration so distinguished an efficiency and greatness. It was not brilliant genius; for his faculties, though powerful and elevated, were not transcendent; it was not the gift of eloquence nor anything persuasive in speech or writing. The capacities of his well-regulated mind, schooled into their utmost efficiency, performed wonderful things; but those capacities in themselves were in few respects greater than those often met with in undistinguished characters. There was indeed a rare power of deliberation and judgment, an unusual faculty of discernment and research, a keen discrimination of truth from error. Yet these were mainly the result of studious habit, and earnest purpose. And herein, in our judgment, lies the grand praise of the late administration. It was by *labour* that it was perfected—conscientious, unceasing, daily labour; by a wakeful anxiety that knew no respite; by a severity of thought, ever busy and ever prolific in the devising of new arrangements, and the perfecting of old. Yet his mind was so beautifully balanced that this unwearied work and never-ceasing tension produced (as in most men it could hardly fail to have done) no irregularity of action, and no fretful or impatient advance. All was even, serene, powerful.'[2]

[1] Oswell, op. cit., p. 192.
[2] W. Muir, *The Honourable James Thomason* (second edition, 1897), pp. 88-9.

Thomason's successful career was largely due to his absolute sincerity and his unremitting devotion to duty—qualities which are the product of a sound education and those which he was anxious to foster among the rising generation of India. He has been called 'the prince of Indian civilians' and has been classed with Elphinstone and Munro, with Malcolm and Metcalfe, as an administrator of the first rank. Even if these claims are somewhat extravagant, it is none the less true that no more noble and selfless Englishman ever gave so much sympathetic consideration to the problem of the education of the Indian masses. In an important minute, written in the month following Thomason's death and recommending the introduction of his scheme of village schools, not only in the North-Western Provinces but also in Bengal, Lord Dalhousie paid a well-deserved tribute to the late Lt-Governor: 'I cannot refrain from recording anew in this place my deep regret that the ear, which would have heard this welcome sanction given with so much joy, is now dull in death. I desire at the same time to add to the expression of my feelings, that even though Mr Thomason had left no other memorial of his public life behind him, this system of general vernacular education, which is all his own, would have sufficed to build up for him a noble and abiding monument of his earthly career.'[1] Then followed Wood's Dispatch which eulogized the great services he had rendered to the people of his own province and held up his system of elementary education as a pattern for the rest of India. These appreciative references serve to fix Thomason's place in the history of modern Indian education and to commemorate 'his eminent merits' more fittingly than even that 'enduring memorial'[2]—the College of Engineering, Roorkee—which continues to bear his honoured name.

[1] Richey, op. cit., p. 267.   [2] ibid., p. 361.

SIR SYED AHMED KHAN

SIR SYED AHMED KHAN, 1817-98

MUSLIM EDUCATIONAL REFORMER

FOR many years after effective political control had passed into the hands of the East India Company, a titular Emperor continued to hold court at Delhi, to bestow honours and titles and to wield nominal sway over vast territories. Even up to 1835 the Company's coinage bore the name and titles of the Mogul Emperor, then commonly called the King of Delhi. These outward marks of a phantom sovereignty did not blind the Mohammedans of India to the realities of their unenviable position; they looked with resentment upon the European 'who had so unceremoniously helped himself to the empire of their fathers';[1] they looked with contempt upon the Hindu who had thrown in his lot with the new rulers and, for the sake of office and material gain, had abandoned the pursuit of that culture which Muslims considered their most precious heritage and their most valuable gift to the land of their adoption. Not only was the loss of power bitterly felt, but the growing apprehension that their culture might be altogether submerged created an atmosphere of pessimism. Cut off from contact with the foreigners and infidels, who had become rulers of the land, and from the followers of Hinduism, who had recently been their subjects and servants, Muslims looked back with pride to the glories which had vanished and with hopelessness to the calamities which the future held in store.

With the passing of the years things became worse rather than better. In the early days of British supremacy, no sweeping administrative changes were introduced and no attempts were made to substitute Western for Persian and Arabic learning or to overthrow the established system of education. Indeed, for the first seventy years of British rule, this system was used to train officials for the conduct of civil administration[2] and Hindus showed little reluctance to continue their Persian studies. By degrees, a new system of public instruction was introduced and one

---

[1] J. N. Farquhar, *Modern Religious Movements in India* (1929), p. 91.

[2] W. W. Hunter, *The Indian Musalmans* (1871), p. 175.

of the results of the spread of Western learning was the substitution of English for Persian as the language of official business. Mohammedans viewed with dismay the displacement of Persian and they held themselves aloof from a movement which had dealt a heavy blow to their culture and was even calculated to undermine their faith. Hindus, on the other hand, were more adaptable and far-seeing; they readily availed themselves of the facilities offered for the acquisition of Western knowledge and they managed to secure a disproportionate share of administrative and judicial appointments. In consequence, 'the relative positions of the Hindu and Muhammadan communities steadily changed, the former rising in knowledge, wealth and influence, the latter declining'.[1]

This reversal of fortune, not unnaturally, made a proud and sensitive people sullen and despondent, and they came to regard themselves as 'a race ruined under British rule'.[2]   They complained, with some justification, that the new system of public instruction was 'opposed to the traditions, unsuited to the requirements, and hateful to the religion, of the Mussalmans';[3] they recalled that a comparatively short time ago their own system of education had been the basis of their intellectual and material supremacy, as well as the medium by which Hindus had proved their fitness to wield authority in their own country. Dr (afterwards Sir William) Hunter put the Muslim point of view very clearly when he wrote: 'The truth is, that our system of Public Instruction ignores the three most powerful instincts of the Musalman heart. In the first place, it conducts education in the vernacular, a language which educated Muhammadans despise, and through Hindu teachers, whom the whole Muhammadan community hates. . . . In the second place, our rural schools seldom enable a Musalman to learn the tongues necessary for his holding a responsible position in life, and for the performance of his religious duties. . . . In the third place, our system of Public Instruction makes no provision for the religious education of Muhammadan youth.'[4]   In the circumstances, 'the Maulvis, the religious leaders of the people, from a mistaken loyalty to Islam, forbade their people from acquiring the learning of the *Firanghi* [Franks, i.e. Europeans]';[5]

[1] Farquhar, op. cit., p. 91.   [2] Hunter, op. cit., p. 149.   [3] ibid., p. 174.
[4] ibid., pp. 178-9.   [5] J. Cumming (Editor), *Political India* (1932), p. 87.

the consequences were disastrous because, while Hindus, 'inspired by the arts and sciences of Europe, were experiencing an intellectual and moral renaissance, the Muslims all over India were falling into a state of material indigence and intellectual decay'.[1] As another writer says, 'owing to loss of power and dignity, loss of honourable employment and the comforts of material life, owing to poverty and injured pride, there was a degradation in Muslim standards';[2] by degrees even the purity of the religion of Islam became tainted by corruptions from within and accretions from without.

It is not necessary to enter into doctrinal questions concerning the alleged declensions from the teachings of the Prophet nor to describe the subsequent movements for reform, which are loosely labelled 'Back to the Koran'. It is, however, desirable to point out that the Mutiny (1857) rendered the pitiable condition of the Muslims more intolerable than ever. Historians have discussed *ad nauseam* the various causes of the sepoy revolt; from the cultural point of view, it is difficult to dissent from Vincent Smith's verdict that 'the movement was a revolt of the old against the new, of Indian conservatism against aggressive European innovation'.[3] Whatever may have been the causes of the outbreak, and they were many, there is no doubt that this tragic episode led to a still greater estrangement between Britisher and Muslim. As a contemporary puts it, 'during, and for a long time after, the Mutiny, the Mohammadans were under a cloud. To them were attributed all the horrors and calamities of that terrible time'.[4] Sir Theodore Morison writes, 'in 1857 came the catastrophe of the Mutiny, for which the English believed, wrongly, that the Muslims were mainly to blame'.[5] Hunter in the last chapter of his book, *The Indian Musalmans*, regrets the bitter feelings which the Mutiny engendered and deplores the vindictive measures which were taken to eradicate the old Muslim educational

[1] ibid., p. 87.

[2] L. L. S. O'Malley (Editor), *Modern India and the West* (1941), p. 396.

[3] *Oxford History of India* (1919), p. 725.

[4] G. F. J. Graham, *The Life and Work of Sir Syed Ahmed Khan, K.C.S.I.* (revised edition, 1909), p. 40.

[5] Cumming, op. cit., p. 87.

system.[1]   In a still more recent book it is claimed that, once the
Mutiny had been quelled, the Muslims suffered more than any
other people because 'the rebellion was regarded, quite unjustly,
as having had its origin among them'; the authors go on to say
that 'the one man who broke the spell of this desperate state of
affairs was Sir Syed Ahmed Khan'.[2]   This, however, is only one
of the achievements of a great Muslim leader, whose name will
long hold a prominent place in the history of modern Indian
education.

Syed Ahmed Khan, who was born in Delhi in 1817, belonged
to a family which had been very influential in Mogul times.
His paternal grandfather was a general on whom Alamgir II
had bestowed many titles, while his grandfather on his mother's
side was the Prime Minister of Akbar II.   His father, however,
attached more value and importance to things spiritual than to
the pomp and gaiety of the Court and, having politely refused to
accept the titles[3] which the Emperor wished to confer on him,
he became a religious recluse.   His mother was equally devout
and the influence of a deeply religious home left a lasting
impression on one who, in later life, advocated reforms which
were bitterly opposed by orthodox Muslims.

Although he received no regular schooling, and learnt no
English, the Syed was given the education which was traditionally
due to Mohammedan boys of good family.   Under the guidance
of maulvis, who worked under parental supervision, he acquired
a good knowledge of Persian and Arabic, not to mention Urdu,
and an intimate acquaintance with the religious teachings of
Islam.   In 1836 his father died and he was invested by Bahadur
Shah, the last of the Moguls, with his grandfather's titles; it seemed
reasonable to anticipate that he would carry on the family tradition
and soon occupy a position of importance at Court.   Syed Ahmed,
however, decided to enter the British Service and this decision,

---

[1] As soon as the British system of education 'had trained up a generation
of men in the new plan, we flung aside the old Muhammadan system, and the
Musalman youth found every avenue of public life closed in their faces'
(Hunter, op. cit., p. 175).

[2] C. F. Andrews and Girija Mukerji, *The Rise and Growth of the Congress
in India* (1938), p. 87.

[3] i.e. his father's titles; titles were not hereditary under the Moguls.

taken against the wishes of his family, marked a turning-point in his life.

He was first appointed *Sheristadar* (Reader) of the Sadr Court in Delhi; a couple of years later he was transferred to Agra, and in 1841 he was promoted *Munsif*, or Subordinate Judge, at Fatehpur Sikri, Akbar's former capital. His assiduous devotion to duty and his strict impartiality won official recognition and one of the fruits of his efforts to qualify himself for promotion in the Legal Department was the publication of his *Transcript and Analysis of the Regulations*. In his spare time he devoted himself to serious study and in 1844 published the *Archaeological History of the Ruins of Delhi*.[1] At the time this book attracted little notice, but when it was translated into French by M. Garcin de Tassy a second edition was called for, and it was on the strength of this work that Syed Ahmed Khan was elected (1864) an Honorary Member of the Royal Asiatic Society, a distinction of which he was very proud.

Meantime, he had weathered the storm of the Mutiny, which had burst over Northern India in 1857. He was then stationed at Bijnore, a District headquarters town about midway between Meerut and Roorkee. When bands of disaffected troops swept through, on their way from Roorkee to Bareilly, an attempt was made to release the prisoners from the local jail, but the Syed rallied the guards and only a few convicts managed to escape. A little later, a Rohilla chieftain, Nawab Mahmud Khan, at the head of some 800 men, surrounded the Collector's bungalow in which a handful of English officials, with a few wives and children, had taken refuge. As soon as this news reached Syed Ahmed he resolved to take immediate action: he slipped through the Rohilla lines undetected and held a hurried conference with the beleaguered inmates. The upshot was that the intrepid Munsif volunteered to interview Mahmud Khan and to intercede on their behalf. With the utmost presence of mind, he strolled unarmed into the Rohilla camp and proposed that the Nawab should allow the Europeans to depart unmolested, on condition that a deed were signed transferring to him the right to rule the District until 'the English returned to claim it'. These terms

[1] So called by Graham, his biographer; the correct title is *Asar-us-Sanadid* (Traces of the Great).

proved acceptable and were embodied in a document, quickly drawn up in Persian by the Syed himself, signed and sealed by the Collector, Mr Shakespeare, and duly delivered to Mahmud Khan. Early the following morning the English residents left under escort and reached Meerut in safety. Syed Ahmed remained behind and for a time administered the District on behalf of the Nawab; within a few weeks further disturbances arose and he had to flee for his life. With the aid of some friends he, too, managed to reach Meerut after several weeks of exposure and danger. In an official letter written to the Commissioner of Rohilkhand soon after the restoration of peace, Mr Shakespeare paid a glowing tribute to three Indian officials, all of them Muslims, who (at considerable personal risk) had afforded him every assistance at a period of incessant anxiety and danger; he added: 'If I were required to draw a distinction, I should do so in favour of Syed Ahmed Khan, whose clear sound judgment, and rare uprightness and zeal, could scarcely be surpassed.'[1]

Syed Ahmed's courage and loyalty cost him dearly. Soon after the fall of Delhi he decided to visit his home and there he found that his property had been pillaged by the rebels and that his uncle and cousin, whose house adjoined his own, had been done to death by infuriated Sikhs. He then discovered that his mother had taken refuge, with a female servant, in a stable and that for five days she had been living on the horses' grain and that for three days she had not had a drop of water. He took her back with him to Meerut, but the horrors of the massacre and siege had proved too much and within a month she died of shock. As a reward for his loyalty, the Syed received, among other marks of distinction, a special pension of two hundred rupees a month, a pearl necklace and sword of honour. He returned to his post at Bijnore, but was soon transferred to Moradabad, where he started a school for the study of modern history.

The distressing experiences which he had undergone during the Mutiny had a profound effect on Syed Ahmed and turned his thoughts to the deeper issues of social and political life. He set himself to examine the causes which had led up to the tragic revolt, and the conclusions at which he arrived were

[1] Graham, op. cit., p. 23.

embodied in an Urdu pamphlet, *The Causes of the Indian Mutiny* (1858). This was not published until five years later and, of the 500 copies originally printed for private circulation, no less than 498 were sent for distribution in England and one was sent to the Government of India; one copy was retained by the author himself and not a single copy circulated in India.[1] If this is so, it is clear that the Syed's methods of voicing his views were very different from those which are usually employed nowadays. It was not until 1873 that the pamphlet was translated into English by Sir Auckland Colvin and Col. (later Major-General) Graham, who became the Syed's intimate friend and biographer. It is a document of very great value, for it is written by one who had had first-hand experience of the horrors of the Mutiny and was penned at a time when the conflagration was still smouldering and when martial law was still in force; also, it gives us an insight into the mind of one of the ablest and most advanced Mohammedans of his day.

He held that the Mutiny was not a political conspiracy—that it was a popular movement rather than a movement headed by princes and ruling chiefs. He made light of the Russian bogey, the intrigues of Afghanistan and the annexation of Oudh. The root cause, he maintained, was simply misunderstanding by the masses of the motives of the Government. This was reflected in the passing of laws and regulations which ran counter to Indian traditions and sentiments and in the ignorance of the English rulers of the general conditions in which the people lived and of their prevailing outlook on life. The pamphlet is a powerful plea, written with sincerity and candour, for mutual understanding between the rulers and the ruled. In one passage he argues: 'Most men agree that it is highly conducive to the welfare and prosperity of Government, indeed, is essential to its stability—that the people should have a voice in its councils. It is from the voice of the people only that Government can learn whether its projects are likely to be well received. . . . This voice, however, can never be heard, this security never acquired, unless the people are allowed a share in the consultations of Government. . . . The security of Government is founded on its knowledge of the character of the governed, as well as on its careful observance of

[1] Mohammad Noman, *Muslim India* (1942), p. 33.

their rights and privileges.'[1]   Historians are now agreed that the suspicions of the people who revolted were not altogether without foundation.   Although the East India Company had long professed the doctrine of religious neutrality, had been careful to avoid any interference with ceremonial practices and had been reluctant to encourage missionary activity within their territories, there had been clear indications, in the years immediately preceding the Mutiny, that the Government were embarking on a policy of innovation.   Suttee and thuggee had been abolished, Western education had been introduced, Sanskrit and Arabic had been discouraged in Government schools and colleges, and missionary institutions, where Christianity was openly taught, had been patronized; even the validity of many land tenures had been questioned and vexatious litigation had resulted.   It may be argued that these reforms had been introduced for the good of the people, but neither they nor their leaders had been consulted, and so there was some justification for the popular apprehension that the Government's intentions were directed against established religion; this was the cause of much anxiety to orthodox Hindus as well as to orthodox Mohammedans.   To restore and consolidate 'mutual understanding' the Syed advocated the nomination of an Indian to the Governor-General's Council, a mild measure of reform which was not introduced until political agitation had begun to clamour for something more drastic.

In 1862 Syed Ahmed Khan was posted to Ghazipur, where he first met Col. Graham, who was then Assistant Superintendent of Police.   It was here that he commenced the first commentary on the Bible ever written by a Muslim.   The labour involved was immense, for the Syed knew hardly any English and had to have various theological works translated into Urdu.   But, once he had made up his mind to follow a certain course of action, difficulties, however great, never deterred Syed Ahmed.   He continued his biblical studies for years and eventually published three commentaries—one on the Bible as a whole, one on the first eleven chapters of Genesis and one on the Gospel of St Matthew. Farquhar claims that his 'fragment of a *Commentary on Genesis* has been of real service in opening Muhammadan minds'.[2]   Before leaving Moradabad he had written a pamphlet on *The Loyal*

---

[1] Graham, op. cit., pp. 26-7.   [2] Farquhar, op. cit., p. 97.

Mohammedans of India (1860), in which he strove to rehabilitate
the reputation of his co-religionists, whose share in the uprising,
and the excesses which followed, had brought about their unpopularity in official circles. He gave examples of the valuable
services which had been rendered by many Muslims, high and
low, and of the rewards which they had received for their bravery
and loyalty; he regretted the growing tendency to refrain from
making any allusion, either in the press or from the public plat-
form, to facts which were beyond dispute, and he regarded this
tendency as a slur on his community. The Syed had reason to
be proud of what staunch Muslims had done during those days
of indescribable horror and it galled him that the authorities
were reluctant to give credit where credit was due. But the more
he pondered over the Mutiny, and the events which had led up
to it, the more clearly he realized that his co-religionists had fallen
into a desperately backward state and that 'if they were not to
lose ground which they might never be able to regain, they must
make their account with things as they were'.[1] As Farquhar
puts it: 'The Mutiny showed him, as by a flash of lightning,
the frightful danger in which his community stood. He had
early grasped the value of British rule in India and had thereby
been led to believe that it would prove stable, in spite of any
such storm as the Mutiny. He now saw clearly that the
Muhammadans of India must absorb the science and education of
the West and must also introduce social reform among themselves,
or else fall into complete helplessness and ruin.'[2]

He, therefore, set about making plans for persuading his
brethren of the truth of his ideas. He talked incessantly to his
personal friends, he published pamphlets and formed an association for the study of Western science. He frankly confessed
that 'all the religious learning in Muhammadan libraries is of no
avail'[3] and, so, he established English schools and struggled in
every possible way to convince his community of the wisdom
of learning English and of absorbing the culture of the West. He
himself had the greatest admiration for Islamic culture, but he
saw that the extreme conservatism of their leaders was an insuper-
able barrier to the well-being and progress of Muslims. As he

[1] O'Malley, op. cit., p. 158.   [2] Farquhar, op. cit., p.92.   [3] ibid.

said in a letter written from England some years later (1869), 'the fatal shroud of self-complacency is wrapt around the Mohammedan community; they remember the old folk-tales of their ancestors and think that there are none like themselves'.[1] He took as his motto 'Educate, educate, educate,' and once said to Graham, 'All the socio-political diseases may be cured by this treatment'.[2] In 1864 he formed at Ghazipur, with the help of some Indian and English friends, a Translation Society which was instrumental in having translated into Urdu many English books on history, economics and science and which, later, developed into the Scientific Society of Aligarh.

The year 1866 is memorable in the Syed's life, for he was then transferred to Aligarh, a place which will ever remain associated with his name. In the city and neighbourhood there resided many old and aristocratic Muslim families, amongst whom were men of great learning, well versed in Islamic culture. Syed Ahmed determined to attack conservatism in one of its greatest strongholds, and his zeal and enthusiasm were so infectious that he succeeded in making many converts to his enlightened views; they proved to be influential supporters of his schemes for engrafting modern knowledge upon Islamic learning. His efforts to promote modern education in the Muslim community were officially recognized in 1866 when the Viceroy, Lord Lawrence, decorated him with a gold medal and presented him with a complete set of the works of Lord Macaulay.

Three years later, after a brief spell of official duty at Benares, Syed Ahmed, on the suggestion of Col. Graham, decided to accompany his two sons to England. The elder, Syed Mahmood, was the first Muslim to be awarded a State scholarship to enable him to complete his studies abroad; he subsequently became a distinguished judge of the High Court, Allahabad, Secretary of the Mohammedan Anglo-Oriental College, Aligarh, and author of an authoritative *History of Education in India* (1895). The younger, Syed Hamid, entered the Indian Police and rose to be District Superintendent in his own province. On 10 April 1869 father and sons sailed from Bombay in S.S. *Poona*. They thoroughly enjoyed the voyage and made friends with several passengers, including Miss Mary Carpenter, an admirer of Ram

[1] Graham, op. cit., p. 129.   [2] ibid., p. 48.

Mohun Roy and one of the staunchest of the early champions of female education in India. Another interesting fellow-traveller, who came aboard at Suez, was M. de Lesseps, builder of the Suez Canal, with whom the Syed conversed in Arabic. He eventually decided to settle in London and there he met many distinguished men, including Carlyle with whom he 'talked long and earnestly over *Heroes and Hero-Worship*, especially about Mohammed . . . and also about Syed Ahmed's *Essays on the Life of Mohammed*, then in the Press'.[1] He was present at the last public reading given by Charles Dickens, and among former Indian officials he renewed his acquaintance with Lord Lawrence. He was cordially welcomed by the Secretary of State for India, the Duke of Argyll, who presented him with the insignia of the Companion of the Star of India. His financial worries were greatly relieved by a special grant of £250 per annum (for two years), which was in addition to the ordinary furlough pay to which he was entitled.

While in England he contributed a series of letters, in Urdu, which were published in the *Aligarh Literary Gazette*; they show that Syed Ahmed Khan was a shrewd observer of men and things and that he had a keen sense of humour. Apart from his visits to the spacious mansions of the great, he saw museums, engineering works, ship-building yards, gun factories, vessels of war and the like; he was so impressed with what he was shown that he had to confess that 'without flattering the English' he was convinced that they were far ahead of his own countrymen 'in education, manners and uprightness'.[2] He was particularly impressed by the efficiency of English schools and universities and by the comparatively high standard of education among the masses. He was amazed that his landlady should take an intelligent interest in politics, that the maid-servant should read newspapers, that even cabmen should keep papers, or books, under their driving-seats and read them while they were waiting to pick up a fare. 'Until the education of the masses', he observes, 'is pushed on as it is here, it is impossible for a native [of India] to become civilized and honoured'; again, 'the cause of England's civilisation is that all the arts and sciences are in the language of the country. . . . Those who are bent on bettering and improving

---

[1] ibid., p. 65.   [2] ibid., p. 125.

India must remember that the only way of compassing this is by having the whole of the arts and sciences translated into their own language. I should like to have this written in gigantic letters on the Himalayas, for the remembrance of future generations'.[1] A modern writer is careful to point out that 'at one time Sir Saiyid Ahmad Khan protested against the domination of English and urged that government should provide access to the stores of western knowledge through the media of the languages of the Indian people, but his was a voice crying in the wilderness'.[2] At any rate, his visit to England confirmed two beliefs which the Syed had long cherished: (1) that the higher-class Muslims must pursue modern learning, imparted in their own language and animated by the spirit of Islam, and in institutions established and controlled by Muslims; and (2) that elementary education must be spread among the masses through the medium of the mother-tongue. Force of circumstances compelled him to make a start from above, for he knew full well that, unless the lower classes were given a lead by those to whom they looked up for guidance, ignorance and bigotry would defeat every effort to spread what he vaguely called 'civilization' among the masses of his co-religionists.

In 1870 Syed Ahmed, after an absence of about eighteen months, returned to India and resumed his post at Benares. In the same year there appeared in London his volume of *Essays on the Life of Mohammed* which, in the words of his biographer, 'show an extraordinary depth of learning, great toleration of other religions, great veneration for the essential principles of true Christianity'.[3] In this book the Syed came to grips with his old friend Sir William Muir, over certain statements in the latter's well-known *Life of Mahomet*, and he took particular pains to refute the popular accusation that Mohammedanism is a religion of the sword. He wrote: 'The remark that "the sword is the inevitable penalty for the denial of Islam" is one of the gravest charges imputed to this faith by the professors of other religions, and arises from the utter ignorance of those who make this accusation. Islam inculcates and demands a hearty and sincere belief in all that it teaches; and that genuine faith which proceeds from a person's heart cannot be obtained by force or violence.

[1] ibid., p. 132.   [2] O'Malley, op. cit., p. 661.   [3] Graham, op. cit., p. 70

Judicious readers will not fail to observe that the above-quoted remark is entirely contrary to the fundamental principles of the Moslem faith, wherein it is inculcated in the clearest language possible: "Let there be no foreign in religion; the right way has been clearly made distinguishable from the wrong way".[1] Copies of these *Essays* were sent to the Sultan of Turkey and the Khedive of Egypt but, although they attracted the notice of scholars, they did little, if anything, to dispel the popular belief that Islam was a militant religion.

Meantime, Syed Ahmed had heralded his return to India by another literary venture: he started a monthly periodical called *Tahzib-ul-Akhlaq* (Social, or Moral, Reformer) in which he combated, with his usual candour, prejudices against Western knowledge and advocated greater social freedom. 'He urged that there was no religious reason why Muslims should not dine with Europeans, provided there was no forbidden food on the table, and boldly put his teaching into practice, living in European style, receiving Englishmen as his guests and accepting their hospitality in return. In consequence, he was excommunicated, slandered and persecuted. He was called atheist, renegade, anti-Christ.'[2] The Syed was not a man to be overawed by threats or slander and for several years, in spite of violent opposition from orthodox quarters, he continued to carry on his vigorous campaign for social and religious reform.

In 1872 Dr (afterwards Sir) William Hunter published a book which attracted considerable attention—*The Indian Musalmans—Are they Bound in Conscience to Rebel against the Queen?* Syed Ahmed quickly entered the arena and showed that Muslims had not a more courageous and outspoken supporter. He published a rejoinder—*Review on Dr Hunter's Indian Musalmans* (1872)—to prove that loyalty to established Government was an integral part of the Islamic faith. 'So long', he wrote, 'as Musalmans can preach the unity of God in perfect peace no Musalman can, according to his religion, wage war against the rulers of that country, of whatever creed they be.'[3] It would seem that regarding doctrinal issues Dr Hunter was singularly badly informed and that the Syed was justified in stating that the author 'has, throughout his work, relied upon

---

[1] ibid., p. 71.   [2] Farquhar, op. cit., p. 93.
[3] Graham, op. cit., p. 153.

15

very weak authorities when treating of Mohammedan creeds. He
has shown little discretion in not sifting more carefully the chaff
from the wheat'.[1]   Hunter's attack on Islam appears to have had
its origin in the Wahabi trials in Bengal, which caused a sensation
at the time and led some people to fear a serious fanatical uprising.
Admittedly, Syed Ahmed had come under the influence of the
Wahabis,[2] a puritanical reforming sect which believed in the
immediate access of the soul to God, and repudiated miracles,
priestcraft and saint-worship.

In his eagerness to defend Wahabiism from bigoted and
partisan attacks, Syed Ahmed gave further evidence of his religious
beliefs; this did not win the approval of orthodox Muslims but,
rather, intensified the hostility which his articles in the *Social
Reformer* had stirred up.   The views which gained him so much
unpopularity and led to threats on his life seem to the outsider,
whether right or wrong, to have been very harmless; at most,
they appear to be a mild expression of the modern rationalistic
spirit which had begun to influence Indian thought.   The most
explicit statement of the Syed's beliefs is to be found in his
Tafsir-al-Quran (Commentary on the Koran), which was never
completed.   He held that in the Koran, as in the Bible, there
is a human element as well as a divine, and that the Koran, like
the Bible, is not verbally inspired, but can be interpreted by the
light of reason.   As Farquhar says: 'He made much of reason.
One of his phrases was "Reason alone is a sufficient guide".
He wrote and spoke in favour of Natural Religion.   Hence his
followers are called *Naturis*.   The word has been corrupted into
Necharis.'[3]   The chief difference between him and the more
orthodox theologians was that he advocated rational explanations
of passages from the Holy Book, while his opponents thought
that such explanations were hazardous in that they ultimately
depended on individual whim and might be used to undermine
the essentials of the faith.   Professor W. Cantwell Smith sums
up the whole issue in these words: 'The religion which was
fashioned by Sir Sayyid was as he intended that it should be,

[1] ibid., p. 151.
[2] For fuller details see Syed Ahmad Khan, *Review on Dr Hunter's Indian
Musalmans* (1872).
[3] Farquhar, op. cit., p. 97.

explicitly and in fact an Islām thoroughly compatible with progress, and specifically with that progress which consisted in adopting . . . the culture of nineteenth-century Britain, with its new learning, its liberal and humanitarian morality, and its scientific rationalism.'[1] If this view is accepted, it is not difficult to see that the Syed's beliefs were sufficiently revolutionary to arouse opposition in the ranks of the conservatives, who resented his attitude towards inspiration, miracles and priestly authority.

The substitution of reason for authority in the interpretation of the Koran was considered by the orthodox as little short of downright heresy. The conservative point of view may be illustrated by a remark which a maulvi made to the Syed: 'We don't object to English education or to your wearing English clothes. What we do object to is that you learn natural theology; that you try to interpret the Koran in ways that we cannot understand; that you throw aside the authority of the commentators and take your stand upon the text as interpreted by your own intelligence.'[2] Organized opposition, however, was carried too far; certain *ulemas* (theologians) denounced Syed Ahmed as a *kafir* (infidel) and one extremist went to the length of taking to Mecca a document of denunciation, or excommunication. He brought back a *fatwa* (religious edict) with the seal of a learned mullah denouncing the Syed as a 'renegade' and hoping that 'he would be severely chastised'—even that 'God would destroy him'.[3] Although these machinations boded ill and threatened the success of the college on which he had set his heart, they did not deter the Syed from carrying bravely on with his educational plans nor from working without fear or trembling for the betterment of the community to which he belonged.

His visit to England had given definite shape to rough plans which he had already made for the encouragement of higher Muslim education and, on his return, he decided to establish a residential college at Aligarh, on the pattern of those at Oxford and Cambridge. He had come to the conclusion that a good modern education, supplemented by wise Islamic teaching, would produce young men of character and capacity, who would be

[1] W. C. Smith, *Modern Islam in India* (1943), p. 15.
[2] O'Malley, op. cit., p. 774.   [3] Graham, op. cit., p. 138.

able to play an important part in public life. Before taking steps to carry his plans into execution, he formed a committee of the more enlightened members of his community—A Committee for the Better Diffusion and Advancement of Learning Among the Mohammedans of India; its object was to investigate the causes of the intellectual backwardness of Muslims and to suggest ways and means of reconciling them to the study of Western arts and sciences.   After some preliminary discussions, the committee decided to offer prizes for the best essays on the backward state of Muslim education and it is interesting to note that among the reasons assigned in the more thoughtful essays were:

(1) The general disinclination of well-to-do parents to let their children associate with boys of humbler birth, and the apathy and lethargy of children brought up in comfortable homes where standards of discipline were not high.

(2) Aversion to English education because of the apprehension that it might undermine the foundations of faith and, also, resentment because the teaching of Muslim tradition and theology was not included in the curriculum.

(3) Neglect of Arabic and Muslim philosophy in English schools; also, the non-observance of Mohammedan festivals coupled with the alleged indifference of Hindu and Christian teachers towards Mohammedan boys.

(4) The contempt shown by Mohammedans for learning and clerical pursuits and their preference for military careers, or lives of ease and indulgence.[1]

The committee were satisfied that sufficient evidence had been adduced to show that advanced Muslim opinion not only was beginning to realize the sad plight to which Mohammedans had been reduced, but that the time had come to restore the community to its rightful place in the life of the country. Syed Ahmed decided that energetic measures must be taken for the betterment of his co-religionists and, in 1872, he formed the Mohammedan Anglo-Oriental College Fund Committee. The response to his appeal for funds was so liberal that three years later Sir William

[1] This admirable summary is taken from D. N. Bannerjea's *India's Nation Builders* (1919) which contains a sympathetic study of the Syed's life and work.

Muir, who had become Governor of the North-Western Provinces, performed the opening ceremony of an institution which began in a small way with the formation of a few school classes. The Syed boldly declared that the avowed purpose of the college was to turn out men who would 'preach the gospel of free enquiry, of large-hearted tolerance and of pure morality';[1] this statement was, in itself, enough to break down active opposition and to stifle adverse criticism.

In 1876 Syed Ahmed retired on pension; he made Aligarh his home, so that he could devote the rest of his life to the care and development of the institution which he had conceived, and for the building and endowment of which he had collected funds. In January 1877 the foundation stone of the new buildings, which were to house the college proper, were laid by the Viceroy, Lord Lytton, and so materialized 'the first independent educational effort of any magnitude made by the Muslims since the establishment of British rule more than a century before'.[2]   In the address of welcome to the Viceroy, Syed Mahmood stressed this point when he said: 'There have before been schools and colleges founded and endowed by private individuals. There have been others built by sovereigns and supported by the revenues of the State. But this is the first time in the history of the Mohammedans of India that a college owes its establishment, not to the charity or love of learning of an individual, but to the combined wishes and united efforts of a whole community. It has its origin in causes which the history of this country has never witnessed before. It is based on principles of toleration and progress such as find no parallel in the history of the East.'[3]   The most eloquent passage in the Viceroy's reply is deserving of quotation: 'You will, I am sure, be the last to admit that anything in the creed of Islam is incompatible with the highest forms of intellectual culture. The greatest and most enduring conquests of the Mohammedan races have all been achieved in the fields of science, literature and art. Not only have they given to a large portion of this continent an architecture which is the wonder and admiration of the world, but in an age when the Christian societies of Europe had barely emerged out of intellectual darkness and social barbarism, they

---

[1] O'Malley, op. cit., p. 93.   [2] ibid., p. 773.
[3] Graham, op. cit., p. 178

covered the whole Iberian Peninsula with schools of medicine, of mathematics, and philosophy far in advance of all contemporary science. . . . But Providence has not confided to any single race a permanent initiative in the direction of human thought or the development of social life. The modern culture of the West is now in a position to repay the great debt owed by it to the early wisdom of the East. It is to the activity of Western ideas, and the application of Western science, that we must now look for the social and political progress of this Indian empire; and it is in the absorption of those ideas and the mastery of that science that I exhort the Mohammedans of India to seek and find new fields of conquest, and fresh opportunities for the achievement of a noble ambition.'[1]   At last the fondest dream of Syed Ahmed Khan had been realized and as one of the speakers, Mr H. G. Keene, a distinguished civil servant and author of *Fall of the Mogal Empire* (1876), said, 'the ceremony they had that day witnessed was not merely the foundation of a school, but marked an epoch in the history of the country'.[2]   It is universally acknowledged that the crowning work of Syed Ahmed's life—that for which he will be long remembered and that in which he took a legitimate pride—was the foundation of the great college which in 1920 developed into the Muslim University of Aligarh and which continues to exist 'for the propagation of Western learning with a strong bias of Islamic teaching, consistent with the ideas and information imported from without'.[3]   There, to quote the original prospectus,[4] 'Musalmans may acquire an English education without prejudice to their religion,' and, consequently, students flock to Aligarh from all over India and even from as far abroad as Java, Zanzibar and Mombasa. The spirit of the indomitable Syed still pervades this great institution, which bids fair to fulfil the hope that it will be 'an intellectual capital for Indian Muslims commanding the same respect in the world of letters as Berlin or Oxford, Leipzig or Paris'.[5]

The initial success of the college cannot be attributed to the ample resources, which provided beautiful buildings and adequate

[1] ibid., p. 181.   [2] ibid., p. 187.
[3] O'Malley, op. cit., p. 317.
[4] Extracts are given by Farquhar, op. cit., p. 94.
[5] O'Malley, op., cit., 773-4.

equipment, nor, even, to the lofty ideals which the founders set before them; it was largely due to the appointment of a staff of Indian and English scholars who, from the very start, made it their aim to reach and maintain the highest academic standards. The first Principal was Theodore Beck, who came out from Cambridge with a great reputation and proved himself to be a born administrator; his early death at Simla cut short a career of great promise. He was succeeded by Professor (afterwards Sir) Theodore Morison, who for six years guided the destinies of the college with tact and skill; he was the author of several scholarly books and subsequently became Member of the Council of State for India and, later still, Principal of Armstrong College, New-castle-on-Tyne. Another notable figure was Professor (afterwards Sir) Thomas Arnold, who established a reputation as an Arabic scholar and, on retirement, joined the staff of the School of Oriental Studies, London. Other distinguished scholars who served the Aligarh College in its early days were Harold Cox, who was editor of the *Edinburgh Review* from 1912-29, and Professor (later Sir) Walter Raleigh,[1] who became Professor of English Literature at Oxford in 1904 and whose name is a household one among students of English literature. Of the Muslim scholars whose names are associated with the beginnings of the Mohammedan Anglo-Oriental College, the most notable are Hali, the poet and author of an Urdu biography of Sir Syed, and Shibli, famous for his scholarly life of the Great Prophet of Islam, Maulvi Nazir Ahmad and Nawab Muhsinal Mulk; it was men of their calibre who caught Syed Ahmed's inspiration and paved the way for the elevation of the college to the status of a University.

In 1878 Syed Ahmed Khan was appointed by Lord Lytton a Member of the Imperial Legislative Council—a rare distinction in those days for a Muslim who had started his official career on the lowest rung of the ladder and who had never earned promotion to gazetted rank. He was renominated in 1880 by Lord Ripon for a further period of two years; in his speeches on the Deccan Agricultural Relief Bill and on the Compulsory

---

[1] Interesting, and often amusing, details of his Aligarh days will be found in *The Letters of Sir Walter Raleigh, 1879-1922*, Edited by Lady Raleigh, I (1922), pp. 28 ff.

Vaccination Bill he advocated the rights of his fellow-countrymen in his usual outspoken and fearless manner.   More interesting, perhaps, is the fact that he was appointed a member of the Indian Education Commission (1882), which was presided over by Dr William Hunter, his former literary antagonist with whom he had long before settled his differences.   Of the non-official members the most distinguished were Mr T. K. Telang,[1] afterwards Vice-Chancellor and Judge of the High Court, Bombay, and the Rev. Principal Miller, Christian College, Madras, and subsequently Vice-Chancellor of the local University.   The Syed's evidence covers more than thirty printed pages, but only a few important extracts need be quoted.   On the subject of the State's obligations in the matter of education he advanced a view which was not commonly accepted at the time: 'I am personally of the opinion that the duty of Government, in relation to public instruction, is not to provide education to the people, but to aid the people in procuring it for themselves. . . . It would, therefore, be more beneficial to the country if Government should leave the entire management of their education to the people and withdraw its own interference.'[2]   Regarding the reasons for Muslim educational backwardness, he said that 'the causes which had kept the Mohammedans aloof from education may be briefly traced to four sources—to their political traditions, social customs, religious beliefs and poverty';[3] he went on to blame his co-religionists for their reluctance to take advantage of Government schools and colleges and explained that this might, in some measure, be ascribed to the fact that these institutions 'included among their pupils some of those whom the Mohammedans, with an undue pride and unreasonable self-conceit and vanity, regarded with social contempt.   They could never be brought to admit that sound and useful learning existed in any language except Arabic and Persian'.[4]   He reminded the members of the Commission that he still remembered 'the days when, in respectable families, the study of English, with the object of obtaining a post in Government

---

[1] Who wrote a long and important Minute of Dissent (*Report*, pp. 606 ff.).

[2] Graham, op. cit., p. 219.

[3] ibid., p. 220. In the body of the *Report* (p. 483) Muslim backwardness is attributed to 'pride of race, a memory of bygone superiority, religious fears and a not unnatural attachment to the learning of Islam'.

[4] ibid., p. 221.

service, or of securing any other lucrative employment, was considered highly discreditable. The prejudice has now, however, much slackened'.[1] Modesty prevented him from adding that this slackening had been due to his own personal efforts more than to any other agency, individual or, even, corporate.

As regards the education of Muslim girls, the Syed pointed out that it was a popular misconception that 'Mohammedan ladies of respectable families were quite ignorant'; he emphasized that poverty was the chief cause of the decline of female education and confessed that he sympathized with the disinclination of Muslims to send their daughters to Government girls' schools, which were far inferior to the corresponding institutions he had seen in England; he added: 'The fact is that no satisfactory education can be provided for Mohammedan females until a large number of Mohammedan males receive a sound education. The present state of Mohammedan education is, in my opinion, enough for domestic happiness, considering the social and economic condition of the Mohammedans in India. What the Government at present ought to do is to concentrate its efforts in adopting measures for the education of Mohammedan boys. When the present generation of Mohammedan men is well educated and enlightened, the circumstance will necessarily have a powerful, though indirect, effect on the education of Mohammedan women, for enlightened fathers, brothers and husbands will naturally be most anxious to educate their female relations.'[2] About fifty years earlier almost precisely the same views were held, and forcibly expressed, by Dr Duff, although he had Hindus, rather than Muslims, particularly in mind. Considering, however, the difficulties which Syed Ahmed had to overcome before he succeeded in winning over his co-religionists to support modern education for boys, it would be ungenerous to brand him as a reactionary in the matter of female education. Mayhew, however, holds that, despite the fact that Western learning has had a marked effect on the Muslim who has imbibed modern knowledge, the attitude of the orthodox Mohammedan towards the education of his womenfolk 'is a sign that his social system and family life has not been saturated and transformed by European ideas'.[3]

[1] ibid., p. 221.   [2] ibid., pp. 223-4.
[3] *The Education of India* (1926), p. 47.

Syed Ahmed Khan's evidence was taken in his own college, for Dr Hunter, in recognition of the Syed's work for the advancement of Muslim education, decided that the first session of the Education Commission in the North-Western Provinces should be held at Aligarh. In a remarkable speech at the opening meeting, Dr Hunter said that he hoped that their presence there would be taken as a 'public tribute of admiration to this splendid example of self-help' and added that those who had built the college would bequeath to posterity 'a noble memorial not of the discord, but of the reconciliation of races'. He went on: 'This College at Aligarh not only provides an education for the Mohammedans of the North-Western Provinces, but it stands forth as an example to all India as a Mohammedan institution which combines the secular and religious aspects of education. . . . This is a noble work to have done upon earth. And, here beside me, see the brave and liberal-hearted man who, by twenty years of patient effort, has accomplished it. I hope that centuries after our generation, with its cares and hopes and ambitions, has passed away, the memory of Syed Ahmed will be honoured afresh each year, as the pious founder of the noblest Mohammedan seat of learning which this age has bequeathed to posterity.'[1] Not even the generous words of Lord Ripon, who visited the college a couple of years later on the eve of his departure from India, gave the Syed so much satisfaction as those of Dr Hunter, who had become one of his closest friends.

After a short period Syed Ahmed resigned his membership of the Education Commission and his place was taken by his son, Syed Mahmood. The Commission, having toured the various provinces, heard the evidence of nearly two hundred witnesses, and read some three hundred written memorials, issued its report in 1893. It is a voluminous document, running to more than 600 foolscap pages and containing no less than 222 resolutions, of which 180 were carried unanimously. Though its importance does not rest on its mere bulk, the Hunter Commission's Report is by far the most noteworthy official document concerning Indian education to have been published between the issue of Wood's Dispatch and the end of the century. The Commissioners were not slow to realize that the existing educational system had become

[1] Graham, op. cit., p. 225.

top-heavy and 'to redress the balance they recommended the gradual withdrawal of the Government from the field of higher education and its transference to semi-official and private bodies, which were to be given liberal grants-in-aid. The main object of these proposals was to curtail Government's expenditure on secondary schools and colleges and so make available more money for the spread of primary education, which was held to have "an almost exclusive claim on public revenues". In order to encourage the establishment of private high schools and colleges, they went so far as to recommend that these institutions should charge fees lower than those charged in similar institutions controlled by the Government'.[1] These recommendations, though plausible on the surface, were based on the mistaken assumption that efficient educational establishments could be run on the low fees which Indian parents could afford to pay, supplemented by small grants-in-aid. Unfortunate and unforeseen results followed: (1) there was a multiplication of inefficient secondary schools and colleges, badly staffed and inadequately equipped; (2) local Governments, in order to prevent missionary bodies from gaining too much control over secondary schools and colleges, instead of withdrawing from the field of higher education, concentrated their attention on the improvement of their own institutions and increased their number; (3) in course of time, an unworkable system of dual control sprung up whereby the Universities (with no funds at their disposal and no machinery for inspection) were empowered to grant recognition to schools, many of which were unable to satisfy the requirements of Provincial Departments of Public Instruction. 'By their terms of reference the Commission were precluded from dealing with the universities, but one of their most important recommendations indicates that they viewed with alarm the stereotyped literary education imparted in high schools already dominated by the requirements of Matriculation: they proposed that in the upper classes there should be bifurcation, "one division leading to Matriculation and the other of a more practical character to fit youths for commercial and non-literary pursuits". The Government gave this recommendation their blessing, but no steps were taken to implement it, even in their

[1] Oxford Pamphlets on Indian Affairs, No. 15, *The Educational System* (1943), pp. 25-6.

own schools, while private, including missionary, institutions were unable to meet the expenditure involved by the provision of modern equipment and the employment of expert teachers.'[1]

On the subjects of female education and Muslim education the recommendations of the Commission, if not original, were sound and practicable; things, however, were allowed to drift, and the twentieth century was well advanced before determined efforts were made to carry these proposals into effect.   Indeed, for a long time to come, higher English education, of the purely literary type, continued to enjoy popular support and the patronage of the Government; it seemed convenient to overlook one of the most important of the recommendations of the Hunter Commission, which ran as follows: 'That, while every branch of education can justly claim the fostering care of the State, it is desirable in the present circumstances of the country to declare the elementary education of the masses, its provision, extension and improvement, to be that part of the educational system to which the strenuous efforts of the State should now be directed, in a still larger measure than ever before' (p. 174).

Meanwhile, Syed Ahmed, who had not been intoxicated by early success nor carried away by the plaudits of admirers, continued to devote his failing energies to the welfare of his college. In 1884 he made a tour of the Punjab; his old unpopularity had long died down and he was received everywhere with the greatest cordiality.   He was presented with many congratulatory addresses, but what pleased him most were the liberal subscriptions which poured in for the endowment of his college.   In 1886 he started the Mohammedan Educational Society, originally an adjunct of his college, which has since been a powerful influence in the spread of educational propaganda.   It continues to hold its annual meetings in important cities and it has been responsible for the establishment of many schools and colleges throughout the country. Two years later (1888) he was created a Knight Commander of the Star of India and this was a fitting culmination to a career of public service which has no parallel in modern Indian history.

He had still another ten years to live and, residing in his comfortable home at Aligarh, he watched with pride the rapid growth and development of the institution which he had founded

[1] ibid., p. 26.

and which he continued to cherish with fatherly affection. If ever a man had reason to feel satisfied with what he considered to be his life-work, surely that man was Syed Ahmed Khan! At the ripe age of 81 he passed quietly away (1898) mourned by his fellow-countrymen without distinction of class or creed. As was right and fitting, he was laid to rest within the precincts of the college and a simple epitaph was erected to commemorate the many and great services he had rendered to his community and country. At his funeral a lifelong friend said: 'Other men have written books and founded colleges; but to arrest, as with a wall, the degeneration of a whole people, that is the work of a prophet.' Many years later Sir Theodore Morison wrote, 'that remark conveys, in my opinion, a correct judgement of Sir Syed's personality and of the quality of his work. For myself I can say that I have never met a man so great as he'.[1] C. F. Andrews, a close and sympathetic observer of Indian social and political life, strikes the same note when he writes: 'There are few more impressive facts in modern history than this conversion of a great people in a single generation by the steady pressure of higher education combined with the influence of a commanding personality'.[2]

Few would dissent from Morison when he states that, among the many sterling qualities of the Syed's character, the most outstanding was fearless moral courage. 'Sir Syed', he writes, 'was violently attacked for his courageous opinions and suffered much from social persecution; but no persecution could daunt his leonine courage; his great personality prevailed at length over opposition and misrepresentation and in the last years of his life he exercised a marvellous influence over Muslim opinion.'[3] In his pamphlet on the Mutiny he had reproached the English for their aloofness and in the *Social Reformer* he had frequently upbraided Muslims for their backwardness; in his evidence before the Hunter Commission he had accused English officials of lack of sympathy with movements for educational reform and blamed his co-religionists for their adherence to outworn customs and beliefs. Once he had made up his mind, nothing deterred him from giving

---

[1] Cumming, op. cit., p. 88.
[2] C. F. Andrews, *The Renaissance in India* (1912), p. 125.
[3] Cumming, op. cit., p. 88.

expression to what he thought—'even', to quote his own words, 'at the risk of it being found distasteful'.

It has been suggested, however, that the disconcerting candour with which he was ready to discuss matters of religion, education and social reform, forsook him when he came to deal with political issues such as national and local self-government. It has been urged that, at one time, he held progressive views on Indian politics and sympathized with the leaders of the Indian National Congress (founded in 1885); but, having fallen a victim to official patronage, his detractors say that he recanted and warned Muslims of the evils they would suffer from majority rule. Sir Henry Cotton in *New India* (1885) accuses him of what amounts to apostasy and other writers have not been slow to follow up this clue. It is extremely doubtful, however, whether the charge can be sustained. As early as 1869 he wrote, in a letter from England, that praiseworthy as were the progressive tendencies of Bengalis and Parsis, 'their pace is so fast that there is danger of their falling'.[1] Twenty years later he publicly deplored the estrangement between Muslim and Hindu and appealed, in the national interest, for reconciliation and mutual co-operation. 'There is no person', he stated, 'who desires more than I that friendship and union should exist between the two peoples of India and that one should help the other. I have often said that India is like a bride whose two eyes are the Hindus and Muslims. Her beauty consists in this—that her two eyes be of equal lustre.'[2] These are not the words of a fanatical communalist; even if it be admitted that the Syed's sympathy with progressive political thought dwindled as the years went on, the explanation is not that he was willing to shed his patriotism in order to curry official favour; such an imputation can come only from those who are unfamiliar with the life and work of a man whose sincerity, outside the troubled sphere of politics, has never been questioned. If he condemned Congress activities, it was because he thought that it was more essential for Muslims to concentrate on making good their deficiencies in education. In short, 'he abstained from political propaganda, which he condemned as dangerous to the country and undesirable for his own people, because it was likely

[1] Graham, op. cit., p. 129.
[2] Cumming, op. cit., p. 89.

to deflect them from the task of moral and intellectual regeneration
—the only thing that mattered'.[1]

There seems no reasonable doubt that Sir Syed Ahmed's
attitude towards the Congress has been grossly misunderstood and
wilfully misrepresented; his patriotism has been called in question
and he has even been accused of having encouraged separatist
tendencies.   Perhaps the best refutation of these charges is that
the doors of the Mohammedan Anglo-Oriental College have always
been thrown open freely to Hindu students and that many
distinguished Hindu scholars have been appointed members of
the staff; again, many Hindu and other non-Muslim benefactors
have been among the most liberal donors to the institution which
will ever remain as the greatest memorial of that fearless advocate
of progress, 'who achieved for the social and educational betterment
of the Muslims of India' what the illustrious Rajah Ram Mohun
Roy achieved for 'the moral and intellectual rejuvenation of the
Hindus'.[2]

[1] Cumming, op. cit., p. 89.
[2] Bannerjea, op. cit., p. 95.

BIBLIOGRAPHY

CHARLES GRANT

MORRIS, HENRY ... *The Life of Charles Grant,* (1904).
The standard life.

MORRIS, HENRY ... *Heroes of Our Indian Empire.* 2 vols. (1908).
Contains a readable biographical sketch based on the complete life.

SMITH, GEORGE ... *Twelve Indian Statesmen,* (1898).
The opening sketch emphasizes the importance of Grant's educational work and of his services to missions.

SHARP, H. (EDITOR) ... *Selections from Educational Records, Part I, 1781–1839,* (1920).
An indispensable work of reference for all students of the beginnings of education in India under British rule.

MAHMOOD, SYED ... *A History of English Education in India, 1781–1893,* (1894).
Particularly good on the early period and on the development of modern Muslim education.

MARSHMAN, J. C. ... *Life and Times of Carey, Marshman and Ward.* 2 vols. (1859).
Covers a much wider range than the title would indicate; despite a missionary bias ·(easily understandable) the author is reliable in his accounts of early movements for social and educational reform.

GRANT, CHARLES ... *Observations on the state of Society among the Asiatic Subjects of Great Britain, particularly with respect to Morals; and on the means of Improving it,* (1832).*
Very difficult to procure; many important extracts will be found in Syed Mahmood's *History.*

*Printed in full in *Report from the Committee of the House of Commons on the Affairs of the East India Company, 16th August 1832. General Appendix I,* pp. 3-89.

RAM MOHUN ROY

COLLETT, SOPHIA   ... *Life and Letters of Ram Mohun Roy,* (1913).
The standard English life, published privately in 1900; a new and enlarged edition (edited by H. M. Sarkar) appeared in 1913 and was reprinted in 1933.

BALL, U. N.   ... *Ram Mohun Roy—A Study of his Life, Works and Thoughts,* (1933).
A judicious estimate, based on original sources.

GANGULY, N. C.   ... *Raja Ram Mohun Roy,* (1934).
By far the best of the many short lives; well written and fully documented.

CARPENTER, MARY   ... *The Last Days in England of the Rajah Ram Mohun Roy,* (1866).
Limited in scope and generally disappointing; useful only for reference.

CHANDA, R. AND
MAJMUDAR, J. K.   ... *Selections from Official Letters and Documents Relating to the Life of Raja Rammohun Roy,* vol. I, (1938).
A compilation of records, most of them tedious and unimportant, relating to Ram Mohun's private affairs and law-suits in which he was involved; contains an introductory memoir.

CHAKRAVARTI, S. C. ... *The Father of Modern India,* (1935).
Commemorative Volume of the Centenary Celebrations of 1933; Part II includes Amal Home's *Ram Mohun, The Man and his Work.*

GHOSE, J. C.   ... *The English Works of Raja Rammohun Roy,* (Panini edition, 1906).
Two volumes in one; the most complete edition available.

NATESAN, G. A.   ... *Raja Ram Mohun Roy—His Life, Writings and Speeches,* (n.d.).
A representative selection of Ram Mohun Roy's works, preceded by a short biographical sketch.

FARQUHAR, J. N.   ... *Modern Religious Movements in India,* (1929).
A book of the utmost importance, for it has no rival in its own sphere.

BUCH, M. A.   ... *Rise and Growth of Indian Liberalism (from Ram Mohun Roy to Gokhale),* (1938).
Stresses the importance of Ram Mohun Roy as the leader of the first liberal movement in Hindu religious thought.

MAJUMDAR, B.   ... *History of Political Thought from Rammohun to Dayananda (1821–84),* (1934).
Contains an appreciation of Ram Mohun's work and influence as a political and social reformer.

DAVID HARE

MITTRA, P. C.   ... *A Biographical Sketch of David Hare,* (1877).
Inadequate in many respects, but still the main source for the events of Hare's life.

KERR, J.   ... *A Review of Public Instruction in the Bengal Presidency from 1835 to 1851.* 2 vols. (1853).
Gives a good account of the early days of the Hindu College and of Hare's leadership.

HOWELL, A. P.   ... *Education in British India prior to 1854,* (1872).
One of the earliest, and still one of the best, histories of Indian education in the first half of the nineteenth century.

GHOSH, J.   ... *Higher Education in Bengal under British Rule,* (1926).
An authoritative and scholarly book, which deserves to be better known; excellent on the Anglicist-Orientalist controversy.

THOMAS, F. W.   ... *History and Prospects of British Education in India,* (1891).
The Le Bas Prize Essay for 1890, which remained for many years the standard history; contains a few inaccuracies which have found their way into later books.

RONALDSHAY, THE EARL
OF   ... *The Heart of Aryavarta,* (1925).
This study of Indian unrest is critical of the educational system and deals sympathetically with the revolt against Western culture.

EDWARDS, T.   ... *Henry Derozio, the Eurasian Poet,* (1884).
The standard life.

BRADLEY-BIRT, F. B.   *Poems of Henry Louis Vivian Derozio,* (1923).
A representative selection of Derozio's poems, preceded by a short biographical sketch.

DOVER, CEDRIC   ... *Half Caste,* (1937).
Includes a brief but interesting account of Derozio's work and influence.

ALEXANDER DUFF

SMITH, G. ... *The Life of Alexander Duff, D.D., LL.D.* 2 vols. (1879).
The standard life, written in Dr Smith's usual pontifical style. The author's zeal leads him to make extravagant statements, many of which, unfortunately, have found their way into subsequent books.

SMITH, G. ... *The Life of Alexander Duff, D.D., LL.D.,* (1881).
An abridged edition of the standard life; it omits much that is of interest to the educationist, e.g. the account of Duff's controversy with Lord Auckland.

PATON, W. ... *Alexander Duff—Pioneer of Missionary Education,* (1923).
An admirable short life—accurate and well balanced; should be read as a corrective to Dr Smith.

DAY, LAL BEHARI ... *Recollections of Dr Duff,* (1879).
A pious tribute by one of Duff's earliest converts; he was ordained in 1855 and, subsequently, became Professor of English Literature at the Hooghly College.

OGILVIE, G. ... *The Apostles of India,* (1915).
The Baird Lecture for 1915; contains a good short account of Duff's educational and missionary work. The chapters on Schwartz and Carey should also be consulted.

TREVELYAN, C. E. ... *On the Education of the People of India,* (1838).
An early and authoritative work which champions the policy of the Anglicists.

RICHTER, J. ... *The History of Missions in India,* (1910).
A standard work and easily the best short history of missions in India; not always fair, however, to Roman Catholic or Anglican missionary enterprise.

ANDREWS, C. F. ... *The Renaissance in India—Its Missionary Aspects,* (1912).
Deals in a popular way with the changes brought about as a result of the study of English and Western science and of the influence of Christianity; contains several illustrations and a useful bibliography.

WHITEHEAD, H.   ... *Indian Problems in Religion, Education, Politics,* (1924).

Before becoming Bishop of Madras, the author was for many years Superior of the Oxford Mission and Principal of Bishop's College, Calcutta; he writes from first-hand experience of educational and missionary work and his book is marked by learning, wisdom and tolerance.

MYLNE, L. G.   ... *Missions to Hindus,* (1908).

Pays a generous tribute to Duff as the founder of educational missions.

DUFF, A.   ... *India and India Missions,* (1879).

Duff's best known work, once very popular; it is inspired by a burning religious zeal which blinds him to the nobler side of Hinduism.

SIR THOMAS MUNRO

GLEIG, G. R.   ... *The Life of Major-General Sir Thomas Munro, Bart.* 3 vols. (1830); 2nd edition, 2 vols. (1831).

A voluminous and tedious life; redeemed mainly by copious quotations from Munro's letters and official writings.

GLEIG, G. R.   ... *Life of Sir Thomas Munro,* (1849).

A short and revised edition of the larger work; it has gained rather than lost by condensation.

BRADSHAW, J.   ... *Sir Thomas Munro (and the British Settlement of the Madras Presidency),* (1894).

An admirable short life; accurate and readable.

ARBUTHNOT, A. J.   ... *Major-General Sir Thomas Munro—A Memoir,* (1889).

A reprint, with a few minor alterations, of the memoir prefixed to the author's compilation of Munro's Minutes.

SATTHIANADHAN, S.   ... *History of Education in the Madras Presidency,* (1894).

Contains much valuable information not easily available elsewhere; authoritative and well documented.

SHARP, H. (EDITOR)   ... *Selections from Educational Records, Part I, 1781–1839,* (1920).

Includes Munro's Minute of 1826 and stresses his importance as an educational reformer.

RICHEY, J. A. (EDITOR) ... *Selections from Educational ·Records, Part II, 1840–59*, (1922).
Reproduces many important official documents relating to the failure of Munro's educational plans.

SEN, J. M. ... *History of Elementary Education in India*, (1933).
The best book of its kind and very useful for reference; contains a good bibliography but no index.

HARTOG, SIR PHILIP *Some Aspects of Indian Education Past and Present*, (1939).
Argues that Munro, almost certainly, over-estimated the number of schools and of pupils in Madras (1822); vide Memorandum A, pp 72–5.

O'MALLEY, L. S. S. (EDITOR) ... *Modern India and the West*, (1941).
A very important book in which various writers pay tribute to Munro's eminence as an administrator and educational reformer.

MOUNTSTUART ELPHINSTONE

COLEBROOKE, T. E. ... *Life of the Honourable Mountstuart Elphinstone*. 2 vols. (1884).
The standard life; there is now room for a new full-dress biography.

COTTON, J. S. ... *Mountstuart Elphinstone (and the Making of Western India)*, (1894).
An excellent short life, based mainly on Colebrooke.

KAYE, J. W. ... *Lives of Indian Officers*. 3 vols. (1873–5).
The first volume contains an admirable sketch of Elphinstone's career in India; it lays particular emphasis on his opposition to the policy of wholesale innovation.

FORREST, G. W. ... *Selections from the Minutes and other official Writings of the Honourable Mountstuart Elphinstone*, (1884).
Includes Elphinstone's *Educational Minute* (1824) and his *Report on the Territories Conquered from the Peshwa* (1819); preceded by a good biographical sketch.

BHAGWAT, R. B. ... *A Short History of the Elphinstone High School*, (1925).
A slim and inadequate centenary volume; it contains, however, an interesting *Sketch of Elphinstone High School, 1824-1856*, by A. L. Covernton, a former Principal of the Elphinstone College.

DOUGLAS, J. ... *Bombay and Western India*. 2 vols. (1893).
A series of stray papers on old Bombay; vol. II includes short sketches of Elphinstone and Wilson.

SMITH, G. ... *The Life of John Wilson, D.D., F.R.S.*, (1879).
Suffers from the author's characteristic faults; should be consulted by those interested in the development of education in Western India from 1832 until the establishment of the University of Bombay (1857).

RICHEY, J. A. (EDITOR) ... *Selections from Educational Records, Part II, 1840-59*, (1922).
Reproduces documents dealing with the Anglo-Vernacularist controversy, the decline of Elphinstone's elementary schools and the ultimate triumph of the Anglicists.

SEN, J. M. ... *History of Elementary Education in India*, (1933).
A good account, reliable and well documented.

O'MALLEY, L. S. S. (EDITOR) ... *Modern India and the West*, (1941).
A very important study of the interactions between Eastern and Western civilizations; one section is devoted to Education.

MASANI, R. P. ... *Dadabhai Naoroji—The Grand Old Man of India*, (1939).
A sympathetic study of the first Indian to be appointed to an 'Elphinstone Professorship'.

JAMES THOMASON

TEMPLE, SIR RICHARD *James Thomason*, (1893).
A good short biography, which lays particular emphasis on the lofty ideals which inspired Thomason.

OSWELL, G. D. ... *Sketches of the Rulers of India; vol II.—The Company's Governors*, (1908).
Summarizes accurately in about twenty pages the main events in Thomason's life; contains, also, less satisfactory sketches of Munro and Elphinstone, whose careers were too long and varied for such short treatment.

248   BIBLIOGRAPHY

MUIR, SIR WILLIAM   *The Honourable James Thomason,* (1879).
A readable memoir by a distinguished official who began his career under Thomason.

SARGENT, J.   ... *Life of the Rev. T. T. Thomason,* (2nd edition, 1834).
Contains interesting details of Thomason's early life and of the 'evangelical chaplains'.

THOMASON, J.   ... *Despatches; Selections from the Records of the Government of the North-Western Provinces.* 2 vols. (1856–8).
Vol. I contains Thomason's account of village schools and of his plans to improve them; vol. II is the best source for the early history of the Engineering College, Roorkee.

RICHEY, J. A. (EDITOR)   ... *Selections from Educational Records, Part II, 1840–59,* (1922).
Reproduces (chap. VI) the more important passages in Thomason's official writings on education; traces, also, (chap. VII) the beginnings of state education in the Punjab.

SEN, J. M.   ... *History of Elementary Education in India,* (1933).
Gives a good short account of Thomason's efforts to promote elementary education in northern India.

LEITNER, G. W.   ... *History of Education in the Punjab since Annexation and in 1882,* (1882).
An important work based on the study of original documents; some of the author's conclusions are of doubtful validity.

GODLEY, J. C.   ... *The Beginning of Western Education in the Punjab,* (1917).
A reproduction, almost complete, of W. D. Arnold's *Reports on Public Instruction for the year 1856-57*; not previously published and already out of print.

SIR SYED AHMED KHAN

GRAHAM, G. F. L. ... *The Life and Work of Sir Syed Ahmed Khan,*
(1885—new and revised edition, 1909).
The only detailed repository in English of the
facts of the Syed's career; a badly constructed
work, though it contains most of the material
for the full-length biography that is long overdue.

BANNERJEE, D. N. ... *India's Nation Builders,* (1919).
Contains an excellent short sketch of the Syed's
life and influence.

RUSHBROOK WILLIAMS,
L. F. (EDITOR) ... *Great Men of India,* (n.d.).
Includes a good biographical sketch of Sir Syed
Ahmed by Sir Abdul Qadir.

MAHMOOD, SYED ... *A History of English Education in India,
1781-1893,* (1894).
Traces the growth and development of Muslim
education; modesty prevents the author from
doing justice to the influence of his illustrious
father.

FARQUHAR, J. N. ... *Modern Religious Movements in India,* (1929).
An invaluable book which stresses the Syed's
importance as a social and religious reformer.

HUNTER, W. W. ... *The Indian Musalmans,* (1871—3rd edition,
1876).
Still well worth reading; the concluding chapter
is of particular interest to the educationist.

O'MALLEY, L. S. S. ... *Modern India and the West,* (1941).
(EDITOR) Emphasizes the importance of Sir Syed Ahmed's
contribution to the advancement of Muslim
education.

CUMMING, SIR JOHN. ... *Political India, 1832-1932,* (1932).
(EDITOR) Contains a valuable contribution by Sir Theodore
Morison on *Muhammadan Movements;* its
importance is out of all proportion to its length.

SMITH, W. C. ... *Modern Islam in India,* (1943).
A recent book which should be consulted by all
who are interested in the Aligarh movement.

NOMAN, MOHAMMAD ... *Muslim India,* (1942).
A history of the rise and growth of the All India
Muslim League; the opening chapters are devot-
ed mainly to Sir Syed Ahmed Khan.

CHRONOLOGICAL TABLE

1781 Warren Hastings founds the Calcutta Madrassa.

1792 Jonathan Duncan founds the Sanskrit College, Benares.

1793 Renewal of Company's Charter and rejection of the 'pious clauses'.

1800 Fort William College, Calcutta.

1808 Court of Directors declare policy of 'strict religious neutrality'.

1811 Lord Minto's Minute on the decay of learning in India.

1813 Publication of Grant's *Observations* (written in 1792).

„   Renewal of Charter; Parliament sanctions first educational grant for India.

1814 The Directors issue their first Educational Dispatch.

1815 Lord Moira's Minute on Judicial Administration.

1817 Opening of the Vidyalaya (Hindu, or Anglo-Indian, College), Calcutta.

1818 Foundation of Serampore College (granted Danish Royal Charter in 1827).

1822 Establishment of Bombay Native Education Society.

„   Munro's Educational Survey, Madras.

1823 Appointment of General Committee of Public Instruction, Calcutta.

„   Mountstuart Elphinstone's Educational Survey, Bombay.

„   Ram Mohun Roy's letter on educational policy addressed to the Governor-General (Lord Amherst).

1824 Mountstuart Elphinstone's Minute on Education.

„   Opening of Bombay Native Education Society's Central School (later, Elphinstone Institution).

1826 Munro's Educational Minute.

1830 Foundation of Duff's College (General Assembly's Institution).

1833 Renewal of Charter; employment under the Company thrown open to Indians without distinction of class or creed.

1835 Macaulay's Minute and Bentinck's Resolution on English education.

„   Foundation of Medical College, Calcutta.

1835 -38 Adam's *Reports on Vernacular Education in Bengal and Behar.*

1839 Lord Auckland's Minute on English education and Oriental learning.

1840 Board of Education, Bombay.

„   University Board, Madras (superseded in 1845 by Council of Education).

1841 Lord Elphinstone inaugurates the Madras 'University'.

1842 Council of Education, Calcutta.

1844 Lord Hardinge's Proclamation on the employment of educated Indians.
1845 Grant Medical College, Bombay.
„ Hardinge's *halkabandi* schools, Bengal.
1847 Thomason establishes College of Civil Engineering, Roorkee.
1849 Bethune's Female School, Calcutta; the Directors sanction the 'Thomason plan'.
1850 Lord Dalhousie's Minute on female education.
1854 Wood's Dispatch.
1855 Establishment of provincial Departments of Public Instruction.
1857 Universities of Calcutta, Bombay and Madras.
„ Arnold's *Report on Public Instruction for 1856-57*, (Punjab).
1858 Government of India transferred to Crown; Queen Victoria's Proclamation.
1859 First Educational Dispatch of Secretary of State (Lord Stanley).
1875 Foundation, as a school, of the Mohammedan Anglo-Oriental College, Aligarh.
1882 Punjab University.
1883 Report of the Indian Education (Hunter) Commission.
1887 University of Allahabad.
1902 Report of the Indian University Commission.

INDEX

Adam, J., 160, 191
Adam, W., 33, 101, 103, 198, 200, 203
AHMED KHAN, SIR SYED, **213-39.**
Birth and education, 216; enters Govt. Service, 217; experiences during the Mutiny, 217-18; views on political unrest, 218-21; advocates m o d e r n education, 221-2; visits England, 222-4; defends Islam and supports social reform, 224-7; forms committees to further Muslim education, 228-9; establishes M.A.O. C o l l e g e, 229-31; Member of Legislative Council and of Education Committee, 231-2; e v i d e n c e before Hunter Commission, 232-5; active interest in development of his College, 236-8; political views, 238-9
Alexander, Mr, 201-2
Amherst, Lord, 41, 53
Anderson, J., 97, 155
Andrews, C. F., 30, 216, 237
Anglicist - Orientalist controversy, 42, 43, 54, 65, 103, 104, 163
Anglicist-Vernacularist controversy, 163, 181
Anglo-Indian College, see Hindu College
Arbuthnot, Sir A., 134, 143, 152
Archer, W., 1
Arnold, Sir T., 231
Arnold, W. D., 206-8
Arpooly (Hare's) School, 76-7
Asiatic Society (Bengal), 19, 41, 73
Auckland, Lord, 102, 103, 155, 180

Ballantyne, J. R., 209
Banerjea, K. M., 105, 119, 209
Becher, R., 4, 5
Beck, T., 231
Bentinck, Lord William, 30, 42, 49, 50, 72, 74, 80, 82, 97, 98, 100, 101, 103, 129, 142, 145
Bethune, Sir W., 75, 78, 116
Bishop's College, 40, 71, 87, 89
Bird, R. M., 194
Bombay Education Society, 157, 160, 173, 174
Bombay Native Education Society, 160, 161, 171, 176, 180

Brown, D., 7
Bryce, J., 45, 48, 86, 87
Buchanan, C., 187

Calcutta School Society, 36, 76, 77, 78
Calcutta School Book Society, 36, 76, 77, 189
Cameron, C. H., 108, 110, 170
Campbell, R. D., 53, 136
Canning, G., 132
Canning, Lord, 205
Carey, W., 10, 13, 19, 36, 37, 86, 89
Carpenter, L., 53
Carpenter, Miss Mary, 222
Chalmers, T., 85, 109
Chambers, W., 5, 7
Chaplin, Mr, 163
Charter (1793), Renewal of, 8, 14-16
   „   (1813)   „ 9, 19ff., 129, 130
   „   (1833)   „ 50ff.
   „   (1853)   „ 109ff.
Christian College (Madras), 155
Clapham Sect, 8, 18
Clerk, Sir G. R., 197
C. M. S., 7, 10, 35, 78, 183, 210
Cobbe, R., 157
Colebrooke, H. T., 19
Colebrooke, Sir T. E. 158, 186
Collett, Miss Sophia, 28, 49
Colvin, Sir A., 219
Committee of Public Instruction, 41ff., 46, 53, 61, 65, 66, 73, 74, 101, 102, 104
Congress, Indian National, 238, 239
Cooke, Miss (Mrs Wilson), 78
Cornwallis, Lord, 6, 7, 8
Corrie, Archdeacon, 86, 94
Cotton, Bishop, 120
Cotton, Sir H., 238
Cotton, J. S., 164
Council of Education, 104, 106ff.
Cox, H., 231
Cust, R. N., 207

Dalhousie, Lord, 78, 108, 112, 116, 193, 212
Deb, Radhakant, 77, 78, 101
Deccan College (Poona), 177
Derozio, H. L. V., 66ff., 79, 95, 96
Dubois, Abbé, 88
DUFF, ALEXANDER, **85-125.** Birth and education, 85; establishes the 'educational mission' in Calcutta, 86-8; makes Bible